AF698900

RECENT DEVELOPMENTS IN THE CHINESE ECONOMY

RECENT DEVELOPMENTS IN THE CHINESE ECONOMY

ALMAS HESHMATI
EDITOR

Nova Science Publishers, Inc.
New York

Copyright © 2007 by Nova Science Publishers, Inc.

All rights reserved. No part of this book may be reproduced, stored in a retrieval system or transmitted in any form or by any means: electronic, electrostatic, magnetic, tape, mechanical photocopying, recording or otherwise without the written permission of the Publisher.

For permission to use material from this book please contact us:
Telephone 631-231-7269; Fax 631-231-8175
Web Site: http://www.novapublishers.com

NOTICE TO THE READER

The Publisher has taken reasonable care in the preparation of this book, but makes no expressed or implied warranty of any kind and assumes no responsibility for any errors or omissions. No liability is assumed for incidental or consequential damages in connection with or arising out of information contained in this book. The Publisher shall not be liable for any special, consequential, or exemplary damages resulting, in whole or in part, from the readers' use of, or reliance upon, this material.

Independent verification should be sought for any data, advice or recommendations contained in this book. In addition, no responsibility is assumed by the publisher for any injury and/or damage to persons or property arising from any methods, products, instructions, ideas or otherwise contained in this publication.

This publication is designed to provide accurate and authoritative information with regard to the subject matter covered herein. It is sold with the clear understanding that the Publisher is not engaged in rendering legal or any other professional services. If legal or any other expert assistance is required, the services of a competent person should be sought. FROM A DECLARATION OF PARTICIPANTS JOINTLY ADOPTED BY A COMMITTEE OF THE AMERICAN BAR ASSOCIATION AND A COMMITTEE OF PUBLISHERS.

LIBRARY OF CONGRESS CATALOGING-IN-PUBLICATION DATA

Recent developments in the Chinese economy / [edited by] Almas Heshmati.
p. cm.
Includes bibliographical references and index.
ISBN-13: 978-1-60021-449-3
ISBN-10: 1-60021-449-5 (alk. paper)
1. China--Economic policy--2000- . 2. Investments, Foreign --China. 3. China--Commerce. I. Heshmati, Almas.
HC427.95.R43 2006
330.951--dc22 2006029828

Published by Nova Science Publishers, Inc. ✢ New York

DEDICATION

To my daughters:
Emma-Shirin, Sara-Shilan and Lisa-Sharmin

CONTENTS

ACKNOWLEDGEMENTS

In addition to the individual contributors, this volume is the result of the work of several organizations and individuals. I owe special thank to Wang Qingshi and Wang Weiguo at the Dongbei University of Economic and Finance (DUFE), Dalian, China for hosting me in 2004 and my dear friend Ms. Huihua Zhao who was the source of my interest for studies of the Chinese economy. First, I would like to acknowledge the key role played by the Techno-Economics and Policy Program, Seoul National University for hosting the contributors and to the Ministry of Industry, Commerce and Energy of Korea for financing their research. Second, I would like to thank Tai-Yoo Kim, Jeong-Dong Lee, Junseok Hwang, Nils Karlson, Niclas Berggren and Dan Johansson for providing research facilities at Techno-Economic and Policy Program (TEPP) and RATIO Research Institute while preparing the manuscript. Third, my special thanks go to Mrs. Dianah Ngui, Mr. Guy Wallbank and Dr. Rhona Davis for their careful reading of the manuscript and editorial improvements of the text. Fourth, support from Mrs. Maya Columbus at Nova Science Publisher has been crucial to facilitate smooth process of publication of the volume. Fifth, at home, my daughters Emma-Shirin, Sara-Shilan and Lisa-Sharmin Heshmati, have gracefully put up with my extended stay in East Asia. I owe them a special thank you. In the end, none of the organizations and individuals mentioned here is responsible for my and the authors errors and omissions

ABBREVIATIONS

ACF	Autocorrelation Function
APEC	The Asia-Pacific Economic Cooperation
DEA	Data Envelopment Analysis
DUFE	Dongbei University of Finance and Economic
EU	European Union
FDI	Foreign Direct Investment
FE	Fixed Effects
FEM	Fixed Effects Model
GDP	Gross Domestic Product
GINI	Gini Coefficient
GLS	Generalized Least Square
GNP	Gross National Product
HEIs	Higher Education Institutes
IASP	International Association of Science Parks
ICT	Information and Communication Technology
IIT	Intra-Industry Trade
IMF	International Monetary Fund
LS	Least Square
LSDV	Least Square Dummy Variable
MNCs	Multinational Corporations
MNEs	Multinational Enterprises
NIEs	Newly Industrialized Economies
NTBF	New Technology-Based Firms
OECD	Organization for Economic Co-operation and Development
OLS	Ordinary Least Square
PACF	Partial Autocorrelation Function
R&D	Research and Development
RE	Random Effects
REM	Random Effect Model
RMB	Renminbi
RTC	Rate of Technical Change
RTS	Return To Scale
SEZ	State Economic-development Zone
SP	Science Parks

TC	Technical Change
TCI	Trade Complementarity Index
TEC	Technical Efficiency Change
TEPP	Techno-Economic and Policy Program
TFP	Total Factor Productivity
T-L	Trans-logarithm
TP	Technological Progress
UK	United Kingdom
USA	United States of America
USSR	Union of Soviet Socialist Republics
VAR	Vector Autoregression
WFOEs	Wholly Foreign Owned Enterprises
WIID	World Income Inequality Database
WTO	World Trade Organization
2SLS	Two Stage Least Square
3SLS	Three Stage Least Square

CONTRIBUTORS
(BY THE ALPHABETICAL ORDER OF THEIR LAST NAMES)

Feng, Yi, Director of Nuclear Safety Division, Department of System Engineering, China Atomic Energy Authority, Beijing, China, Contact: fysnu@yahoo.com.cn

Heshmati, Almas, Professor of Economics, University of Kurdistan Hawler, Erbil and Techno-Economics and Policy Program, College of Engineering at Seoul National University and Research Fellow member of the Institute for the Study of Labor (IZA), Bonn, German Institute for Economic Research (DIW), Berlin, RATIO Institute, Stockholm, and Center for Excellence for Science and Innovation Studies (CECIS), The Royal Institute of Technology (KTH), Stockholm, Sweden. His earlier positions include Professor of Economics at the MTT Economic Research, Helsinki, Finland and Research Fellow at the World Institute for Development Economics Research (WIDER), The United Nations University (UNU), Helsinki during 2001-2004. From 1998 until 2001, he was Associate Professor of Economics at the Stockholm School of Economics. Homepages: http://tepp.snu.ac.kr/, http://www.ratio.se and http://www.iza.org/.

Contact: heshmati@snu.ac.kr and almas.heshmati@hotmail.com

Wang, Boyong, Chief Clerk, Department of Asia, Ministry of Commerce, Beijing, China and Graduate Student, Techno-Economics & Policy Program, College of Engineering, Seoul National University, Seoul 151-742, Korea, Contact: wangboyong_ren@hotmail.com

Zheng, Yu, Chief Clerk, Department of Law Enforcement and Supervision, General Administration of Quality Supervision, Inspection and Quarantine of People's Republic of China, Beijing and Graduate Student, Techno-Economics & Policy Program, College of Engineering, Seoul National University, Seoul 151-742, Korea, Contact: fishead001@hotmail.com

Zhu, Zhengang, Director, Department of Foreign Trade, Ministry of Commerce, Beijing, China, Contact: zhuzg@ec.com.cn or froster515@hotmail.com

In: Recent Developments in the Chinese Economy
Editor: Almas Heshmati, pp. 1-34
ISBN: 1-60021-449-5
© 2007 Nova Science Publishers, Inc.

Chapter 1

RECENT DEVELOPMENTS IN THE CHINESE ECONOMY: ANALYSIS OF SCIENCE PARKS, FDI, ECONOMIC GROWTH, BILATERAL TRADE AND INCOME INEQUALITY

Almas Heshmati
University of Kurdistan Hawler and
Seoul National University

INTRODUCTION

There are a number of key factors crucial to the development of welfare in any nation. China, following its radical economic reform has developed rapidly in recent decades with annual economic growth rates in nearly double figures. China has experienced a major transformation in its transition from a centrally planned economy to a developed and relatively well-functioning market economy. This has been facilitated through vision, strategy, planning, management and skillful implementation of such comprehensive transition. The planning and implementation of the policy of reforming the economy has affected every aspect of life in China. It has implied organizational reforms, changes in production technology and trade relations. The policy changes have required an enormous amount of resources in various forms particularly in the energy sector, education and different public and private infrastructures and their organizations. Efforts have been made successfully to attract foreign direct investment in competition with alternative investments in countries with a well-functioning financial market, security and an educated productive labour force.

This volume does not aim to analyse the reform process, the policy and different incentives for implementing a successful policy but at providing an up-to-date and in depth analysis of five factors crucial to the success of the policy and current state of the economy. These include: economic growth, bilateral trade relations, science and technology, the flow of foreign direct investment and income inequality. The latter is seen in a negative perspective. Each of the five studies included in this volume are to be seen as separate comprehensive studies but yet integrated in many ways. All together they provide a complete and comprehensive picture of the recent developments in the Chinese economy and its path of reform and transition from a centrally planned economy to a modern and, from development and productivity perspectives, quite well-functioning market economy. The development has been a great source of admiration to competitors, politicians, economists and investors around the world, as well as to many international and non-governmental organizations, banks and the international financial market.

The existing literature about the Chinese economy is growing rapidly, yet it is far from being sufficient to provide a complete picture of the development. The paucity of literature is a result of inadequate and lacking relevant high quality data sources at different levels of aggregation and covering various sectors of the economy, as well as researchers with the necessary skill to conduct high quality evaluation research. Thus, this volume makes a significant contribution to the growing stock of databases under construction, their analysis and to the literature. It is a unique work in that it creates a number of databases assembled from published statistics and other secondary data sources to conduct the research. The data covers the entire reform period and up-to-date policies and developments. In analyzing the Chinese economy, the contributors utilise up-to-date methodologies and data in their computations and data analysis.

The volume has a high academic level, and it bridges researchers, academics and practitioners. The target readers are: researchers, decision makers, governmental and non-governmental organisations, graduate students and the general public. It is a perfect basic text to teach a topic-based graduate course on the Chinese economy and development economics. The primary market consists of segments of individual researchers, research institutes, libraries, decision makers, governmental and non-governmental organizations, undergraduate and graduate students. The secondary market includes the general public with an interest in technology, globalisation, foreign direct investment, development, and outsourcing at the national, regional and global levels. The analysis of each area is conducted by experts in the field with deep insight in the reform design and process. A brief summary of each area of study is given below.

The volume is organized as follows. In Section 1.1 of this introductory chapter, the readers are introduced to some basic facts about the Chinese economy and its development after the economic reform initiated in the second half of 1970s. The remaining sections 1.2 to 1.6 present a summary of each of the five studies outlined in detailed form in Chapters 2 to 6. These are inflow of FDI, Science and Technology parks, economic growth, bilateral trade relations and income inequality. Each chapter contains a comprehensive section summarising the study and provides suggestions for further research and discusses the policy implications of the results. The key conclusions of the five chapters are also summarised in the last section of this chapter, Section 1.7.

1.1. Development and Correlation Between Important Economic Indicators

Here I will discuss the developments of the key time series reported in Table 1. The information includes the development of: GDP level, GDP per capita, annual growth rate of the Chinese economy, trade volume, private investment expenditure, research and development investment, public investment, labour productivity, inflow of foreign direct investment, population, number of scientists and engineers and income inequality. The data on an irregular basis covers the period from 1978 until 2004. The monetary values expressed in Chinese RMB units are transformed to fixed 2000 prices by using producer price index. All indicators (with the exception of annual economic growth) show positive and rapid development over time. The annual growth rate varies in the interval 3.8 and 15.2. It is on average higher before 1995 than after. In order to produce simple descriptive statistics of the data and to make different series comparable, a correlation matrix and a number of graphs are produced whereby in the latter case, several variables are reported and normalized to the base year 2000 in each graph (Figure 1-3).

The correlation matrix (Table 2) shows correlation among the indicators. It should be noted that the numbers are unconditional correlation among the indicators. Multiple regression analysis provides conditional relationship between different indicators. The cost of using multiple regression analysis might be high. The costs are related to identification of the direction of causal relationships, strong assumptions about the distribution of indicators, and the problem of multicollinearity and subsequent difficulties to separate the effects. Multiple regression analysis based on modeled relationship between some sets of the indicators is reported and discussed in the individual chapters of this volume.

All indicators are positively correlated with time indicating a positive trend in each indicator's development. One exception is the annual economic growth which is negatively correlated over time. The growth rate during the entire period is positive and exceptionally high, although the rate is somewhat lower in the second half of the period. The GDP level and GDP per capita are highly correlated indicating low population growth. The two GDP variables and several other indicators are negatively correlated with the economic growth. Economic growth is positively correlated only with labour productivity and income inequality. However, none of the coefficients regardless of their sign are statistically significant. The series are of different lengths affecting their relationships. Labour productivity is highly correlated with GDP per capita. The association of the former is lower with income inequality.

Among the investment variables, the general private and public investments show a more positive association with GDP than R&D investment, inflow of FDI and the number of scientists and engineers. The pay-off from basic investment and investment in infrastructure so far seems to have been more effective for China's economic development. Investment in R&D has not been a strong conditional factor for the country's development. The driving force has been the skilled and low cost labour with high labour productivity and the essential good infrastructure enhancing production and trade. We do not find that economic growth increases income inequality, but inequality is positively related to the level of GDP and GDP per capita. The same positive association is found in relation with other indicators with an exception of the number of scientists and engineers. Since all indicators are increasing over time, their correlation coefficients are positive and highly significant. The correlation should not be interpreted as pure causal relationships among the indicators.

Table 1. Development of key indicators of the Chinese economy, 1978-2004, Unit: RMB 1 billion

Year	GDP level	GDP per Capita (RMB)	Annual Growth %	Trade Volume	Invest. Expend.	R&D Investment	Public Investment	Labor Prod. RMB	FDI Inflow	Population in million	Scientist and Eng In 1000	Income Inequality (GINI)
1978	360.56	379	11.7	35.5	137.79	.	.	911	.	962.59	.	22.5
1979	407.40	417	7.6	.	147.42	.	.	.	.	969.01	.	23.7
1980	455.13	460	7.8	57.00	159.00	.	.	1084	.	987.05	.	29.4
1981	490.14	489	5.2	.	158.10	.	.	.	0.64	993.86	.	19.7
1982	548.92	525	9.1	.	176.02	.	.	.	0.83	1008.60	.	23.6
1983	607.63	580	10.9	.	200.50	.	.	.	1.26	1023.29	.	24.4
1984	716.44	692	15.2	.	246.86	.	.	.	2.93	1036.80	.	23.4
1985	879.21	853	13.5	206.67	338.60	.	.	1828	4.88	1058.51	.	29.8
1986	1013.28	956	8.8	258.04	384.60	.	.	.	6.47	1066.76	.	27.3
1987	1178.47	1104	11.6	308.42	432.20	.	.	.	8.61	1084.00	.	28.0
1988	1470.40	1355	11.3	382.18	549.50	.	.	.	11.89	1101.60	.	31.9
1989	1646.60	1512	4.1	415.60	609.50	.	.	3084	12.77	1127.04	.	29.8
1990	1831.95	1634	3.8	556.01	644.40	40.33	.	3310	16.68	1143.33	.	32.0
1991	2128.04	1879	9.2	722.58	751.70	.	.	.	23.24	1158.23	.	31.0
1992	2586.37	2287	14.2	911.96	963.60	.	.	.	60.60	1171.71	.	33.0
1993	3450.07	2939	13.5	1127.10	1499.80	68.58	.	.	158.54	1185.17	1355	29.5
1994	4669.07	3923	12.6	2038.19	1926.06	71.85	961.58	.	291.03	1198.50	1532	31.5
1995	5851.05	4854	10.5	2349.99	2387.70	96.25	1089.82	9408	313.34	1211.21	1554	35.4
1996	6833.04	5576	9.6	2413.38	2686.72	104.32	1200.62	9963	346.92	1223.89	1688	28.3
1997	7489.42	6054	8.8	2696.72	2845.76	118.19	1309.17	10732	375.17	1236.26	1668	29.3
1998	7900.33	6308	7.8	2684.97	2954.59	128.98	1536.93	11349	376.39	1247.61	1490	40.3
1999	8267.31	6551	7.1	2989.62	3070.16	146.06	1594.78	11604	333.77	1257.86	1595	.
2000	8934.09	7086	8.0	3927.32	3249.98	234.67	1650.44	12566	337.06	1267.43	2046	.
2001	9859.29	7651	7.5	4218.36	3746.08	258.94	1760.70	13222	388.01	1276.27	2072	.
2002	10789.76	8214	8.3	5137.82	4230.49	293.80	1887.74	14211	436.55	1284.53	2172	.
2003	12173.03	9111	9.5	7048.35	5155.47	345.91	2166.10	16863	442.86	1292.27	2255	.
2004	14239.42	10561	9.5	9553.91	6287.53	432.89	2502.76	18295	501.82	1299.88	2252	.

Source: China's Statistical Yearbook, various issues. GINI coefficient is from the Chapter of Income inequality of China.

Table 2. Correlation among key indicators of the Chinese economy, 1978-2004, 11-27 observations

Varia-bles	Time	GDP Level	GDP/ Capita	Annual Growth	Trade Volume	Invest Expend.	R&D Invest.	Public Invest.	Labor Prod.	FDI Inflow	Popula-tion	Scientist and Eng	Income Ineq.
Time	1.00												
GDP Level	0.936a	1.000											
GDP/ capita	0.946a	0.999a	1.000										
Annual Growth	-0.109	-0.154	-0.151	1.000									
Trade volume	0.849a	0.957a	0.944a	-0.136	1.000								
Invest. Exp.	0.921a	0.996a	0.992a	-0.128	0.978a	1.000							
RandD Invest.	0.932a	0.950a	0.935a	-0.067	0.974a	0.961a	1.000						
Public Invest.	0.978a	0.993a	0.992a	-0.398	0.944a	0.975a	0.968a	1.000					
Labor Prod.	0.959a	0.997a	0.998a	0.019	0.932a	0.988a	0.925a	0.988a	1.000				
FDI Inflow	0.937a	0.966a	0.973a	-0.136	0.859a	0.953a	0.767a	0.915a	0.962a	1.000			
Polula-tion	0.996a	0.906a	0.920a	-0.105	0.797a	0.890a	0.887a	0.963a	0.935a	0.915a	1.000		
ScientistandEng	0.918a	0.905a	0.902a	-0.434	0.874a	0.886a	0.941a	0.851a	0.871a	0.804a	0.897a	1.000	
Income Ineq.	0.769a	0.648a	0.656a	0.005	0.633b	0.641a	0.353	0.497	0.579c	0.537b	0.776a	-0.287	1.000

Note: Significant at the less than 1% (a), 1-5% (b) and 6-10% (c) levels of significance.

The development of GDP level, population and income inequality are shown in Figure 1. The variables are normalized to 100 at year 2000. The population growth has been faster in the second half of the 1980s than during the periods before and after. The time pattern of the GDP level and trade differs. GDP grew faster from 1992-1996 and after 2000, while trade grew fastest during 1993-1995 and the period post 2001. The growth rate of GDP level post 2000 is 60 percent, while that of trade is 143 percent.

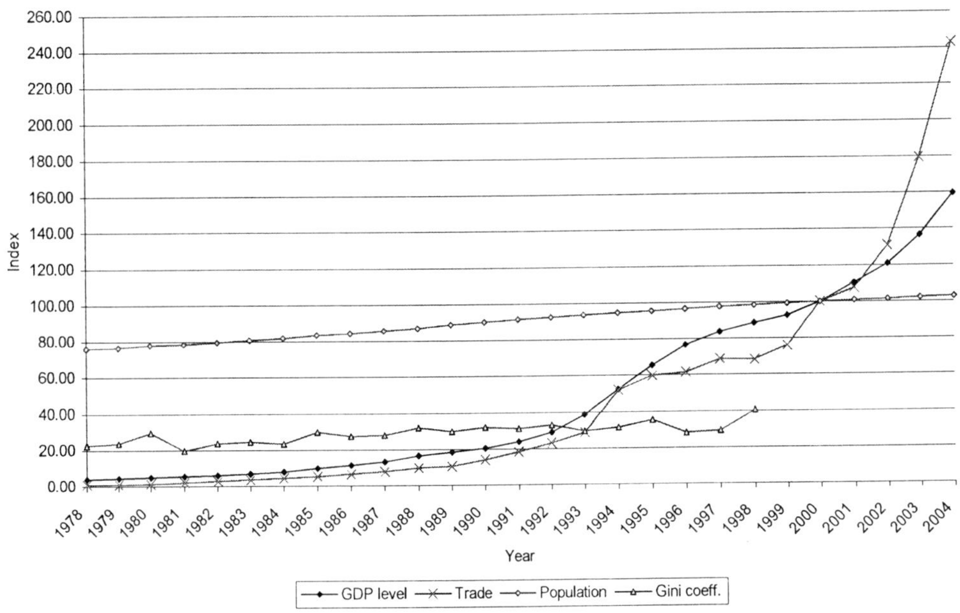

Figure 1. Development of GDP level, Trade, Population and Gini coefficient in China 1978-2004, 2000=100.

Figure 2 shows the development of GDP per capita, annual percentage economic growth, labour productivity and the number of scientists and engineers in China. The annual growth rate is constantly positive with the highest growth rate around 1984-1985 and 1992-1993. There was a sharp decline in economic growth during 1989-1990 due to the economic sanctions following the Tiananmen square events of April 1989. There was a decline in the number of scientists and engineers during 1998 and a rapid recovery during 1999-2000. GDP per capita and labour productivity are growing at the same rate from 1996 onwards. The growth rate in labour productivity was faster during 1990-1995. The two variables grew by more than 45 percent post 2000.

The development of private and public investment variables together with inflow of FDI are shown in Figure 3. To facilitate a better comparison over time, the variables are normalized at the year 2000. The time pattern of the variables differs greatly. The inflow of FDI grew fastest from 1991 until 1994. There was a slowdown from 1998 to 2000. The inflow recovered and reached 45 percent after 2000. There is also disparity in the development of the investment variables in the post-1991 period. Private investment grew fastest followed by public investment. Public investment programmes increased rapidly from 1999 catching up with and bypassing growth in FDI after 2002. The growth rate in public and private investments is around 80-90 percent post 2000.

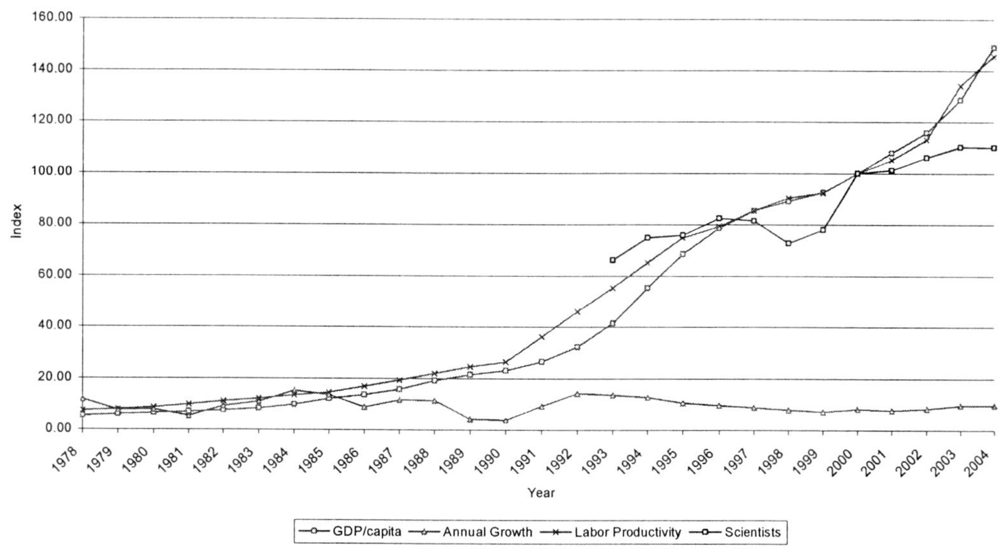

Figure 2. Development of GDP per capita, economic growth, labor productivity and number of scientists in China, 1983-2004, 2000=100.

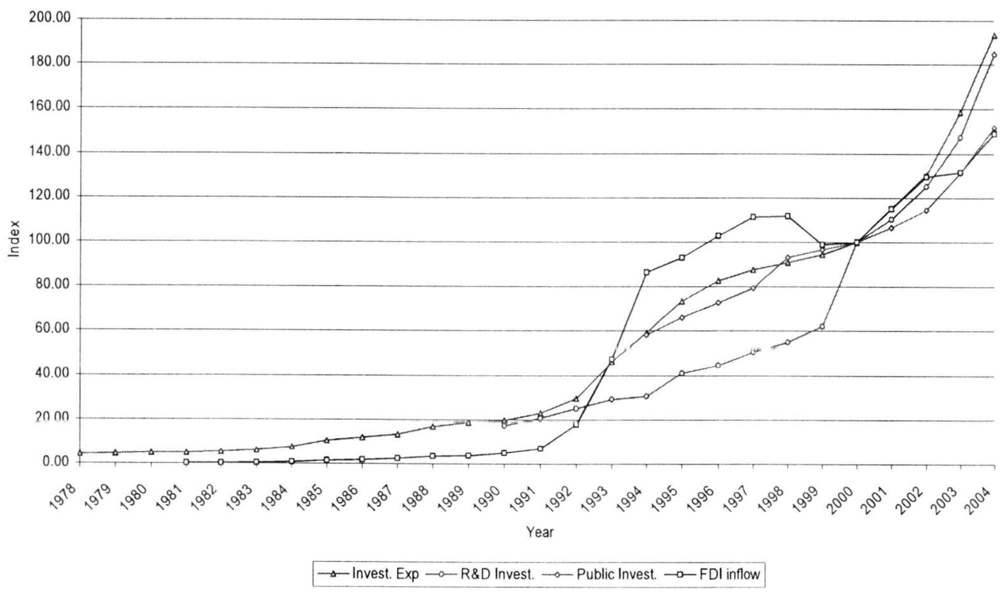

Figure 3. Development of Private and public investment, R&D expenditure and FDI inflows in China 1983-2004, 2000=100.

1.2. Inflow of Foreign Direct Investment

In the literature on economic development and growth, the impact of several factors on growth is often examined. These include: openness, democracy, information and communication technology (ICT), foreign direct investment (FDI), research and development (R&D), human capital, and many other development factors. However, few studies examine the causal relationship between the factors listed above. These results of such examination indicate that there are differences in the direction of causal relationship between the variables among the countries by their levels of development.

For instance, following Gholami, Lee and Heshmati (2006), in developed countries, existing ICT infrastructure attracts FDI, which suggests that ICT contributes to productivity and economic growth indirectly by attracting more FDI. But in developing countries, the direction of causality instead goes from FDI to ICT, which means ICT capacity must be built up in order to attract FDI. The inflow of FDI causes further increases in ICT investment and production capacity building. Blomstrom (1986), Kokko (1994) and Kokko, Tansini and Zejan (1996) find econometric evidence of positive FDI spillovers for several developing countries. While others find evidence that economic growth is a crucial determinant of attracting FDI (Cheng and Kwan, 1998 Coughlin and Segev, 2000; and Fung *et al.*, 2002). Several recent studies provide insights into the causal relationships between FDI and economic growth (Nair-Reichert and Weinhold, 2001; Kumar and Pradhan, 2002; Chowdhury and Mavrotas, 2005; Addison and Heshmati, 2004; Heshmati, 2006; and Shiu and Heshmati, 2006).

Since the start of the process of economic reform, and the opening up of the market to the outside world in 1978, China has become one of the fastest growing economies in the world. Meanwhile, as a result China is now the largest recipient of foreign direct investment in the world. The studies above, with the exception of Shiu and Heshmati (2006), are at the cross country levels. Such causality studies at provincial level are rare. Wang in his study makes a significant contribution in this respect. He examines the causal relationship between China's economic growth and inflow of FDI. In the empirical part, he uses up-to-date and unique data at the provincial level and tests the causal relationship between FDI and economic growth. He focuses on the macroeconomic perspective of growth and its correlation with inflow of FDI. In doing so, he uses fixed effects and instrument variable panel data approaches.

The results suggest that the need to focus on regional heterogeneity on FDI flow and economic growth is in favour of using disaggregated provincial data. This helps to shed light on the extent of provincial heterogeneity and inequality in development in China. The sequence of specification and estimation methods tests indicates that gross domestic product (GDP) and FDI have a bi-directional causal relationship in China, which means inflow of FDI and rapid economic growth have reinforced each other. Openness and government expenditure are also found to have positive effects on GDP and FDI. The results show evidence of significant heterogeneous patterns in development and flow of FDI across provinces in China and also over time.

1.3. SCIENCE AND TECHNOLOGY PARKS

Science parks play a key role and are of growing importance to economic development in many countries and in particular, in newly industrialized countries. From the early 1990s, science parks were introduced in China. In the light of recent decades of rapid economic growth in China, it is interesting to know the performance and contributions of these parks to the Chinese economic growth and how to promote the development and impact of those parks. Yu and Heshmati aim at analysing the growth and performance of 51 science parks in China during the period 1994 to 2003. Chinese Science Parks are built on the condition of intellectual integration of capital, skills and technology in an open entrepreneurship environment. The parks are mainly supported by domestic infrastructure and foreign technology and capital and they maximise the potential transformation from management and technical achievement to actual productivity performance through full absorption of the overseas advanced financial, technology and management resources.

Since Science Parks are in general a quite new phenomenon and especially in China, there is no literature developed on the evaluation of technology parks in general and case studies of China in particular are very rare. Among the few studies on science parks, Castells and Hall (1994) found that science parks provide an important resource network for new technology-based enterprises. Link and Scott (2003) show the link between the growth of a science park and the proximity to universities and other resources. Chan and Lau (2005), focus on meeting the needs of technology firms during their stages of development. Moreover, Hansson, et al. (2005) concludes that the new role of science parks might be to enhance entrepreneurship in networks. Finally, Jussawalla and Taylor (2003) present a collection of descriptive studies discussing information technology parks of the Asia Pacific and their implication for the global digital divide.

Thus, Yu and Heshmati in their study make a number of contributions by studying an important element of the new economic policy in China. They create a new panel data covering the entire population of science parks and their period of existence. For the empirical analysis they use up-to-date panel data methodology to model and estimate the production relationship at the park level accounting for parks, provinces and time heterogeneity and parametrically estimate total factor productivity (TFP) growth rate for each point of the data. In addition to TFP growth, they estimate return to scale and rate of technological change and evaluate their level and variations by provinces, parks and over time. For sensitivity analysis the parametric approach is compared with the non-parametric commonly used Solow's residual growth measure. Finally, they discuss the importance of parks to the Chinese economic growth. Based on the results obtained, they suggest a number of policy recommendations to enhance the parks performance and their contribution to the overall Chinese economic growth.

The results show that Science Parks are productive and have grown rapidly. It is an indication of a successful policy and development strategy in China. There is significant heterogeneity, which is not only a reflection of the failure of some parks, but of differences in the initial conditions and attractiveness of parks. The authors suggest policy measures along: (i) simultaneous improvement in the size and quality of the human resources to benefit the gross output of parks, (ii) to pay more attention to the share of technology progress rather than simple expansion in scale to realise the desired level of economic growth, (iii) information technology as an active applied technology should be strongly pushed to improve the productivity of parks and the economic growth in general, and (iv) that there is great diversity among the parks in both their capacity and growth speeds implying heterogeneous policies to achieve the regional and national targets.

1.4. Productivity Growth in the Chinese Economy and Industry

Productivity is commonly defined as a ratio of some measure of output to some weighted measure of inputs usage (for a survey on productivity in manufacturing and services see Heshmati, 2003). With the increasing recognition that productivity growth is the key to sustained economic expansion, an accurate measure of productivity is becoming important to economists, for policy recommendations and decision making. The pace of economic change in China has been extremely rapid since the start of economic reforms. Economic growth has averaged 9.5% over the past two decades and very likely seems to continue at that pace for some time. Such an increase in output represents one of the most sustained and rapid economic transformations seen in the world economy in the past 50 years.

The manufacturing industries have been the main drivers for the Chinese national economic growth by attracting a huge amount of capital, expanding investment, production, international trade and meeting the needs of domestic consumers. However, there has been an increasing concern related to increasing energy consumption, pollution, upgrading technologies, improving economic efficiencies, lowering resource utilisation, reducing negative environmental externalities, and fully developing human resources. The Chinese government has formulated and implemented a series of programmes for scientific and technological research and development, aimed at improving China's competitiveness in science and technology in the 21st century. Measuring the degree of the technology innovation efforts indirectly at national aggregate and industry level is an essential research strategy. Therefore, it is necessary to conduct empirical research to investigate productivity growth and its development to fill the gap in our knowledge of Chinese economic growth.

The economic theory of productivity measurement goes back to the work of Tinbergen (1942) and to Solow (1957). They formulated productivity measures in a production function context and linked them to the analysis of economic growth. The field has since developed considerably, particularly following major contributions by Jorgenson (1967), Griliches (1995) and Diewert (1981). The study by Yi begins with a comprehensive review of the general literature investigating productivity growth and in particular the China-related empirical research. Then it focuses on empirical measurements of Chinese productivity growth at national aggregate in the midterm (1978-2004) and industry-level in the short term (1998-2003). A flexible Translog aggregate production function model is specified and estimated using panel data methodology. Yi discusses the determinants of Chinese aggregate economic growth post 1978, the productivity change rate of Chinese industrial sectors and the heterogeneity in growth across industrial sectors during 1998-2003. The main contributions of Yi's research compared with previous studies lies in his focus on the Chinese national aggregate in the midterm and industrial sectors in the short term, by utilisation of updated data set and application of state of the arts econometric methods.

Empirical results suggest that in the midterm the Chinese economy enjoyed a rapid and sustainable growth with some cyclical fluctuations during the period of 1978-2004 with an annual real GDP growth rate of 9.0% on average. The mean annual growth rate of Chinese real capital stock varies from 9.2% to 9.3%, while the average annual growth rate of labour working hours is only 2.4%. The capital and labour elasticities indicate increasing returns to scale in production. The mean of Chinese TFP growth rate is from 6.4% to 6.6% during 1979-2004. In the midterm, both factor inputs and TFP growth are the main determinants of Chinese economic growth post 1978. In addition to these, the main sources of TFP growth are technical efficiency change and scale economy due to the combination and gradual accumulation of capital and labour-saving techniques. The negative pure technical change empirically hints insufficient innovation in Chinese aggregate economy during the study period.

Concerning the industry level analysis during 1998-2003, it is noted that the traditional infrastructure, heavy, chemical and textile industrial sectors are the dominant sources of value added among Chinese industrial sectors. The 36 sectors as a whole enjoy a value added increase of 12.7% per year. The main contributors of the rapid growth are the infrastructure sector (especially, ICT), medical and pharmaceutical products, ordinary machinery, etc. As regards the capital input, the infrastructure sectors take the majority of the total stock of capital. The industrial sectors as a whole enjoy a capital stock increase of 8.6% per year. For the labour input, Textile, Basic materials, Transportation equipment, Ordinary machinery, Equipment for special purposes, and Electric supply takes on more labour. However, the industrial sectors as a whole witness 0.4% per year of employee reduction during the period in contrast with the growth of value added and capital stock. It reflects the reforming effect of improving efficiency, the tendency to be fewer job openings, increased capital intensity in production and a labour surplus.

The returns to scale by sector as a whole suggest a decreasing return to scale during the period. However, there are 8 specific sectors with increasing returns to scale. The industrial sectors as a whole enjoy TFP growth of 10.4% per year during the period 1998-2003. In the short term, both the combination of various input and infrastructure factors and technological progress are the main determinants of industrial growth. The decomposition of industrial TFP growth shows that the exogenous rate of technical change is 11.1% per year while the technical efficiency change is –0.6% per year during the period of study. Therefore, the industrial productivity growth attributes much to the exogenous technological change affecting production processes. It shows the positive impacts of the innovation promotion efforts made by the Chinese government and inflow of FDI and, together with it, acquired management and skills. However, the lower technical efficiency rate indicates the existence of room for reallocation of resources to strengthen further the growth rates.

1.5. Chinese Bilateral Trade Flows

In the empirical applications, the Gravity model is a popular model used for the analysis of international trade flows (Deardorff 1995; Krugman 1979; Helpman and Krugman, 1985; Hummels and Levinsohn, 1995; Baltagi et al., 2003, and others). However, there is a continued debate over the consistency of the gravity model with standard economic trade theories and its applications in the context of developing and developed countries trade relations. It is found that the model is consistent with theories of trade based upon models of imperfect competition and with the Heckscher-Ohlin model. It is proved that it is suitable for explaining the trade among developed and developing countries where inter-industry trade is dominant. More recently, increasing similarity in GDPs among OECD country pairs is shown to lead to higher bilateral trade to GDP ratios. Therefore, based on the wide range of empirical findings, the gravity model is found to be able to characterize a large class of nested models.

The discussion above suggests that it is of great necessity to find out the proper trade model that fits China's trade flows. The trade model used in Zhu is an augmented gravity model in that the standard gravity model includes only income and distance variables. Apart from the distance variable, this model also introduces two other explanatory variables, namely overall bilateral country size and similarity in country size. A third additional variable, the Trade Complementarity Index, is calculated to measure the degree of trade complementarities between China and each OECD member. The index is introduced in the augmented gravity model in an attempt to understand the relevance of the complementarities between countries in the determination of trade flows. The model is specified with various degrees of flexibility and estimated by different estimation methods. Results suggest a positive impact of the New Trade Theory variables and a negative impact of the Distance variable on China's trade flows. A significantly positive impact of the Trade Complementarity Index on bilateral trade has been found in all equations at aggregate level. Thus, in conclusion, the gravity equation in this study finds empirical support for the theory that intra-industry trade and inter-industry trade are both equally critical.

In addition to the estimation at aggregate level, Zhu applies the gravity equation to sectoral level data, namely the top ten sectors in China's trade flows. The estimation results show that all the top ten sectors are characterised with monopolistic competition and increasing returns to scale. These results also reinforce the findings from the estimations at the aggregate level. Finally, Zhu applies the gravity equation to China's trade flows in the ICT arena with respect to the growing importance and instrumental role of the ICT sector. All gravity equations whether at aggregate country level or at industrial level, have found to lend empirical support for firms of relatively larger size to have good chances to survive and succeed. Effective strategies should be designed to encourage economies of scale and operation of scale at the firm level. The negative coefficient of the Distance variable implies a two-way direct foreign investment. Firms should invest in product innovation in order to enhance demand for their diversified products. Concerning the importance of factor endowment, China with abundant labour endowment, will continue to export labour-intensive products, such as textiles and clothing, to capital-abundant economies, such as OECD members. Meanwhile, they will import large amounts of capital-intensive and technology-intensive goods to facilitate an effective technology transfer.

In summation, by means of panel data estimation technique, Zhu applies an augmented gravity model to analyze China's trade with 26 OECD members - China's major trading partners, over the period 1996-2003 at three different levels of aggregation. At aggregate level, Zhu finds empirical support for the New Trade Theory and Heckscher-Ohlin Theory. Furthermore, the gravity equation is applied to the bilateral trade of top ten sectors. Lastly, the gravity equation is applied to the bilateral trade in ICT goods. The empirical findings at the sectoral level reinforce the estimation results at the aggregate level. The empirical findings also carry important and meaningful policy implications. The study has made significant contributions in three aspects. Firstly, this is the first time to apply the gravity model to the Chinese data, as a specific country, to explain its trade patterns and determinants. Secondly, in addition to the standard gravity model, a trade complementarity index is calculated and introduced in the gravity equation in an attempt to find out the peculiarity of China's trade patterns. Thirdly, in view of the heated debate upon the theoretical foundation of the gravity equation, this study finds empirical support for appropriate trade theory by applying the gravity model to the bilateral trade between China, the largest developing country, and selected 26 OECD members, the developed world.

1.6. Income Inequality in China

There is a comprehensive literature on income inequality in China mainly at regional and provincial levels (Tusi 1993; Xu and Zou, 2000; Gustafsson and Shi, 2002; Zheng and Kanbur, 2001). Heshmati in his chapter attempts to fill the gap in the existing literature by focusing on the empirical analysis of income inequality in China. He addresses a number of issues crucial to the studies of income inequality. These are the concepts, measurements and decomposition of inequality, the world distribution of income and inequality measured at different levels such as at the global, continental, international, intra-national and regional levels. Other areas of interest are the relationship between macroeconomic variables, inequality and poverty. Experiences gained from the analysis of these issues are then reflected in the discussion of data differences, their impacts on conclusions drawn and on the discussion of income inequality in China. The results are from the review of literature and his findings based on the World Income Inequality Database (WIID). The chapter which is an extraction of Heshmati (2006) provides a good picture of Chinese income inequality and compares it with the regional and global inequalities.

Inequality has different dimensions and in general it is divided into two broad categories of income and non-income dimensions. Heshmati focuses on income dimensions. Several inequality indices derived from the Lorenz diagram are discussed. The most widely used index of inequality is the Gini coefficient. Decomposition of income inequality at different levels of aggregation is discussed. A comprehensive literature on inequality decomposition is developing to measure variations in inequality and associate it with underlying causal factors. Non-parametric methods have been developed to decompose inequality at the micro level by sub-groups, income sources, causal factors and by other characteristics of units of observations. At the aggregate national level, it is decomposed into within-subgroup and between-subgroups components, while at the international level, it is decomposed into within-country and between-country components. Different non-parametric methods of decomposing the changes in poverty into growth, redistribution and poverty standard components are also suggested. Regression-based methods of decomposition of inequality by income sources have also been proposed. Compared with the former unconditional approach, the latter provides possibilities to quantify the conditional roles of various characteristics in a multivariate context and to construct confidence intervals for different components or causal factors contributions to the inequality index.

Heshmati classifies different existing alternative ways to construct world indices of income distribution and to measure global income inequality (Milanovic 2002; Schultz 1998; Quah 2002; Bourguignon and Morrisson 2002; Sala-i-Martin 2002). Few of these studies compare the world's distribution of income at the individual level. A combined micro and macro data where mean income per capita complemented with some measures of income dispersion or income share from household surveys is often used. In these studies economic growth, population growth, life expectancy, and the changes in the structure of income inequality are found to be important factors determining the evolution of world income distribution. Empirical results show that the world inequality measured as Gini coefficient increased and poverty measured as headcount decreased. Inequality within individual countries is not increasing but inequality between countries and regions is increasing with great impact on world income inequality. However, results based on the WIID database show no evidence of a significant global trend in income inequality over the last 50 years. Inequality is found to be volatile prior to 1970 but more stable and slowly increasing in the post 1986 period.

In addition to global, international and national levels Heshmati considers income inequality at regional level defined as continents or sub-continents. He studies decomposition of inequality within and between regions by looking at inter and intra-regional disparity in income distribution between and within regions consisting of a number of countries. The East Asian countries have been successful in coupling growth and equality mainly prior to the 1997 Asian economic crisis. The entry of China into the world market and the advent of new technology biased against unskilled workers did have major impacts on the inter-regional development of inequality. Results based on WIID database shows large inter-regional heterogeneity in both the level and the development of regional income distribution and income inequality over time. Inequality in Latin America, Eastern Europe and Former Soviet Republics showed increasing trends in the recent decades.

The within-country income inequality at the regional level in a selection of large countries including China, Russia, India and the USA with regional division is examined by Heshmati. The results are based on the second half of the 20th century. Empirical results suggest that the level and development of inequality has differed greatly between geographical locations and economic sectors. China has experienced a rapid economic growth since the economic reform initiated in 1978, accompanied by significant increases within and between regional inequality. In a number of studies, attempts have been made to identify the determinants of inequality across different provinces. There is an indication that regional polarization has been driven by structural differences between regions. Results based on the WIID database show that inequality in US has increased slightly over time. The trend in inequality in India is negative but varies over time. There is a positive trend in inequality in China and Russia during their post-economic reform periods.

In his discussion of data issues, Heshmati (2006) refers to a number of databases that are frequently used in applied global, international, regional and also in national growth and inequality research. Despite these database benefits, limitations and differences by objectives, composition of countries, country coverage, sources, unit of measurement and income definitions, each of them play an important and complementary role in inequality studies. The choice of data is found to affect the conclusion drawn about the trends in inequality for a single country or groups of countries and over time. Quality, consistency, income definition and measurement, changing population and household size and various adjustment procedures are among important data issues discussed by Heshmati. The existing empirical results and conclusions drawn are found to be quite sensitive to the factors mentioned above.

Heshmati, in his summary of the income inequality, emphasises that rising global or national inequality, although undesirable, is not inevitable, as individuals, regions and countries differ in initial conditions, goals and in performance and development potential. It is evident that the wealthy and advanced nations in their capacity as technology leaders and the driving force of development are the main beneficiaries of economic development. Despite such persisting difference, the current world's social situation underlines the argument that, although living standards have improved in many places, poverty remains a serious issue of concern. This, and as a result of the existing technology gap, the global power struggle and tensions will widen further the gap between the rich and the poor calling for immediate action. Growth is considered as an effective means of reducing poverty and achieving the Millennium Development Goals. However, focusing only on economic growth is not an optimal approach to achieve development and equality. Redistribution is often a neglected measure in the debate about the country's development strategy. The multidimensionality of inequality and its overall impact on the poor in form of inequality in income, wealth, opportunity, health, gender issues and education should not be neglected.

1.7. Summary of Key Conclusions and Policy Implications

This volume aims at providing an up-to-date and in-depth analysis of five factors crucial to the success of the policy and current state of the Chinese economy. These include: economic growth, bilateral trade relations, science and technology, flow of foreign direct investment and income (in)equality. Each of the five studies included are to be seen as separate comprehensive studies but yet integrated in many ways. Together they provide a complete and comprehensive picture of the recent developments in the Chinese economy and its path of reform and transition from a centrally planned economy to a modern, and from a development and productivity perspective, well functioning market economy. This volume makes a significant contribution to the existing literature about the Chinese economy. The analyses are based on unique data sets at low levels of aggregation and the use of advanced methods. The data covers the entire reform period and policies and developments. In summary, this volume provides an up-to-date and complete picture of the country's development.

A preliminary analysis of development of key indicators was conducted. The series included: GDP level, GDP per capita, annual growth rate of the Chinese economy, trade volume, private investment expenditure, research and development investment, public investment, labour productivity, inflow of foreign direct investment, population, number of scientists and engineers and income inequality covering the period from 1978 until 2004. Simple descriptive statistics of the data and comparison of the normalized series reveals interesting information. All indicators are positively correlated with time indicating a positive trend in each indicator's development. One exception is the annual economic growth which is negatively correlated over time. The series are of different lengths which affect their relationships. Labour productivity is highly correlated with GDP per capita but it shows a lower association with income inequality.

Since the starting of the process of economic reform, and opening up of the market to the outside world, China has become one of the fastest growing economies in the world. As a result China is now the largest recipient of foreign direct investment in the world. Previous studies of causal relationship between inflow of FDI and economics growth are mainly at the aggregate national level. Studies of determinants of flow of FDI at the provincial level are rare. This volume makes a significant contribution in this respect by examining the causal relationship between China's economic growth and inflow of FDI at the provincial level. Results suggest that the need to focus on regional heterogeneity on FDI flows and economic growth is in favour of using disaggregated provincial data. This helps to shed light on the extent of provincial heterogeneity and inequality in development in China. The estimation results indicate that GDP and FDI have a bi-directional causal relationship. This is interpreted as that the inflow of FDI and rapid economic growth have reinforced each other. Openness and government expenditure are two other factors that are found to have positive effects on GDP and FDI. The overall results show evidence of significant heterogeneous patterns in development and flow of FDI across provinces in China and also over time.

Science parks play a key role and are of growing importance to the economic development particularly to the newly industrialised economies. In this volume, the performance and contributions of these parks to the Chinese economic growth is investigated. Chinese Science Parks are mainly supported by domestic infrastructure and foreign technology and capital. Since Science Parks are in general a quite new phenomenon and especially in China, there is no evaluation of their performance and effects on economic growth. The study here makes a number of contributions by studying an important element of the new economic policy in China. Estimation results show that Science Parks are productive and have grown rapidly which is an indication of a successful science park policy in China. There is significant heterogeneity in parks performance, which is mainly a reflection of differences in their initial conditions and attractiveness to investors. The development enhancing policy measures suggested here include: improvements in the size and quality of the human resources, to pay more attention to the share of technology progress, information technology as an active applied technology should be strongly pushed to improve the productivity of parks, and there are great diversities among the parks in both their capacity and growth speeds implying application of heterogeneous policies to achieve the regional and national targets.

Productivity is increasingly recognized as the key to sustained economic expansion. The pace of economic change in China has been extremely rapid since the start of economic reforms. The manufacturing industries have been the main drivers for the Chinese national economic growth by attracting foreign capital, expanding investment, production, international trade and domestic market. The study in this volume focuses on empirical measurements of Chinese productivity growth at national level in the midterm and at the industrial level in the short term and discusses the determinants of aggregate economic growth and the heterogeneity in growth across industrial sectors. Empirical results suggest that in the midterm, the Chinese economy enjoys a rapid and sustainable growth with some cyclical fluctuations. In the midterm both factor inputs and TFP growth are the main determinants of economic growth. The main sources of TFP growth are technical efficiency change due to the combination and gradual accumulation of capital and saving labour. The negative pure technical change hints at insufficient innovation in Chinese aggregate economy. Concerning the industry level analysis, it is noted that the traditional infrastructure, heavy, chemical and textile industrial sectors are the dominant sources of value added. The main contributors of the rapid growth are infrastructure sector, medical and pharmaceutical products and ordinary machinery. In the case of capital input, the infrastructure sectors absorb the majority of the stock of capital. The industrial sectors as a whole enjoy a high rate of capital stock increase and witness a minor employee reduction. This reflects the reform effect of improving efficiency, increased capital intensity, and tendency for labour surplus. In the short term, both the combination of various input and infrastructure factors and technological progress are the main determinants of industrial growth. The industrial productivity growth attributes much to the exogenous technological change affecting production processes. The lower technical efficiency rate indicates potential for reallocation of resources to strengthen further the economic growth rates of the industrial sector in China.

An attempt was made to find a proper trade model that fits China's trade flows. The Gravity model is a popular model used for analysis of international trade. The model was augmented so that in addition to income and distance variables, overall bilateral country size, similarity in country size and trade complementarity index are included. The model was applied to Chinese trade with its mains OECD trade partners. The model was specified with various degrees of flexibility and estimated by different estimation methods. Results suggest a positive impact of the New Trade Theory variables, a negative impact of the Distance variable and significantly positive impact of the Trade Complementarity Index on bilateral trade at the aggregate level. The results lend support for the theory that intra-industry trade and inter-industry trade are both equally critical to the China's trade flows. In addition to the estimation at the aggregate level, the gravity equation is applied to sectoral level data. The estimation results show that all the top ten sectors are characterized with monopolistic competition and increasing returns to scale. Finally, the model is applied to China's trade flows in ICT arena. All gravity equations lend empirical support for firms of relatively larger size to have good chances to survive and to succeed. Effective strategies should be designed to encourage economies of scale at the firm level. The negative coefficient of Distance variable implies preference for a two-way direct foreign investment. Firms should invest in product innovation in order to enhance demand for their diversified products. Concerning the importance of factor endowment, China with its abundant labour endowment, will continue to export labour-intensive products to capital-abundant OECD economies and it should import a large amount of capital-intensive and technology-intensive goods to facilitate an effective technology transfer.

The increasing income inequality in China has been given great emphasis. This volume addresses a number of issues crucial to the studies of income inequality in China. Results from the review of literature and findings based on the World Income Inequality Database are presented. The study provides a good picture of Chinese income inequality and compares it with the regional and global income inequalities. Several studies show that inequality within individual countries is not increasing but inequality between countries and regions is increasing. However, results based on the WIID database shows no evidence of a significant global trend in income inequality over the last 50 years. The entry of China into the world market and the advent of new technology biased against unskilled workers did have major impacts on the inter-regional development of inequality. Results based on WIID database show large inter-regional heterogeneity in both the level and the development of regional income distribution and income inequality over time. The within-country income inequality at the regional level in a selection of large countries including China, Russia, India and USA with regional (provincial, state or confederation) division is examined. China has experienced a rapid economic growth post the economic reform accompanied by significant increases within and between regional income inequality. In a number of studies, attempts have been made to identify the determinants of inequality across different provinces. There is an indication that regional polarization has been driven by structural differences between regions. There is a positive trend in inequality in China during the post economic reform period. The existing empirical results and conclusions drawn are found to be quite sensitive to data issues. In summary, the rising inequality, although undesirable, is not inevitable, as regions are different in initial conditions and in performance and development potential. Growth is considered as an effective mean of reducing poverty. However, focusing only on economic growth might be sufficient to reduce poverty but not to achieve equality. Redistribution is often a neglected measure in the debate. The multidimensionality of inequality and its overall impact on the poor should not be neglected. The World Bank's shameful one or two dollars per day is not a suitable measure of poverty in a country like China with such economic progress.

REFERENCES

Addison T. and A. Heshmati (2004), The new global determinants of FDI flows to developing countries: the importance of ICT and democratization, Research in Banking and Finance 4, 151-186.

Baltagi B. H., P. Egger and M. Pfaffermayr (2003), A generalized design for bilateral trade flow models, Economics Letters 80(3), 391-397.

Blomstrom M. (1986), Foreign investment and productivity efficiency: the case of Mexico, *Journal of Industrial Economics* 15, 97-110.

Bourguignon F. and C. Morrisson (2002), Inequality among world citizens: 1820-1992, American Economic Reviews 92(4), 727-747.

Castells M. and P. Hall (1994), Technopoles of the World: The Making of 21st Century, Industrial Complexes. London: Routledge.

Cheng L. K. and Y.K. Kwan (1999), Foreign capital stock and its determinants, Foreign Direct Investment and Economic Growth in China, edited by Wu, Y. MPG Books, Great Britain.

Chowdhury A. and G. Mavrotas (2005), FDI and growth: a causal relationship, Research Paper of World Institute for Development Economics Research, United Nations University, No. 2005/25.

Coughlin C. C. and E. Segev (2000), Foreign direct investment in China: A Spatial econometric study, World Economy 21(1), 1-23.

Deardorff A.V. (1995), Determinants of Bilateral Trade: Does Gravity Work in a Neoclassical World?, NBER Working Papers 5377, National Bureau of Economic Research.

Diewert W. E. (1981), The theory of total factor productivity measurement in regulated industries. In T. G. Cowing and R. E. Stevenson (eds), Productivity measurement in regulated industries, Academic Press, New York.

Fung K. C., Iizaka, H., Lin, C. and Shiu, A. (2002), An econometric estimation of locational choices of foreign direct investment: The case of Hong Kong and U.S. firms in China. Asian Development Bank Institute.

Gholami R., Tom Lee S-Y. and A. Heshmati (2006), The Causal Relationship Between Information and Communication Technology and Foreign Direct Investment, *The World Economy* 29(1), 43-62.

Gustafsson B. and L. Shi (2002), Income inequality within and across counties in rural China 1988 and 1995, *Journal of Development Economics* 69(1), 179-204.

Hansson F., K. Husted and J. Vestergaard (2005), Second generation science parks: from structural holes jockeys to social capital catalysts of the knowledge society, Technovation 25, 1039–1049.

Helpman E. and P.R. Krugman (1985), Market structure and foreign trade: Increasing returns, imperfect competition and the international economy, Cambridge, MA, MIT Press.

Heshmati A. (2003), Productivity Growth, Efficiency and Outsourcing in Manufacturing and Services, *Journal of Economic Surveys* 17(1), 79-112.

Heshmati A. (2006), Global Trends in Income Inequality, Nova Science Publishers.

Hummels D. and J. Levinsohn (1995), Monopolistic competition and international trade: Reconsidering the evidence, *The Quarterly Journal of Economics* 110(3), 799-836.

Jorgenson D. W. and Z. Griliches (1967), The explanation of productivity change, *Review of Economic Studies* 34(3), 249-284.

Jussawalla M. and R.D. Taylor (2003), Eds. Information Technology Parks of the Asia Pacific: Lessons for the Regional Digital Divide, M.E. Sharpe, Armonk, New York.

Kokko A. (1994), Technology, market characteristics, and spillovers, *Journal of Development Economics* 43, 279-293.

Kokko A., R. Tansini and M. Zejan (1996), Local technological capability and spillovers from FDI in the Uruguayan manufacturing sector, *Journal of Development Studies* 34, 601-611.

Krugman P. (1979), Increasing returns to scale, monopolistic competition and international trade, *Journal of International Economics* 9(4), 469-479.

Kumar N. and J. P. Pradhan (2002), Foreign direct investment, externalities, and economic growth in developing countries: some empirical explorations and implications for WTO negotiations on investment, RIS discussion papers, Research and Information System for Non-aligned and Other Developing Countries.

Link A. N. and J. T. Scott (2003), U.S. science parks: the diffusion of an innovation and its effects on the academic missions of universities, *International Journal of Industrial Organization* 21, 1323–1356.

Milanovic B. (2002), True world income distribution, 1988 and 1993: First calculation based on household surveys alone, *Economic Journal* 112(476), 51-92.

Nair-Reichert U. and D. Weinhold (2001), Causality tests for cross-country panels: a new look at FDI and economic growth in developing countries, *Oxford Bulletin of Economics and Statistics* 63(2), 153-171.

Quah D. (2002), One third of the world's growth and inequality, LSE, Economics Department, CEPR Discussion Paper 2002:3316.

Sala-i-Martin X. (2002), The world distribution of income, NBER Working Paper 8933.

Schultz T.P. (1998), Inequality in distribution of personal income in the world: how is it changing and why?, *Journal of Population Economics* 11(3), 307-344.

Shiu A. and A. Heshmati (2006), Technical Change and Total Factor Productivity for Chinese Provinces: A Panel Data Analysis, *IZA Discussion Paper* 2006:2133.

Solow R. M. (1957), Technical change and the aggregate production function, *Review of Economics and Statistics* 39, 312-320.

Tinbergen J. (1942), Zur theorie der langfritigen wirtschaftsenwicklung, Weltwirt-shaftliches Archiv 55, 511-549.

Tsui K-Y. (1993), Decomposition of China's regional inequalities, *Journal of Comparative Economics* 17(3), 600-627.

Xu L.C. and H-F. Zou (2000), Explaining the changes of income distribution in China, *China Economic Review* 11, 149-170.

Zhang X. and R. Kanbur (2001), What difference do polarisation measures make? An application to China, *Journal of Development Studies* 37(3), 85-98.

In: Recent Developments in the Chinese Economy
Editor: Almas Heshmati, pp. 35-53
ISBN: 1-60021-449-5
© 2007 Nova Science Publishers, Inc.

Chapter 2

THE CAUSAL RELATIONSHIP BETWEEN FDI AND ECONOMIC GROWTH: RESULTS BASED ON CHINESE PROVINCIAL DATA*

Wang Boyong[1]
Techno-Economics and Policy Program
College of Engineering, Seoul National University
San 56-1, Shinlim-dong, Kwanak-gu
Seoul 151-742, Korea

ABSTRACT

Since the start of the process of economic reform, and opening up of the market to the outside world in 1978, China has become one of the fastest growing economies in the world. As a result, China is now the largest recipient of FDI in the world. In this paper, I examine the causal relationship between China's economic growth and inflow of FDI using fixed effects and instrumental variables panel data approaches. For the empirical analysis, data at the provincial level is used. The sequence of specification and estimation methods tests indicates that GDP and FDI have a bi-directional causal relationship in China, which means that inflow of FDI and rapid economic growth have reinforced each other. Openness and government expenditure are also found to have positive effects on GDP and FDI. The results show evidence of significant heterogeneous patterns in development and flow of FDI across provinces and over time.

Keywords: FDI, economic growth, causality testing, China

---

* I would like to express my appreciation to Professor Heshmati, who provided precious instructions and strong support to this paper.
[1] E-mail: wangboyong_ren@hotmail.com

1. INTRODUCTION

There is no consensus on the relationship between foreign direct investment (FDI) and economic growth. However, there is a growing view in recent years that FDI is positively correlated with growth. Theoretically, this view has been supported by recent developments in growth theory, which highlight the importance of improvements in technology, efficiency, and productivity in stimulating growth. In this regard, FDI's contribution to growth comes through its role as a channel for transferring advanced technology from the industrialized to the developing economies. For instance, Findlay (1978) postulates that FDI increases the rate of technical progress in the host country through a "contagion" effect from the more advanced technology and management practices used by foreign firms.

This contagion or knowledge diffusion (often referred to as "spillovers") can lead to improvements in productivity and efficiency of local firms in several ways. FDI may provide better access to technologies for the local economy. Moreover, FDI can also lead to indirect productivity gains through spillovers. For instance, multinational firms may increase the degree of competition in host-country markets, which will force existing inefficient firms to invest more in physical or human capital. Multinational corporations (MNCs) may also provide training of labor and management, which may make them become productive forces to the economy in general. Another possible channel for spillovers is the training of local suppliers of intermediate products to meet the higher standards of production and managerial standard.

Empirically, there appears to be good evidence that FDI efficiency spillovers exist. For developed countries, the evidence available indicates fairly consistently that the productivity of domestically owned firms is positively related to the presence of foreign firms (Caves, 1974; Xu, 2000; Globerman, Kokko, and Sjoholm, 2000). For developing countries, the results are also generally positive, although somewhat mixed, with a number of studies showing a higher foreign presence increasing productivity in host country sectors, but others pointing to limited or no efficiency spillovers. For instance, Blomstrom (1986) and Kokko (1994) find econometric evidence of positive FDI spillovers for Mexico; Kokko, Tansiniand Zejan (1996), for Uruguay; and Sjoholm (1999) for Indonesia. Aitken, Hanson, and Harrison (1997) find that in general, foreign manufacturing investors in Mexico act as export catalysts for domestic firms—the probability of a Mexican-owned plant engaging in exports is positively correlated with its proximity to MNCs, after controlling for various other factors. As such, they conclude that the export spillovers they observe must spring directly or indirectly from ways in which the foreign investors act as a conduit for technology, management, distribution services, and information about foreign markets. However, Aitken and Harrison (1991) find only limited or no evidence for Venezuela; and Harrison (1996) finds that while joint ventures in Morocco and Venezuela exhibit higher productivity levels than their domestic counterparts, there is no evidence of positive short run spillovers from foreign to domestic firms. Harrison (1996) suggests that in the short run FDI may adversely affect domestic firms by taking away market share and leading to reduced capacity utilization for the firms, although that does not rule out positive spillovers over the longer run.

Meanwhile, there is evidence that economic growth is a crucial determinant of attracting FDI (Cheng and Kwan 1998, Dee 1998, Coughlin and Segev 2000, Fung *et al*, 2002). The outcomes of rapid economic growth are the emergence of huge domestic markets and increased per capita income along with the emergence of a large middle class in urban and rural areas. This could be an important reason to attracted foreign investments.

There is a growing number of researches conducting causal test of the relationship between FDI and economic growth, especially for developing countries, to provide the straightforward insights.

Nair-Reichert and Weinhold (2001) use a panel of 24 developing countries from 1971 to 1995 to analyze the dynamic relationship between FDI and economic growth. They find that the relationship between investment, both foreign and domestic, and economic growth in developing countries is highly heterogeneous. There is some evidence that the efficacy of FDI in raising future growth rates is higher in more open economies.

Kumar and Pradhan (2002) analyze the relationships between FDI, growth and domestic investment for a sample of 107 developing countries for the period of 1980-1999. Panel data estimations in a production function framework suggest a positive effect of FDI on growth. However, tests of causality find that in a majority of cases the direction of causation is not pronounced and in a substantial number of cases the direction of causation actually runs from growth to FDI.

Chowdhury and Mavrotas (2005) examine the causal relationship between FDI and economic growth by studying the direction of causality between the two variables. They use time-series data covering the period 1969-2000 for three developing countries, namely Chile, Malaysia and Thailand, all of them major recipients of FDI with a different history of macroeconomic episodes, policy regimes and growth patterns. Their empirical findings clearly suggest that in the case of Chile, it is GDP that causes FDI and not vice versa. While for both Malaysia and Thailand, there is a strong evidence of a bi-directional causality between the two variables.

The world is rapidly moving toward an information-based economy. Thus the new factors for FDI, for instance information and communication technology (ICT), are introduced in some literatures recently. Addison and Heshmati (2004) examine the determinants of FDI, using a large sample of countries. Their findings suggest that ICT increases inflows of FDI to developing countries mainly because ICT lowers the transaction and production costs of foreign investors, as well as improving their access to information on alternative investment opportunities in poorer economies.

Gholami, Lee and Heshmati (2006) examine the relationship between FDI and ICT with time-series and panel data analysis methods including least square dummy variables and instrumental variable estimation methods. Results from the Granger causality test indicate that there is a significant short-run causal relationship between the variables among the countries. However, the results differ according to the country's level of development. In developed countries, existing ICT infrastructure attracts FDI, which suggests that ICT contributes to productivity and economic growth indirectly by attracting more FDI. But in developing countries the direction of causality instead goes from FDI to ICT, which means ICT capacity must be built up in order to attract FDI. The inflow of FDI causes further increases in ICT investment and production capacity building.

Shiu and Heshmati (2006) estimate the rate of technical change and total factor productivity (TFP) growth of 30 Chinese provinces during the period of 1993 to 2003. The random effects model with heteroscedastic variances has been used for the estimation of the translog production functions. Two alternative formulations of technical change measured by the single time trend and the general index approach are used. Based on the measures of technical change, estimates of TFP growth are obtained and its determinants examined using regression analysis. TFP has recorded positive growth for all provinces during the sample period. Foreign direct investment and information and communication technology investment are found to be significant factors contributing to the TFP difference. While these two factors are found to have significant influence on TFP, their influence on production is relatively small compared to traditional inputs of production.

To my knowledge, such causality studies at provincial level are rare. The contribution of this paper is that I use a panel of 29 provinces of China to test the causal relationship between FDI and economic growth. The need to focus on regional heterogeneity on FDI-flow and economic growth is in favor of using disaggregated data. This will help to shed light on the extent of provincial inequality in China. This paper focuses on the macroeconomic perspective of growth and its correlation with inflow FDI. I use fixed effects and instrument variable panel data approaches in the latter part of this paper.

The organization of the paper is as follows. In section 2, I review the current state of FDI in China. I explain the methodology and data in section 3 and 4. Section 5 presents the estimation results, followed by the conclusion in the final section.

2. FDI IN CHINA

An important part of the economic reform process in China has been the promotion of FDI inflow. After more than twenty years of active economic reform, China has become one of the most important destinations for cross-border direct investment among both developing and developed countries.

2.1 Evolution of China's FDI Policy

2.1.1. The Initial Phase (1979-1985)

The promulgation of the Equity Joint Venture Law (Sino-foreign Joint Ventures) in July 1979 formally opened up China's market to the world. The law provided the legal framework for foreign investors to form equity joint ventures with Chinese partners. A number of related laws and regulations in regard to labor management, taxation, registration and foreign exchange were soon formulated.

Later in 1979, Guangdong and Fujian were granted special autonomy in dealing with foreign trade and investment by the central government. Furthermore, four Special Economic Zones (SEZs) were established within the two provinces in 1980. The authorities of local government in the SEZs had independent power to draw up and implement development plans, examine and approve investment projects, issue licenses and land-use permits, and coordinate the work of banking, taxation, customs and frontier inspection (Fu, 2000), the establishment of the SEZs had four objectives:

- To attract not only foreign capital, but also advanced technology, both hardware and software;
- To promote export-led growth, in other words, to accelerate exports, create local employment, and generate foreign exchange;
- To serve as 'policy laboratories', where policies can be tested which, if successful, could then be adopted elsewhere in China; and
- To enhance the link of Hong Kong, Macao and Taiwan with mainland China.

In 1984, the government announced 14 coastal port cities would open to foreign trade and development. The state government further decentralized its power to these open cities. The local governments of the 14 open cities were allowed autonomy to plan the legal framework and regulations for foreign investment.

2.1.2. Development Phase (1986-1991)

In 1986, the state promulgated the "Law on Enterprises Operated Exclusively with Foreign Capital" and the "Provision on Encouraging Foreign Investment" with regard to wholly foreign owned enterprises (WFOEs). These policies lifted the restrictions on foreign ownership, and implemented new incentives and removed uncertainties for foreign investors. For joint ventures involving advanced technology, developing new products and producing export substitutes could lead to additional tax benefits.

After the new policies and incentives were promulgated in 1986, investments into China increased dramatically. Between 1986 and 1991, the total foreign investment actually used was US$33.2 billion, an average of US$6.6 billion per year. These figures increased by 142 percent compared with the previous period.

2.1.3. High-Growth Period (1992 onwards)

After the southern tour of former leader Deng Xiaoping in 1992, a large amount inflow of foreign capital surged into China in the period of high growth. He urged the country to accelerate economic reform and open up further. The reform policy in the 1990s shifted from coastal regions to western and mid areas. This was mainly because the large amounts of foreign investment in the coastal areas caused remarkable income inequality between the east and west of China. The Chinese government began to open up more inland cities and regions to foreign investment.

In December 2001, China became the 143rd member of WTO. The state government has committed to a wide range of reforms as part of WTO accession in late 1990s and early 2000s, such as enhancing transparency, improving intellectual property protection, continuously reducing tariffs, etc. Foreign investors could now have confidence in investing in China due to the reforms within the nation and the entry to WTO. In the period from 2002 to 2005, the annual realized FDI inflows grew strongly and reached US$50-60 billion. This growth phenomenon is expected to continue in the future.

2.2. Current Situation of FDI in China

As a result of the active government promotion through various policy measures, FDI in China has grown rapidly since the 1978, especially in the 1990s. From early 1980s to 2003, contracted FDI inflow to China has grown from about US$ 500 million a year to more than US$ 100 billion a year in 2003 (see Table 1). During the same period, China's actual use of FDI has grown from about US$ 9 million to more than US$ 50 billion per year.

Table 1. FDI Stock as of Year-end

Unit: US$1 billion

Year	No. of Projects	Contractual Value	Realized Value
1979-1990	29,525	40.615	20.692
1991	12,978	11.977	4.366
1992	48,764	58.124	11.008
1993	83,437	111.436	27.515
1994	47,549	82.680	33.767
1995	37,011	91.282	37.521
1996	24,556	73.276	41.726
1997	21,001	51.003	45.257
1998	19,799	52.102	45.463
1999	16,918	41.223	40.319
2000	22,347	62.380	40.715
2001	26,140	69.195	46.878
2002	34,171	82.768	52.743
2003	41,081	115.070	53.505
Total	465,277	943.129	499.760

Source: FDI Statistic, Ministry of Commerce, current value.

* There are gaps between contractual and realized values. When the investment projects are implemented, the contractual value becomes realized value. Contractual value indicates the potential of FDI-flow in the near future.

Table 2. Inflow of FDI by region in 2001

Unit: US$1 billion

Region	Value	Global share%
World Total	735.146	100.00
Developed countries	503.144	68.44
European Union	322.954	43.93
Other Western Europe	13.256	1.80
North America	151.900	20.66
Other developed countries	15.034	2.05
Developing countries	204.801	27.86
Africa	17.165	2.33
Latin America	85.373	11.61
Asia	102.066	13.88
West Asia	4.133	0.56
Central Asia	3.569	0.49
East, South and Southeast Asia	94.365	12.84
The Pacific	0.198	0.03
Central and Eastern Europe	27.200	3.70

Source: the *World Investment Report* of the UN, current value

China has been the world's largest FDI recipient among developing countries since the early 1990s. In recent years, FDI to China accounts for 1/4 to 1/3 of total FDI inflow to developing countries. (See Table 2)

In China, the main sector in which MNCs invest is manufacturing sector, where foreign equity capital mainly consists of fixed assets, such as machine equipments, houses, etc. Table 3 shows that the proportion of actual utilized FDI in total fixed assets investment raised dramatically in the early 1990s, and declined steadily since 1994. In recent years, this proportion has maintained constant at the level of slightly more than 10 percent. While in 2003, there was a sharp drop due to the total investment in fixed assets' rapidly rising.

Table 3. FDI to China as a percentage of total investment in fixed assets for 1992-2003

Unit: US$1 billion

Year	Total Investment in Fixed Assets		Realized FDI	Share in Fixed Asset Investment
	RMB 1 billion	$US Equivalent	in $1 bil.	(%)
1992	808.01	146.522	11.008	7.51
1993	1307.23	226.871	27.515	12.13
1994	1704.23	197.734	33.767	17.08
1995	2001.93	239.723	37.521	15.65
1996	2297.40	276.322	41.726	15.10
1997	2530.00	305.997	45.257	14.79
1998	2845.70	343.729	45.462	13.23
1999	2897.60	360.800	40.318	11.17
2000	3261.90	394.426	40.715	10.32
2001	3689.80	445.811	46.846	10.51
2002	4320.20	522.394	52.743	10.10
2003	5556.70	671.342	53.505	7.97

Source: China's Statistical Yearbook, FDI Statistic

Note: $US Equivalents are based on the average exchange rate of the year concerned

Many people believe that foreign capital in China has played a large positive role in China's economic development during the reform period. They argue that FDI can generate more benefits than just helping to solve the capital shortage problem in a developing country like China. More so, FDI's contagion or spillover effect can lead to improvements in productivity and efficiency in indigenous firms, thus promoting the economic growth.

From Figure 1, we can see that FDI growth fluctuates more than GDP, especially during the period of 1992-1994. For the rest of the time, they seem to have similar trends. Actually the watershed of FDI came in 1992, when Deng Xiaoping gave his famous speech endorsing continued market reforms and rapid growth, and the size of FDI flows into China soon accelerated, especially from industrialized countries. It was also at this time that the Chinese domestic market became more open to foreign firms. The rollback of FDI appeared in 1994 due to the Chinese government's cooling an overheating economy and discouraging FDI in real estate.

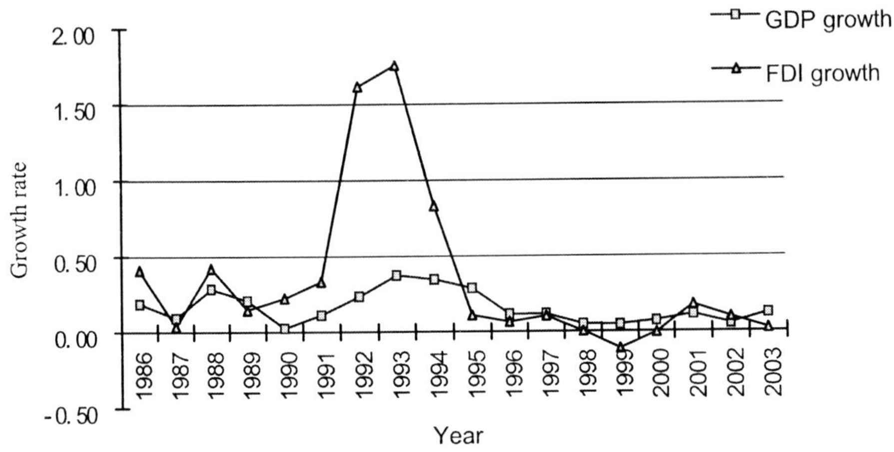

Figure 1. Growth rate of GDP and FDI (1986-2003).

2.3. Studies of China's FDI

Many researchers believe that FDI may raise productivity levels among local firms in the industries, which they enter by improving the allocation of resources in those industries. MNCs may develop new products and technologies earlier than local firms, and may exert competitive pressure on them and force them to imitate or innovate. The threat of competition may also spur firms, which might otherwise have been laggards to adopt best practice technology. As a result, the presence of MNCs may speed up the process or lower the cost of technology transfer. MNCs always try to preserve their proprietary rights over knowledge and technology, but spillovers through 'learning by doing' or 'learning by watching' may induce domestic firms to attain higher levels of technical efficiency. Another route for the diffusion of new ideas is the movement of labor from foreign subsidiaries to locally owned firms.

FDI is believed to promote exports, which in turn will promote economic development and growth in the host country. If there are substantial differences in factor endowments between the host and home countries, the capital-abundant country tends to export capital-intensive services (e.g. R&D and marketing) and intermediate inputs to their subsidiaries in the labor-abundant country in exchange for finished varieties of differentiated goods and homogeneous goods. Thus, FDI generates complementary trade flows. For all these reasons, FDI is recognized as a major source of growth, especially in developing countries.

The growth of FDI has been accompanied by China's outstanding progress in foreign trade and economic growth. During the period 1978-2003, China achieved an average GDP growth rate of around 9 per cent per annum. Foreign trade also expanded dramatically. In the world league tables for international trade, China ranked 32nd in 1978, however, it dramatically moved up to become the 4th largest trading country in 2003.

Meanwhile, there are also concerns that FDI may bring detrimental effect to the Chinese economy. Some people claim that foreign capital inflows can have a negative impact on China's development by substituting for domestic savings. The severe competition that followed by the entrance of MNCs may bring negative effects to domestic corporations. Some also consider that the presence of FDI will in a sense eliminate domestic R&D and have a negative impact in the long term on local capabilities.

There are a number of studies focusing on the effects of inward FDI on economic development or growth in China. Some are largely descriptive supported by simple statistical or enterprise survey data, while others are based on econometric analyses.

Based on the Porter-Dunning Diamond model of international competitiveness, Liu and Song (1997) argue that FDI promotes China's economic growth via its influence on demand and supply conditions, business strategy and competition. The economic reform and open-door policy has enabled China to translate its natural comparative advantage into economic growth and international competitiveness in a wide range of labor-intensive commodities. China needs to link its economy more closely not only to the Asian Newly Industrialized Economies (NIEs) but also to other economies, especially those of the triad (Japan, Europe, and North America) and develop higher order competitiveness ahead of the current factor endowments.

Dayal-Gulati and Husain (2000) and Zhang (2001) attempted to identify possible structural variations over time. The authors conduct panel and/or cross-sectional studies for three sub-periods. In Dayal-Gulati and Husain, it seems that FDI had a much more positive and significant impact on China's economic growth during 1993-97 period than during 1983-87, but it had no significant effects during 1988-92. In Zhang (2001), over the periods of 1984-88, 1989-93 and 1994-98, the impact of FDI on growth appeared to increase, with growth in FDI. Liu (2002), using data on 29 manufacturing industries over the period from 1993 to 1998 in the Shenzhen Special Economic Zone of China, finds that FDI has large and significant spillover effects in that it raises both the level and growth rate of productivity of manufacturing industries, and domestic sectors are the main beneficiaries.

One problem with these studies is that they treat FDI as an exogenous variable in the regression equations. Actually China's fast economic growth may have induced large volumes of FDI into China as it has rendered China attractive to foreign investors. Failure to consider the endogeneity issue may lead to ambiguous results.

Shan, Tian and Sun (1997) test the causal link between the inflow FDI and real output growth of China, based upon quarterly time series data and a vector autoregression (VAR) model applying the Granger causality procedure. The results emerging from their research indicate a two-way Granger causality running between output growth and FDI inflows, that is, the inflow of FDI and rapid industrial growth in China have reinforced each other.

Liu, Burridge and Sinclair (2002) investigate the causal links between trade, economic growth and FDI in China at the aggregate level. The integration and cointegration properties of quarterly data are analyzed. Long-run relationships between growth, exports, imports and FDI are identified in a cointegration framework, in which they find bi-directional causality between economic growth, FDI and exports. They argue that economic development, exports and FDI appear to be mutually reinforcing under the China's open-door policy.

In this paper, I examine the causal relationship between China's economic growth and inflow of FDI at the provincial level. The advantage of this study compared with the studies discussed above is in capturing regional heterogeneity in FDI inflows and its impacts on economic growth. This heterogeneity is a major source if regional inequality in development and welfare of Chinese citizens.

3. Methodology and Models[2]

The causal relationship between FDI and economic growth is studied using fixed or random effects and instrumental variable panel data approaches. A comparison of the results based on the different approaches would show the sensitivity of causal relationship between the two variables.

3.1 Panel Data Causality Analysis

By using the traditional time series Granger causality test, as a benchmark, the introduction of a panel data dimension allows using both cross-sectional and time-series information to test the causality relationships between two variables y and x. In particular, it provides the researcher with a large number of observations, increasing the degree of freedom and reducing the multi-collinearity among explanatory variables. So, it noticeably improves the efficiency of Granger causality tests. The advantage of pooling cross-sectional units is that the assumption of time stationarity can be relaxed. In estimating the causal relationship I use the following VAR model:

$$GDP_{it} = a_1 + \sum_{m=1}^{M} a_m GDP_{i,t-m} + \sum_{n=1}^{N} b_n FDI_{i,t-n} + \sum_{k=1}^{K} e_k X_{i,t-k} + u_{it} \quad (1)$$

$$FDI_{it} = a_2 + \sum_{m=1}^{M} c_m FDI_{i,t-m} + \sum_{n=1}^{N} d_n GDP_{i,t-n} + \sum_{k=1}^{K} f_k X_{i,t-k} + \omega_{it} \quad (2)$$

where *GDP* is the total volume *GDP* of province i (i = 1,..., N) in period t (t = 1,...,T), u_{it} and ω_{it} are the error terms, *FDI* is the total volume *FDI* of province i (i = 1,..., N). X denotes the control variables, which are economy openness and government expenditure, and are defined as the trade (import plus export) share of GDP, and the percentage of government expenditure to GDP, respectively. The error term follows a two-way error component structure (Baltagi, 2001) and can be broken down into an unobservable country-specific (μ_i), a time-specific (λ_t), and a random error (v_{it}) components as:

$$u_{it} = \mu_i + \lambda_t + v_{it} \quad (3)$$

The random error error component v_{it} represents measurement errors in the dependent variable and omitted explanatory variables and random shocks. It is assumed to be independently and identically distributed with zero mean and constant variance, σ^2. Similar

[2] Section 3, Methodology and models, is based on the study of Gholami, Lee and Heshmati (2006) and Addison and Heshmati (2004). The GDP deflators were also provided by Professor Almas Heshmati.

decomposition applies to ω_{it}. The country and time-specific effects, μ_i and λ_t, are factors representing country heterogeneity and neutral shift in the GDP growth over time respectively and assumed to be independent of each other and of the regressors. In the literature, the unobservable country effects μ_i are represented by country dummies and the time effects λ_t are often replaced with a time trend reducing the two way error component model structure to a one-way error component model.

In the panel literature, the estimation of the model (1) has been developed in two directions, the fixed effect (FE) model where μ_i is assumed to be fixed and can be correlated with explanatory variables, and the random effects (RE) model where μ_i is assumed to be random and not correlated with the explanatory variables. In general and likewise in this study, choosing FE or RE model will depend upon the results of Hausman test.

3.2 A Method of Instrumental Variables

I also apply Holtz-Eakin et al. (1988) model to conduct the causality test. The Holtz-Eakin model is written as:

$$y_{it} = \alpha_0 + \sum_{j=1}^{m} \alpha_j y_{i,t-j} + \sum_{j=1}^{m} \delta_j x_{i,t-j} + f_i + u_{it} \tag{4}$$

where i =1...N. In order to eliminate the fixed effects, f_i, the authors difference the data leading to the first difference model:

$$y_{it} - y_{i,t-1} = \sum_{j=1}^{m} \alpha_j (y_{i,t-j} - y_{i,t-j-1}) + \sum_{j=1}^{m} \delta_j (x_{i,t-j} - x_{i,t-j-1}) + (u_{it} - u_{i,t-1}) \tag{5}$$

This specification wipes out the fixed effects but it introduces a problem of simultaneity because the error term is correlated with the regressor $y_{i,t-j} - y_{i,t-j-1}$. Therefore, a Two Stage Least Square (2SLS) instrumental variables procedure with a time-varying set of instruments is used to estimate the model. The authors then equate the question of whether or not x causes y with a test of the joint hypothesis: H0: $\delta_1 = \delta_2 = ... = \delta_m = 0$

If x and y have bi-direction causal relationship, the instrumental variables method 3SLS will instead be applied to conduct the regression analysis.

Instrumental variables method is used to account for the endogeneity of the regressors. This method can be used when standard regression estimates of the relation of interest are biased because of reverse causality, selection bias, measurement error, or the presence of unmeasured confounding effects. The central idea is to use a third, instrumental variable to extract variation in the variable of interest that is unrelated to the above problems, and to use this variation to estimate its causal effect on an outcome measure. The 2SLS and/or 3SLS estimator increases computational efficiency without detracting significantly from its effectiveness.

4. THE DATA

The data used in this study is a balanced panel consisting of a sample of China's 29 provinces observed for the period 1995-2003. The data is collected from the China's Statistical Yearbooks (1996-2004, China State Statistical Bureau) and China's FDI Statistic (Ministry of Commerce).

This study focuses on the macroeconomic perspective of growth and its correlation with inflow of FDI. I define GDP and FDI as annual total volumes of GDP and FDI of each province, both are in logarithmic forms.

The control variables are openness and government expenditure, which are defined as the trade (import plus export) share of GDP, and the percentage of government expenditure to GDP, respectively.

All variables are transformed to constant values. GDP is deflated using the GDP deflator (1995 prices) of each province for each year, and FDI is revised using Fixed-asset Investment Index[3]. In this study, I use the provincial price indices which are derived from GDP deflator for each province to make the estimation more accurate.

5. ESTIMATION RESULTS

The causal relationship between the likely interdependent variables of GDP and FDI is studied using fixed and random effects, and instrumental variable panel data approaches. The results are discussed below.

5.1 Fixed and Random Effects Models

To conduct the panel data causality test, firstly I should decide whether to use FE or RE models. Hence I use the Hausman test to determine the choice. The result of Hausman test suggest that the FE model is the preferred model, which means that μ_i is assumed to be fixed and possibly correlated with explanatory variables. More so, according to the results of autocorrelation function (ACF) and partial autocorrelation function (PACF), GDP lagged one and two periods have the strongest relationship with present GDP value, the same situation happens with FDI. Therefore equation (1) and (2) can be simplified as:

$$GDP_{it} = a_0 + a_1 GDP_{i,t-1} + a_2 GDP_{i,t-2} + b_1 FDI_{i,t-1} + b_2 FDI_{i,t-2} + \sum_{k=1}^{K} e_k X_{i,t-k} + u_{it} \tag{6}$$

[3] The index of FDI has been included in the Fixed-asset Investment Index in China's Statistical Yearbooks.

$$FDI_{it} = a_3 + c_1 FDI_{i,t-1} + c_2 FDI_{i,t-2} + d_1 GDP_{i,t-1} + d_2 GDP_{i,t-2} + \sum_{k=1}^{K} e_k X_{i,t-k} + \omega_{it} \quad (7)$$

The causality test results of FE panel data based on equation (6) and (7) are shown in Table 4, which shows that FDI lagged 1 period causes GDP and, GDP lagged 1 period causes FDI. That is, GDP and FDI have a bi-direction causal relationship. With regard to the control variables, openness and government expenditure are both positively and significantly affecting GDP. As for the FDI, openness and government expenditure have positive effects too, while only the coefficient of government expenditure is statistically significant.

Table 4. Results from the fixed effects model causality test

	Dependent variables		Causality inference
	GDP (t ratio)	FDI (t ratio)	
FDI lagged 1 period	0.083 (2.114)**	0.184 (3.089)***	FDI→GDP
FDI lagged 2 periods	-0.032 (-0.837)	0.024 (0.444)	
GDP lagged 1 period	0.770 (11.14)***	0.222 (2.026)**	GDP→FDI
GDP lagged 2 periods	0.007 (0.103)	-0.067 (-0.724)	
Openness	0.538 (4.054)***	0.556 (1.210)	
Expenditure	1.890 (1.937)*	4.733 (3.448)***	
Adjusted R square	0.8274	0.9286	
F test	155.61	94.14	
RMSE	0.9501	1.8605	

Notes: ***, **, * indicate 1%, 5% and 10% significance levels respectively. Null hypothesis: row explanatory variables do not cause the column dependent variables.

5.2. Instrumental Variable Method

Firstly, I apply 2SLS to test the causal relationship. The 2SLS method has the advantage of accounting for the endogeneity with estimation of each equation. The result of 2SLS (See Table 5) shows that the first difference of GDP (ΔGDP) and FDI (ΔFDI) also has the bi-direction causal relationship. Therefore I continue to conduct the 3SLS method to test the relationship. The result of 3SLS method is shown in Table 6. Again, GDP and FDI have a two-way causal relationship. Analysis of the result in the subsequent sections will mainly be based on the 3SLS results.

5.3. Discussion of the Results

5.3.1. Causality Relationship

The results from the fixed effects and instrumental variables panel data model all indicate that GDP and FDI have a bi-direction causal relationship for China. In other words, the inflow of FDI and rapid economic growth in China have reinforced each other.

Table 5. Results from 2SLS causality test

	Dependent variables		Causality inference
	ΔGDP (t ratio)	ΔFDI (t ratio)	
ΔFDI	0.143 (2.827)***	0.255 (3.690)***	FDI→GDP
ΔGDP	0.501 (444.283)***	0.887 (3.553)***	GDP→FDI
Openness	-0.084 (-0.847)	0.247 (1.666)*	
Expenditure	0.095 (0.153)	0.460 (0.468)	
Adjusted R square	0.0718	0.1946	
F test	11.58	23.47	
RMSE	0.4352	0.8109	

Notes: ***, **, * 1%, 5% and 10% indicate significance levels respectively. Null hypothesis: row explanatory variables do not cause the column dependent variables.

Table 6. Results from 3SLS causality test

	Dependent variables		Causality inference
	GDP (t ratio)	FDI (t ratio)	
FDI lagged 1 period	0.097 (2.445)**	0.658 (9.657)***	FDI→GDP
FDI lagged 2 periods	-0.055 (-1.390)	0.123 (1.817)*	
GDP lagged 1 period	0.907 (23.997)***	0.313 (4.818)***	GDP→FDI
GDP lagged 2 periods	0.054 (1.383)	-0.120 (-0.822)	
Openness	0.482 (3.519)***	1.741 (7.392)***	
Expenditure	1.265 (2.230)**	2.296 (2.356)**	
Adjusted R square	0.8073	0.8519	
F test	156.56	214.69	
RMSE	0.9466	1.8557	

Notes: ***, **, * 1%, 5% and 10% indicate significance levels respectively. Null hypothesis: row explanatory variables do not cause the column dependent variables.

On one hand, the outstanding economic performance in China during the 1990s was propelled by strong FDI inflow in helping China to access overseas markets, improving technology and supplementing domestic saving and investment. Lemione and Unal-Kesenci (2004) showed that China's outstanding performance is directly linked to its integration into international segmentation of production processes. On the other hand, China has benefited from the very rapid growth of domestic demand and hence a high level of domestic investment which has enabled China to achieve a rapid economic growth. Therefore, the outcomes of this rapid economic growth in China are the emergence of huge domestic markets and increased per capita income along with the emergence of a large middle class in urban and rural areas. This has attracted foreign investments into China to dominate China's huge domestic market and to take advantage of China's natural and labor resources.

The empirical studies, which are in agreement among almost all of the researchers, show that investment, consumption, and export are three major engines for Chinese economic development. FDI eventually enhance export, in particular when firms investing in a foreign country continue to source capital goods and intermediary products from their home country. In recent years, the share of MNE subsidiaries' export volume has accounted for a half of total export turnovers of China. Through the production chains, FDI also help local corporations to access global markets. In addition, the MNE subsidiaries, especially the export-oriented FDI provide a large amount employment positions, and the salary of the employee in MNE subsidiaries are comparably higher than those in domestic companies, therefore FDI could promote domestic consumption indirectly through employment providing and higher salary.

Chinese government hopes to attract FDI using the huge domestic market and to promote the technological progress and managerial levels of domestic enterprises though inflow of FDI. Since the late 1970s, Chinese government has implemented a policy named "trade technology with market". Although Chen et al. (1995), and Young and Lan (1997) indicate that technology transfer from FDI is relatively low. More researchers indicate that there exist technology spillover through FDI, and the effects of the spillover are dependent upon the absorptive capabilities, which consist of domestic R&D, human capital, competition, government policy and infrastructure, etc.

5.3.2. Conditional variables

The control variables, openness and government expenditure, are also found to have positive effects on GDP and FDI. In fixed effects panel data causality test, the positive effects of openness and government expenditure on GDP are statistically significant, and the effect of government expenditure on FDI is significant too. While in the causality test using 3SLS, the effects of openness and government expenditure on both GDP and FDI are significant.

Openness is the indicator that shows the relationship between trade and GDP. Export promotion is a major aim of FDI policy in China. The government has been creating an export-promoting trade regime for FDI with minimum administrative interference. Along with the inflow FDI, the import of foreign investments is also increasing. The share of MNE subsidiaries' export volume on total export turnovers of China has increased substantially during 1990s. It accounted for a half of export volume in recent years. Higher openness can promote export and facilitate foreign investments, thus showing a positive effect to GDP and FDI.

The main structure of government expenditure is to create capital stock, culture, education and health care expenses, and administration expenses. As a developing country whose economy is rapidly growing, government expenditure still plays an important role in domestic investment, especially in infrastructure building areas. As the important part of domestic investment, government expenditure enhances economic growth. More so, better infrastructure, which is built by government expenditure, can also facilitate foreign investments. Furthermore, the expenditure that is allocated into the education sectors improves local human resources. Borensztein, Gregorio, and Lee (1995) suggest that the higher productivity of FDI holds only when the host country has a minimum threshold stock of human capital. Meanwhile, high level of human capital itself is an attractive factor to FDI.

5.3.3. Provincial Heterogeneity

The Chinese economic growth process since 1978 has been accompanied by the evolution of a new economic geography, which is characterized by a steep east-west slope of economic development. The provinces located in China's eastern coast belt have experienced the most dynamic growth processes while the central and even more so the western provinces have been lagging behind in development. The panel data approaches allow for the heterogeneity in responses by different provinces. The GDP and FDI general performances of each province are shrinking following the sequence of eastern, central and western provinces.

Some provinces in the west region, such as Qinghai, Gansu and Guizhou are lacking high skilled human resources, afflicted by environmental problems, and lagging behind in infrastructure development and private investment. These are the main disadvantages for these provinces to attract more FDI. On one hand, these provinces seem to have to enhance the fundamental conditions, such as relevant human resources, infrastructure to attract more FDI. On the other hand, the imbalanced development between provinces in a sense can generate transfer of FDI, since the costs for some investments in eastern areas are increasing and FDI will transfer the investments to other provinces in which the costs are comparably lower enhancing their competitiveness.

In an effort to close this economic gap, the Chinese government launched the policy of "Western Development Strategy" in January 2000. The Strategy is a top-down effort to steer state investment, outside expertise, FDI and private capital into the parts of China most in need but least likely to attract aid on their own. FDI is playing an important role to reduce the inequality in development between provinces, since GDP and FDI reinforce each other. As shown above, the trade openness and government expenditure have positive effects on GDP and FDI. Thus, the western and central provinces should pay more attention to generate higher level of openness, and allocate the expenditure to such areas that can promote human resources and infrastructure to foster the economic growth and inflow of FDI.

6. Conclusions

There is no consensus on the relationship between FDI and economic growth, but there is a growing view in recent years that FDI is positively correlated with growth. Since the starting of the process of economic reform, and opening up to the outside world in 1978, China has become one of the fastest growing economies in the world. In addition, China is now the largest recipient of FDI in the world.

In this study, I have examined the causal relationship between China's economic growth and inflow of FDI using fixed effects and instrumental variables panel data approaches at the provincial level. The sequence of tests conducted indicates that GDP and FDI have a bi-direction causal relationship in China, which means inflow of FDI and rapid economic growth have reinforced each other.

The economic performance in China during the 1990s was propelled by strong FDI inflow in helping China to access to overseas markets, it improved access to technology and supplementing domestic saving and investment. More over, China has benefited from the rapid growth of domestic demand and hence a high level of domestic investment which has enabled China to achieve rapid economic growth. Therefore, the outcomes of this rapid economic growth in China are the emergence of huge domestic markets and increased per capita income along with the emergence of a large middle class in urban and rural areas. This has attracted foreign investments into China to dominate the China's huge domestic market and to take advantage of China's natural and labor resources. The results of this paper suggest the policy of attracting FDI should be enhanced. Attention should be paid in promoting the absorptive capability of foreign investment's technology spillover.

Openness and government expenditure are also found to have positive effects on GDP and FDI. The results suggest that Chinese government should maintain a higher level of openness, and allocate the expenditure to areas that can promote human resources and infrastructure to enhance the economic growth and inflow of FDI.

In similarity with the general guidance given above, the provincial heterogeneity requires that the western provinces, which are lagging behind in both economic growth and FDI inflow, to generate a higher level of openness and, to allocate the expenditure to such areas that could promote human resources development and building up infrastructure to enhance further the economic growth and inflow of FDI.

REFERENCES

Addison T. and A. Heshmati (2004), The new global determinants of FDI flows to developing countries: the importance of ICT and democratization, *Research in Banking and Finance* 4, 151-186.

Aitken B., G. H. Hanson and A. Harrison (1997), Spillovers, foreign investment, and export behaviour, *Journal of International Economics* 43, 103-132.

Aitken B. and A. E. Harrison (1991), Are there spillovers from foreign direct investment? Evidence from panel data for Venezuela, American Economic Review 89, 605-618.

Baltagi B. H (2001), *Econometric Analysis of Panel Data*, 2nd edition, Chichester: John Wiley and Sons Ltd.

Blomstrom M. (1986), Foreign investment and productivity efficiency: the case of Mexico, *Journal of Industrial Economics* 15, 97-110.

Borensztein E, Gregorio J. D. and J. W. Lee (1995), How does foreign direct investment affect economic growth?, *Journal of International Economics* 45, 115-135.

Caves R. E. (1974), Multinational firms, competition, and productivity in host-country markets, *Economica* 41, 176-193.

Chen C., L. Chang, and Y. Zhang (1995), The role of foreign direct investment in China's post-1978 economic development, *World Development* 23(4), 691-703.

Cheng L. K. and Y. K. Kwan (1999), Foreign capital stock and its determinants, *Foreign Direct Investment and Economic Growth in China*, ed. by Wu, Y. MPG Books, Great Britain.

Chowdhury A. and G. Mavrotas (2005), FDI and growth: a causal relationship. *Research Paper of World Institute for Development Economics Research*, United Nations University, No. 2005/25.

Coughlin C. C. and E. Segev. (2000), Foreign direct investment in China: *A Spatial econometric study*, World Economy 21(1): 1-23.

Dayal-Gulati A. and A. M. Husain (2000), Centripetal forces in China's economic take-off. *IMF Working Paper* WP/00/86.

Dees S. (1998), Foreign direct investment in China: Determinants and Effects, *Economics of Planning* 31, 175-194.

Findlay R. (1978), Relative backwardness, direct foreign investment, and the transfer of technology: a simple dynamic model, *Quarterly Journal of Economics* 92, 1-66.

Fu J. (2000), Institutions and investments: foreign direct investment in China during an era of reforms, University of Michigan Press U.S.

Fung K. C., Iizaka, H., Lin, C. and A. Siu (2002), An econometric estimation of locational choices of foreign direct investment: The case of Hong Kong and U.S. firms in China, Asian Development Bank Institute.

Gholami R., Tom-Lee S. Y. and A. Heshmati (2006), The Causal Relationship Between Information and Communication Technology and Foreign Direct Investment, *The World Economy* 29(1), 43-62.

Globerman S., A. Kokko and F. Sjoholm (2000), International technology diffusion: evidence from Swedish patent data, Kyklos 53, 17-38.

Harrison A. (1996), Determinants and effects of direct foreign investment in Cote d'Ivoire, Morocco, and Venezuela. *Industrial Evolution in Developing Countries*, ed. by Mark J. Roberts and James R. Tybout, New York, Oxford University Press.

Holtz-Eakin D., W. Newey and H. S. Rosen (1988), Estimating vector autoregressions with panel data, *Econometrica* 56(6), 1371-1395.

Kokko A. (1994), Technology, market characteristics, and spillovers, *Journal of Development Economics* 43, 279-293.

Kokko A., R. Tansini and M. Zejan (1996), Local technological capability and spillovers from FDI in the Uruguayan manufacturing sector, *Journal of Development Studies* 34, 601-611.

Kumar N. and J. P. Pradhan (2002), Foreign direct investment, externalities, and economic growth in developing countries: some empirical explorations and implications for WTO negotiations on investment. *RIS discussion papers, Research and Information System for Non-aligned and Other Developing Countries.*

Lemione F. and D. Unal-Kesenci (2004), Assembly trade and technology transfer: the case of China, *World Development* 32(5), 829-850.

Liu Z (2002), Foreign direct investment and technology spillover: evidence from China, *Journal of Comparative Economics* 30, 579-602.

Liu X., P. Burridge and P. J. N. Sinclair (2002), Relationships between economic growth, foreign direct investment and trade: evidence from China, *Applied Economics* 34, 1433-1440.

Liu X. and H. Song (1997), China and the multinationals: a winning combination, Long Range Planning 30(1), 74-83.

Nair-Reichert U. and D. Weinhold (2001), Causality tests for cross-country panels: a new look at FDI and economic growth in developing countries, *Oxford Bulletin of Economics and Statistics* 63(2), 153-171.

Shan Jordan, G. G. Tian and F. Sun (1997), The FDI-led growth hypothesis: further econometric evidence from China. Working Paper, Economics Division, Research School of Pacific and Asian Studies, The Australian National University.

Shiu A. and A. Heshmati (2006), Technical Change and Total Factor Productivity for Chinese Provinces: A Panel Data Analysis, *IZA Discussion Paper* 2006:2133.

Sjoholm F. (1999), Technology gap, competition, and spillover from direct foreign investment: evidence from establishment data, *Journal of Development Studies* 36(1), 53-73.

Xu B. (2000), Multinational enterprises, technology diffusion, and host country productivity growth, *Journal of Development Economics* 62, 477-493.

Young S. and P. Lan (1997), Technology transfer to China through foreign direct investment, Regional Studies, 31(7), 669-679.

Zhang K. H. (2001), How does foreign direct investment affect economic growth in China?, *Economics of Transition*, 9(3), 679-693.

In: Recent Developments in the Chinese Economy
Editor: Almas Heshmati, pp. 55-81
ISBN: 1-60021-449-5
© 2007 Nova Science Publishers, Inc.

Chapter 3

GROWTH AND PERFORMANCE OF SCIENCE PARKS IN CHINA

***Zheng Yu*[1] *and Almas Heshmati*[2]**
University of Kurdistan Hawler and
Techno-Economics and Policy Program
College of Engineering
Seoul National University

ABSTRACT

Since their birth in the 1950s, science parks have played a key role and are of growing importance to economic development in many countries. Since the early 1990s, science parks have been introduced into China. In the light of recent decades of rapid economic growth in China it is interesting to understand the performance and contributions of these parks to Chinese economic growth and how to promote these parks. This study aims to analyze the growth and performance of 51 science parks in China from 1994 to 2003. By using panel data methodology a production function is estimated accounting for parks, provinces and time heterogeneity. We estimate total factor productivity, return to scale and rate of technological change and evaluate their level and variations by provinces, parks and over time. Based on the results obtained we suggest policy recommendations to enhance the parks performance and their contribution to overall Chinese economic growth.

Key words: Science parks, China, province, performance, growth

---

1 Zheng Yu, Researcher, Techno-Economics and Policy Program, College of Engineering, Seoul National University, San 56-1 Shinlim-Dong, Kwanak-Gu, Seoul 151-742, South Korea, e-mail: fishead001@hotmail.com,

2 Almas Heshmati, Professor of Economics, University of Kurdistan Hawler and Techno-Economics and Policy Program, College of Engineering, Seoul National University, San 56-1 Shinlim-Dong, Kwanak-Gu, Seoul 151-742, South Korea, e-mail: Heshmati@snu.ac.kr,

1. INTRODUCTION

Since their birth in the 1950s, science or technology parks have played a fundamental impetus role in the promotion of economic transformation, achievement of technological capability, technology transfer, cultivation of innovative high-tech enterprises and entrepreneurs, the gestation of the new technological revolution and emerging industry in the newly industrialized countries and many developing countries. Science or technology parks have become the impulse of new economic development, an effective and important method by which a nation or a region achieves high and new technology industrialization, the promotion of economic growth and the development of welfare of societies.

Castells and Hall (1994) found that science parks provide an important resource network for new technology-based enterprises. They listed three motivations for establishing science parks: reindustrialization, regional development, and synergy creation. In addition other research showed that science parks have been widely recognized for their importance in the development of high-tech industries. For example, the success of Silicon Valley has been the engine of prosperous development of the information industry in the United States. It is of no doubt that firms located in science parks are significantly more likely to have a link with a local university than off-park firms. Link and Scott in 2003 modeled the growth of a science park once established, showing significant effects on growth by the proximity to universities and other resources.

According to Chan and Lau (2005), to meet the needs of technology firms during their stages of development, science parks' services and support should be prioritized in accordance with the development process of the technology firms. Meanwhile Hansson, et al. (2005) came up with the conclusion that the new role of science parks might be to cater for the development of the social capital necessary for enabling and facilitating entrepreneurship in networks.

In the case of China, since early 1991 the State Council of China has successively authorized the establishment of 53 science parks. Later, in August 1998, the National High and New Technology Industrial Development Plan of China (Torch Plan) started. Instauration of high and new technology industrial development parks (hereafter Science Parks) was clearly included as an important element of the Torch Plan, and it saw the start of the very rapid development of Science Parks under the impetus of the Torch Plan. Following a series of measures related to the construction of these parks, they have been developing rapidly, attracting worldwide attention and contributing to a unique development path of industrialization in China.

Chinese science parks are built on the condition of intellectual integration of capital, skills and technology in an open environment. Mainly supported by domestic infrastructure and foreign technology and capital, they maximize the potential transformation from technical achievement to actual productivity through full absorption of overseas advanced technology resources.

By 2005, the total income of those parks has in general amounted to 450 billion dollars while the industrial output was 345 billion dollars. They also contributed to industry added value of 100 billion dollars, tax revenue of 20 billion dollars and exportation of 60 billion dollars. More details on the Survey of Chinese high and new technology industry is found on the Website of the Ministry of Science and Technology of China.

This study aims to analyze the growth and performance of 51 Science Parks in China. The sample consists of the entire population3 of parks observed during 1994 to 2003. By using panel data methodology a production function is specified and estimated accounting for parks, provinces and time heterogeneity. We estimate total factor productivity, various input elasticities, return to scale and rate of technological change and evaluate their level and variations by provinces, parks and over time.

Since Science Parks are a new phenomenon, especially in China, there is no literature developed and evaluation of technology parks in general and case studies of China in particular are very rare. Thus, this study makes a number of contributions to the literature. First, it studies an important element of the new economic policy in China. Second, it creates a new panel data covering the entire Science parks and its period of existence. Third, it uses up-to-date panel data methodology to model and estimate the production relationship at the park level and parametrically estimates total factor productivity growth. Fourth, it compares performance of individual parks and analyses their development over time and across provinces. Fifth, the parametric TFP measure is compared with the commonly used Solow's residual in growth studies. Finally, it discusses the importance of parks to Chinese economic growth and, based on the results obtained, we suggest policy recommendations to enhance the parks performance and their contribution to overall Chinese economic growth.

The rest of the paper is organized as follows. In Section 2 we introduce the readers to the background and development of Science Parks. In section 3 and 4 we review the literature and development of the parks in China. The data and empirical model are presented in Section 5 and 6. Estimation results are discussed in Section 7. The final two sections discuss policy recommendations and conclusions.

2. SCIENCE PARKS

2.1. Definition of Science Parks

According to the IASP (International Association of Science Parks) official definition, a Science Park is an organization managed by specialized professionals, whose main aim is to increase the wealth of its community by promoting the culture of innovation and the competitiveness of its associated businesses and knowledge-based institutions. To enable these goals to be met, a Science Park stimulates and manages the flow of knowledge and technology amongst universities, R&D institutions, companies and markets; it facilitates the creation and growth of innovation-based companies through incubation and spin-off processes; and provides other value-added services together with high quality space and facilities. (IASP International Board, 6 February 2002). In recent years they have played a key role in attracting foreign direct investment and the flow of investment finances to productive activities and in the transfer of management, skills, knowledge and technology to host countries.

The IASP has cross-examined and compared the models and experiences of Science/Technology Parks in the 63 countries throughout which its members are located, to ensure the truly global character of its definition.

3 Two parks are excluded due to missing data at the level of provincial location of the parks.

The IASP definition of "Science Park" encompasses other terms and expressions such as "Technology Park", "Technopolis", "Technopole", "Technology Precinct", "Research Park" etc. Although there may be certain differences between them, projects under these afore-mentioned labels share many goals, elements and methodology and therefore come under the remit of this definition. The IASP does not preclude the existence of more 'specific' definitions for each of these "labels", but will not recognize any project as a "Science Park", "Technology Park", "Technopole", etc. which does not fit within this 'broader' IASP definition.

So, with respect to the characteristics in the definition of Science Park by IASP and the purpose of construction of national high and new technology industrial development parks in China, in the current study to be consistent we will use the label "Science Parks" to address those parks in China.

2.2 Development of Science Parks

The concept of science parks originated back in the late 1950s. The science parks are usually based around universities and interact continuously with them. The idea is to provide the infrastructure of technical, logistic and administrative help that a young firm needs as it struggles to gain a foothold for its product in an increasingly competitive market (Guy, 1996).

The first science park was established in Stanford, California, USA, in the 1950s followed by the Cambridge Science Park, UK, and Sophia Antipolis, France, in the late 1960s. In many European countries it was not until the 1980s and 1990s that significant numbers of science parks were established (Storey and Tether, 1998).

In Asia, Singapore is one of the early pioneers in developing Science Parks. The idea of a science and technology park was officially proposed in September 1979, when the Ministry of Trade and Industry convened a meeting to discuss the development of such a park with the relevant authorities. The Singapore Science Park is now one of the Asia Pacific's most prestigious, addressing R&D and technology. Its campus-like setting provides the ideal location and working environment for an exclusive community of a staff of over 8,000 people working for more than 250 multinational corporations (MNCs), local companies, and research organizations.4

India is quickly emerging as one of leaders in the field of software engineering and Web-based services. More and more multinational companies are outsourcing their software requirements to India to retain their competitive advantage. In 1987, the Ministry of Communication and Information Technology (MCIT) stepped in, through its Software Development Division, and established the Software Technology Parks India (STPI) scheme on June 5, 1990.

In China the Torch Plan was initially approved by the government in 1984. Its original objective was to promote the development of science and education and transform lab

---

4 Jussawalla and Taylor (2003) present a collection of comprehensive studies analyzing information technology parks of the Asia Pacific and their implication for the digital divide with focus on parks located in China, Malaysia, India, Singapore, Taiwan and Hawaii.

projects into commercial products, thus improving China's competitiveness in the international market. The key task of the Torch Plan was to establish science parks. The government saw it as an inevitable step in facing the challenge in general. In addition, science parks accomplished intensive information-gathering and it led to the concentration of financial and technological strength. After fifteen years of development, science parks in China have grown into a large enterprise. By 2000, there were fifty-three science parks in the country, housing 16,000 companies and employing 1.84 million people. The growing number of Science Parks is an indication of their success and positive impact on economic development.

Using an on-line questionnaire, sampling 94 Science/Technology Parks, IASP found that a majority of the currently existing Science and Technology Parks in the world were created during the nineties. However it is interesting to notice that a significant 18% of the existing Science Parks have been launched in the first 2 years of the new century, which confirms (as other indicators show as well) that Science/Technology Parks are a growing phenomenon (see Figure 1).

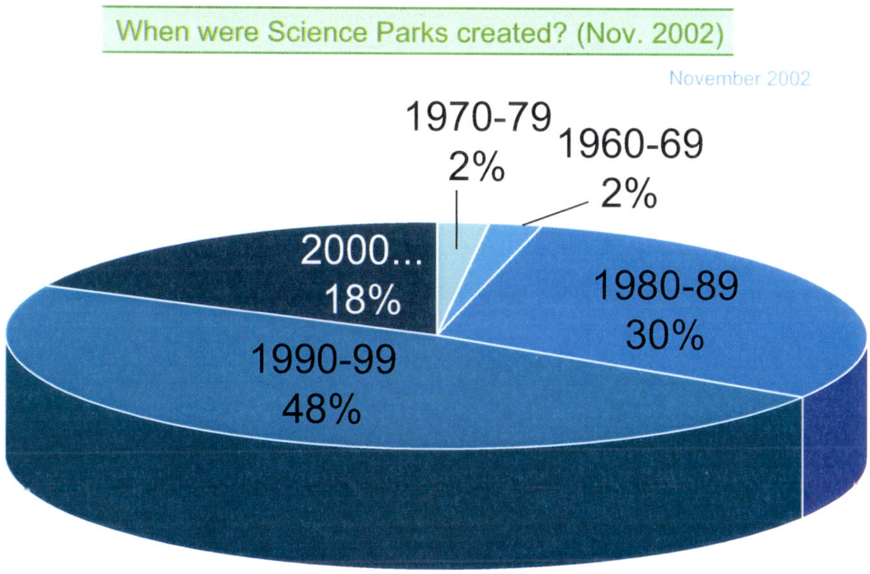

Figure 1. When Science Parks were created.

Moreover, there are four categories of science parks in the world. Big science parks usually occupy a land area of more than 1 million square meters. While the smallest parks, that account for up to 51 percent of the total of science parks, are less than two hundred thousand square meters. In the middle, 5 percent are Medium-Big science parks and 21 percent are Medium-Small science parks (see Figure 2).

For the relation between the general economic growth and the science parks development, see references in Table 1 and Figure 3.

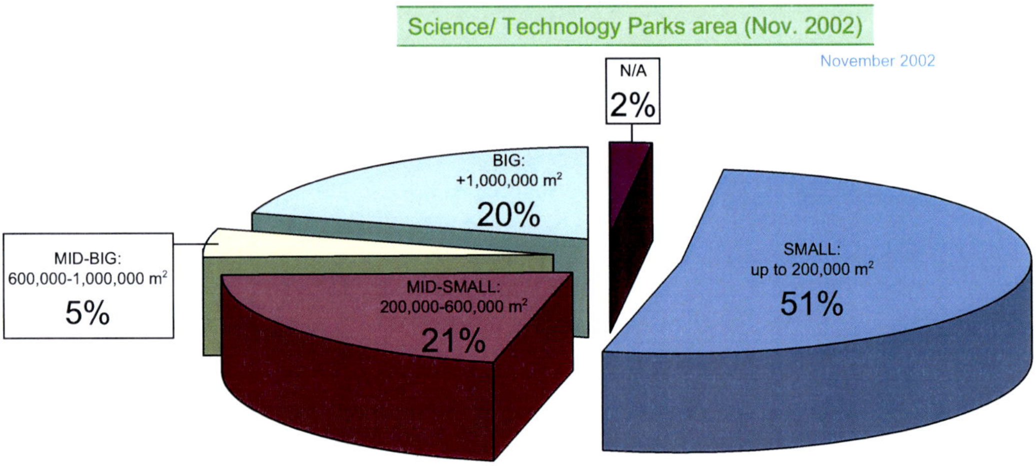

Figure 2. Science Parks area.

Table 1. General Economic Growth and Science Parks Performance

Year	GDP($)	FDI($)	Government Expenditure($)	GDP Growth In %	Parks Production($)	Parks Employee	Parks Growth In %
1994	542.5343	--	67.2099	11.80	0.9622	795976	--
1995	700.2527	37.521	81.7114	10.20	17.9260	1043478	75.56
1996	816.4899	41.726	95.4698	9.70	25.7546	1290980	43.04
1997	898.2436	45.257	111.3846	8.80	37.5098	1475103	45.22
1998	946.3009	45.463	130.4270	7.80	52.3439	1740499	39.37
1999	991.3569	40.319	159.3041	7.10	71.7970	2210487	37.15
2000	1080.7414	40.715	191.9030	8.00	95.9362	2350679	33.62
2001	1175.7255	46.878	228.3748	7.30	144.1152	2761433	50.19
2002	1270.6572	52.743	266.4390	8.00	156.3018	3486686	8.46
2003	1418.2699	53.505	297.8126	9.10	208.4987	3953621	33.39
004	1653.7297	60.63	344.1776	9.50	273.5228	4484387	31.18

*All values are counted by billion dollars.

3. LITERATURE REVIEW

In the literature a number of questions are frequently asked. What contributions to economic growth do science parks actually make? Many researchers have already been absorbed in the study of science and technology parks. But considering the demand of in-depth interpretation of this matter, the expected goal has not been achieved.

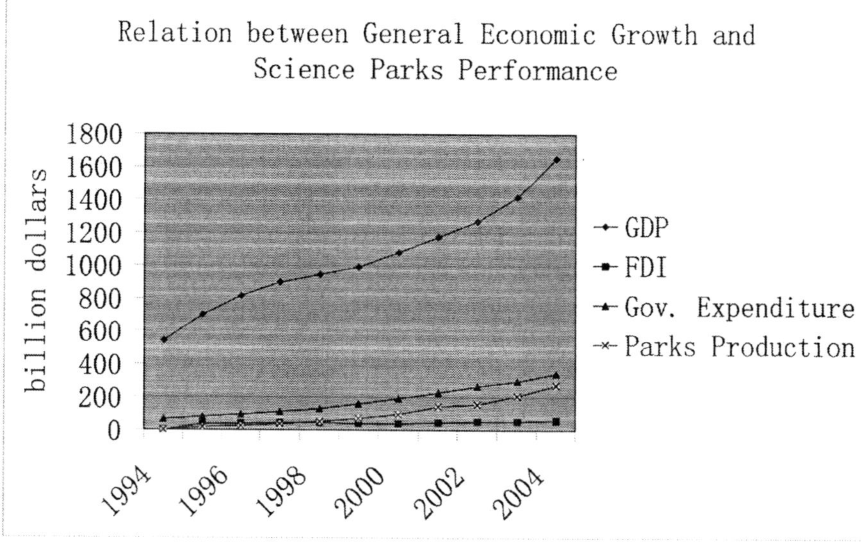

Figure 3. Relation between general economic growth and science parks performance.

Besides, we have not seen a comparatively systematic description about the methodology addressed here. The main motivation for these studies is a review of whether the established science parks have achieved their role, as stated in the above definition, or if they finally constitute prestigious real estate developments.

Lee and Yang (2000) analyzed that, according to the first hi-tech industry development benchmarking model in Taiwan, it has been appreciated that governmental support and human resources are the most essential factors in Hsinchu Science Park's (HSP) performance, and the electronics information related industries (EI) have contributed mutually through improved management strengths. In this paper, the authors wrote their analysis as a simple description and showed the readers the HSP's characteristics as a model for other latecomers in Taiwan.

Siegel, Westhead and Wright (2003), analyzed whether university science parks are alleged to stimulate technological spillovers. However, there was virtually no empirical evidence on the impact of these facilities on research productivity. They then started to fill this gap by examining whether companies located in university science parks in the United Kingdom had higher research productivity than observationally equivalent firms not located in a university science park. The preliminary results appeared to be consistent with the hypothesis and were robust to the use of alternative econometric procedures to assess relative productivity of parks.

Similarly, Hansson, Husted and Vestergaard (2005) reported that several studies had concluded that science parks tended to fail in attracting and developing high-tech companies and had therefore not fulfilled their expected role as catalysts of regional economic growth. Based on two in-depth case studies of science parks in Denmark and the UK, they introduced and discussed alternative mediating roles for science parks in the science–industry relationship. The conclusion was that the new role of science parks might be to cater for the development of the social capital necessary for enabling and facilitating entrepreneurship in networks.

Lai and Shyu (2005) in their study have aimed to explore the innovation capacity in two different science parks across the Taiwan Strait. In both Taiwan and on the Mainland considerable resources are being devoted to science parks as policy instruments, aimed at promoting R&D-based as well as innovation activities. Based on Porter's model for the innovation orientation of the national industrial cluster, they proposed a model to analyze the science parks in their innovation capacity across the Taiwan Strait. Finally they found differences in determinants for innovation capacity between the ZJHP (Zhangjiang High-Tech Park) and HISP (Hsinchu Science-based Industrial Park), such as the basic research infrastructure, sophisticated and demanding local customer base, and the presence of clusters instead of isolated industries.

Chen, Wu and Lin (2006) also found that science parks have been widely recognized for their importance to the development of high-tech industries. However, as the space availability is limited, the selection of firms with better efficiency and/or growth potential in specific high-tech industries to get into the science parks has become a critical issue for the Taiwan government. Accordingly, their study applies Data Envelopment Analysis (DEA), the multiple inputs–multiple outputs evaluation method, to analyze the comparative performances of the six high-tech industries currently developed at Taiwan's Hsinchu Science Park. Malmquist indices of productivity change were also used to analyze the growth potentials of the six high-tech industries. In addition, individual output/input ratio analysis was done to examine the differences in individual productivity levels between efficient and inefficient industries. The results of these analyses provided some policy implications for Taiwan and other countries facing similar problems.

Fukugawa (2006) in his study investigated the value-added contributions of science parks to new technology-based firms (NTBFs). In particular, they focused on whether on-park NTBFs were likely to establish knowledge linkage, represented as joint research, with local higher education institutes (HEIs). Based on a bivariate probit model, they showed that on-park NTBFs exhibit a higher propensity to engage in joint research with research institutes. However, the geographical range of knowledge linkage was not localized as hypothesized. Furthermore, no significant difference was found between science parks and other types of property-based initiatives with regard to the degree of encouragement provided to tenants to establish localized HEI linkage.

Performance measurement of science parks (SP) is becoming paramount and calls for more rigorous approaches. The work of Bigliardi et al. (2005) was aimed at providing a sound and theory-grounded methodological framework to science parks performance measurement and some practical suggestions useful for the design and the implementation of an SP performance evaluation. Following a review of recent literature, it emerged that such a system was drawn up as from the real mission and strategy of the SP, that were influenced by the environment context, the stakeholder's commitment, the life-cycle of the SP, besides their technical and scientific cultures. Based on the analysis of four Italian case studies, the empirical findings partly lent support to previous research output and partly added new elements of discussion to the debate. More specifically, major results were that the evaluation criteria should be aligned with science parks accounting for: (a) actual mission, (b) major stakeholders commitment, (c) economic regional conditions, (d) legal forms, (e) nature of the scientific competence base available within research centers, and (f) SP's life-cycle stages.

In general, the above studies describe the characteristics of science parks from different perspectives, such as performance measurement and innovation capacity. It seems that science parks significantly influence economic growth as well as innovation activities. As science parks play a more and more important role in the economy, further in-depth studies need to be carried out, incorporating both quantity and quality aspects for every country, especially developing countries. However, curently there are few studies about Chinese science parks although they commenced in the early 1990s. Accordingly to compensate for that lack, from the next section we will examine those parks in China systematically. The methodology used here to evaluate performance of Chinese parks differs from that of Bigliardi et al. (2005). We use up-to-date parametric panel data based total factor productivity to measure performance of parks.

4. Technology Policies of Science Parks in China

As Gu mentioned in "China's Industrial Technology: Market Reform and Organizational Change" (1999), China has undergone two decades of economic reform and the achievement has been impressive to outsiders. However, one often wonders to what extent this economic achievement stems from its technological advancement, instead of low labor costs, hence, how sustainable it will be in the long-term.

So, in order to establish and develop a high and new technology industry base, to accelerate the transformation of technology achievements, to deepen reform and in a systematic innovative way to implement technological trade strategy, to raise high and new technology enterprises and entrepreneurs and to transform the traditional industry to modern style, China set up science parks. Those science parks amass technologies involved in Electronics, information technology, bioengineering and new medicine, new materials, advanced manufacturing technology, aerospace technology, oceanographic engineering, nuclear application, new energy and energy saving technologies, environmental protection and advanced agricultural technology.

Especially since 1997, the State Council has successively authorized Beijing, Xi'an, Suzhou, Hefei, Yantai, Wuhan, Shanghai, Shenzhen, Chengdu and Yanglin provinces to link in total ten parks to APEC members, aiming to promote cooperation between APEC members and China in the high and new technology industry.

Chinese science parks take each kind of technical enterprise incubator as a core activity, which utilizes corresponding facilities and organizations in an effective way and provides services including research and development, flow of information information, financial resources, trade, law, guarantees, appraisal, human resources, international exchange and so on to establish a well functioning infrastructure for technological innovation incubating system of China.

The science parks implement the rule of "innovating independently while absorbing innovation as a complement". By the end of 2000, the number of enterprises with a total income exceeding 100 million Yuan has reached 1,252, among which 143 enterprises have income more than 1 billion Yuan. At that moment, the total number of enterprises has reached 20,796 according to a statistical report.

Simultaneously, the science parks gathered 560,000 talented persons. It includes 52,103 persons with master degrees, 9,358 with Ph.D. degrees and 5,615 persons who had a foreign degree. Establishment of a great deal of post-doctorates institutes and 250 high and new technology service centers can also be found.

It is estimated that, in 2010, more than 10 high and new technology industry development belts will vigorously develop, 4 high and new technology industrial districts will make an appearance. The industrial structure of China will be optimal while the value-added and exports of science parks will account for 20% of the total.

5. The Data

The data set used in this study contains two parts. One part is obtained from the CSY (Chinese Statistical yearbook) which is published online at the website of the National Bureau of Statistic of China (NBSC). As an authority, NBSC provides reliable and up-to-date data on an annual basis for the Chinese economy. The other part is from a database at the provincial level, also based on published annual statistics. The first source is at the science park level, while the second is at the province level. Information on location of the parks is used to merge the two data sources.

In total there are 53 science parks in China. However, since there is no information at the province level for Baotou Science Park in Neimenggu province, we excluded this park from the sample. A second park, Yanglin Science Park has been established recently and was subsequently dropped from the sample. Finally, there is full information on the remaining 51 parks during a period of ten years, from 1994 to 2003. It should be mentioned that there is no data collected on Science Parks in 1995. We used the average of 1994 and 1996 to impute the missing year data. The total number of observations is 510. Table 2 presents a summary of data, while Table 3 shows the correlation matrix of the variables.

Table 2. Summary Statistics, NT=510

Variable	Mean	Std. Dev.	Minimum	Maximum
Year	1998.500	2.875	1994.000	2003.000
ICT Investment	240297.465	204595.995	9817.120	961897.115
Capital Stock	112132.211	84694.468	12677.419	536026.786
Investment Expenditure	47567.259	36419.316	4718.478	190985.401
Foreign Direct Investment Inflow	9449473.550	12098564.525	36009.390	43012460.568
Government Expenditure	19005.430	15536.664	1093.151	84104.732
Percent Educated Person	9.298	6.917	2.294	56.872
Openness	0.401	0.480	0.040	2.054
Reform*	43.241	18.760	9.414	88.100
Enterprises of Science Parks	372.936	925.913	6.000	12030.000
Workers of Science Parks	40884.376	42021.606	500.000	488561.000
Value-added of Science Parks	43521055.482	71535875.342	86317.460	673386711.860
Total Income of Science Parks	48475004.665	87552855.837	95650.794	931101774.190
Total Export of Science Parks	5793323.260	13638789.823	1237.374	114210409.090

*Reform= gross industrial value of SOE/total gross industrial value, SOE means state owned enterprises.

Table 3. Correlation Coefficients, N=510 observations, Prob>|r| under H0: Rho=0

	YEAR	VAL	CAP	WOR	ICT	FDI	ENT	INV	GOV	PCNT	OPEN	REFORM	INCOME	EXP
Year	1.0000													
Value Added of Science Parks	0.4499 0.0001	1.0000												
Capital Stock	0.3941 0.0001	0.5927 0.0001	1.0000											
Workers of Science Parks	0.4466 0.0001	0.7714 0.0001	0.3253 0.0001	1.0000										
ICT Investment	0.4209 0.0001	0.3482 0.0001	0.6236 0.0001	0.1770 0.0001	1.0000									
FDI Inflow	0.0575 0.1946	0.2263 0.0001	0.5895 0.0001	-0.0116 0.7943	0.6868 0.0001	1.0000								
Enterprises of Science Parks	0.1357 0.0021	0.6110 0.0001	0.1093 0.0136	0.8492 0.0001	0.0288 0.1567	-0.0544 0.2200	1.0000							
Investment Expenditure	0.4091 0.0001	0.4302 0.0001	0.8641 0.0001	0.2051 0.0001	0.7724 0.0001	0.7758 0.0001	-0.0026 0.9526	1.0000						
Government Expenditure	0.4882 0.0001	0.3527 0.0001	0.7260 0.0001	0.1695 0.0001	0.8586 0.0001	0.6887 0.0001	-0.0322 0.4686	0.8944 0.0001	1.0000					
Percent Educated Person	0.3294 0.0001	0.7157 0.0001	0.4417 0.0001	0.7847 0.0001	0.1192 0.0001	0.0737 0.0966	0.7297 0.0001	0.2260 0.0001	0.1234 0.0053	1.0000				
Openness	0.0028 0.9498	0.2626 0.0001	0.3954 0.0001	0.0659 0.1373	0.6220 0.0001	0.8607 0.0001	0.0939 0.0340	0.5984 0.0001	0.5664 0.0001	0.2049 0.0001	1.0000			
Reform	0.3215 0.0001	-0.0059 0.8937	-0.3134 0.0001	0.1915 0.0001	-0.3160 0.0001	-0.6189 0.0001	0.1039 0.0190	-0.4425 0.0001	-0.3799 0.0001	0.0793 0.0734	-0.5459 0.0001	1.0000		
Total Income of Science Parks	0.4205 0.0001	0.9454 0.0001	0.5444 0.0001	0.8350 0.0001	0.2880 0.0001	0.1888 0.0001	0.7140 0.0001	0.3829 0.0001	0.3039 0.0001	0.7643 0.0001	0.2407 0.0001	0.0144 0.7450	1.0000	
Total Export of Science Parks	0.1414 0.0014	0.5835 0.0001	0.4883 0.0001	0.3193 0.0001	0.3815 0.0001	0.3332 0.0001	0.2497 0.0001	0.3295 0.0001	0.2478 0.0001	0.3576 0.0001	0.3098 0.0001	-0.1710 0.0001	0.4691 0.0001	1.0000

The variables used in this study include output value as dependent variables and number of workers, number of enterprises, total income, total export, ICT investment, investment expenditure, foreign direct investment inflow as independent variables. The monetary variables are transformed to fixed 2000 prices using GDP deflator and producer price index at the province level.

The variables listed above are sufficient to conduct a foundational study of SP and also due to good access to data we include a large number of highly relevant variables. These are used to analyze the relationship between output and inputs and production characteristics variables. In addition we control unobservable park-specific and province-specific effects to account for unobservable science park heterogeneity.

From Table 2 we see large dispersion and ranges among the variables. In particular, the standard deviation and range of the FDI inflow, export and number of enterprises is found to be the largest among the variables. The correlation matrix in Table 3 shows that several variables used in the production model such as Capital-ICT (0.63) and Worker-Enterprises (0.85) are correlated and their effects might be confounded and difficult to separate. The correlation coefficients are higher among the variables such as investment, FDI, government expenditure and openness explaining the variations in the TFP growth rates.

The mean of the variables over time, across individual parks and provinces are reported in Tables 7A, 7B and 7C, respectively. All variables (openness being excepted) show increasing patterns over time (Table 7A). The average level of value added, investment capital and ICT stocks and FDI inflows show significant increases over time. The same is with the number of enterprises and employment. Variations in mean variables by science parks (Appendix Table 7B) and the range of mean values are quite significant. Beijing and Shanghai top the list, while Guiyang, Hainan and Urumqi are ranked as the lowest mean values. Similar tendencies as in the case of Science Parks are observed across the provincial locations (Table 7C). Location and size of parks is not distributed equally across provinces and reflects the preferences and opportunities for investment and the actual development potential heterogeneity. Guandong, Beijing, Shanghai, and Jiangsu attract most FDI, yet Shanghai and Beijing produce the highest value added.

6. THE MODEL

6.1. The Solow Residual

It is quite common, that when analyzing the factors of economic growth, to use the Cobb-Douglas production function as a classical method. The model is written as:

$$Y = AK^{a}L^{1-a}, \quad 0 < a < 1 \tag{1}$$

where Y is output, K is capital, L is labor and A represents a shift in the production function over time due to technological change. The relation in (1) can be transformed to logarithmic form that we can use intuitively and conveniently expressed as:

$$\log Y = \log A + a\log K + (1-a)\log L \tag{2}$$

in a Cobb-Douglas production function, it is often assumed that the production exhibits constant returns to scale. This implies that a proportional change in all inputs will result in a proportional change in output.

The modern study of economic growth starts from the 1950s when Solow and Abramovitz (1953) and Jorgenson (1963) identified the basic inputs of a growing economy as labor, capital and technology. Solow (1957) drew the conclusion that technological change was responsible for most economic growth. However, he did not measure that contribution of technological change to economic growth directly, but rather measured it as an exogenous residual after the contribution of labor and capital were calculated. The Solow residual, labeled as total factor productivity growth (TFP), is obtained at the difference between growth in output and weighted growth in inputs written as:

$$TFP_{SOLOW} = \dot{Y} - a\dot{K} - (1-a)\dot{L} \tag{3}$$

where a dot indicates growth rate of the variables $X = (Y, K, L)$, $\dot{X} = X_t - X_{t-1}$. The weights are unknown and are obtained from an estimation of the Cobb-Douglas production function (2), assuming constant returns to scale. The Solow residual is later compared with parametric estimation of TFP releasing the restrictive assumption of constant returns to scale.

6.2. The Production Model

The production function here is a generalization of the standard production function in (2) but it is specified such that it incorporates some control variables specific to the nature of the Science Parks, as well as controling unobservable Science Park and time specific effects. The latter are important to account for heterogeneity in Park and technology effects. These two effects have been import elements of the unequal development of parks in China and its rapid development of the industry over time. The basic model is specified as:

$$\begin{aligned}\log VA_{it} = \alpha_0 + \alpha_{CAP}\log CAP_{it} + \alpha_{WOR}\log WOR + \alpha_{ICT}\log ICT_{it} \\ + \alpha_{FDI}\log FDI_{it} + \alpha_{ENT}\log ENT_{it} + \varepsilon_{it}\end{aligned} \tag{4}$$

where VA is value added for park i in period t, CAP and WOR are the capital stock and labor force, and the ICT, FDI and ENT are ICT capital stock, FDI inflow and number of enterprises as control variables. These vary across parks and over time. In this specification we separate the capital stock into ICT and non-ICT capital stocks to isolate the effects of ICT on production of value added and TFP growth of parks in China. The residual term follows a two-way error component structure written as:

$$\varepsilon_{it} = \mu_i + \lambda_t + v_{it} \tag{5}$$

where μ is a vector of unobservable park-specific effects capturing systematic but to us unobservable effects such as management, where λ is a vector of unobservable time-specific effects capturing systematic but to us unobservable time effects such as policy and technology changes, and finally ν is a random error term. The vectors of park and time effects are represented by dummy variables.

The panel data literature has been developed in two main directions. The choice depends on the assumptions made about correlation between the effects and the explanatory variables. If we assume that the effects are correlated with the explanatory variable, $E(\mu \mid X) \neq 0$, the model is estimated by least square dummy variable (LSDV) by adding park and time dummies or alternatively within estimation method where the park and time effetcs are transformed out by transformation of the variables to deviation from the mean of the variable by park and year. Within estimation is preferred to the LSDV when the number of parks is large, but the slope coefficients are identical. Alternatively, if we assume that the effects are not correlated with the explanatory variable, $E(\mu \mid X) = 0$, the model is estimated by the generalized least squares method. The choice of a fixed or random effects model will statistically be determined based on Hausman's test. However, in cases where the sample is equal to the population, a fixed effects model is more reasonable and one estimates the effects rather than the parameters of the distribution. Here we use a fixed effect model approach and estimate the model stepwise by (i) pooled least square ignoring the park and time effects, (ii) one-way error component accounting for time effects but ignoring park effects, (iii) one-way error component accounting for park effects but ignoring time effects, (iv) LSDV model accounting for both park and time effects. The four models are nested and by using joint F-test it is possible to determine the final model of choice.

Using the estimation result above, the rate of technical change, returns to scale and TFP are computed. The TFP growth is written as:

$$T\dot{F}P_{it} = T\dot{C}_t + (RTS - 1) \cdot \sum_{j=1}^{J} \hat{\alpha}\dot{X}_{jit} \tag{6}$$

where TC is the rate of technical change estimated as the derivative of the production function (4) with respect to time, RTS is the estimate of returns to scale and is the sum of the input elasticities, and a dot indicates growth rate in factor inputs. The TFP growth here differs from the one by Solow's residual in that here we account for deviation from returns to scale and the returns to scale measure is based on other inputs than capital and labor inputs.

Once we have obtained the estimates of TFP for each observation of the data, one wishes to identify determinants of TFP growth and to estimate their impacts on the TFP growth. In doing so we estimate the following relations:

$$\begin{aligned} T\dot{F}P_{it} = {} & \beta_0 + \beta_{INV} \log INV_{it} + \beta_{FDI} \log FDI_{it} + \beta_{GOV} \log GOV_{it} + \beta_{PCNT} PCNT_{it} \\ & + \beta_{OPEN} \log OPEN_{it} + \beta_{TRN} TRN_{it} + \zeta_{it} \end{aligned} \tag{7}$$

where TFP is estimated parametrically, INV, FDI, GOV, PCNT, OPEN and TRN are investment, foreign direct investment, government expenditure, percentage of the labor force with a university degree, openness and a time trend. These variables are considered as determinants of TFP growth. A positive coefficient suggests that a factor promotes TFP growth, while a negative sign suggests a contraction effect on TFP growth.

7. Estimation Results

Empirical results in this paper are based on the Chinese Bureau of Statistics and data published in CSY (Chinese Statistical Yearbook). The total number of 510 observations used in the estimation steps. In this section we provide a detailed analysis of the results.

7.1. Production Model Results

A number of models and estimation methods are involved in the generation of the results. As mentioned in the previous section, we can estimate the production model by: (i) pooled least square ignoring the park and time effects, (ii) one-way error component accounting for time effects but ignoring park effects, (iii) one-way error component accounting for park effects but ignoring time effects, (iv) LSDV model accounting for both park and time effects.

In Model I, the independent variables are the number of workers, capital stock, ICT investment, FDI inflow and number of enterprises at a park. Parameter estimates show that the coefficients associated with the number of workers, ICT investment and FDI inflow are statistically significant at the less than 1 percent level of significance. So with respect to value added for science parks, the effects of the number of workers, ICT investment and FDI inflow are significant. In Table 4, the biggest coefficient valuing 1.02917 indicates the effect of the number of workers influencing the value added.

Table 4. Parameter Estimation

Parameters	Model I		Model II		Model III	
	Coefficients	Std.Dev.	Coefficients		Coefficients	Std.Dev.
Intercept	-0.38970	0.40129	2.84972***	0.43732	8.55281***	1.86000
Workers	1.02917***	0.04768	0.80857***	0.04539	0.53827***	0.04559
Capital Stock	0.06407	0.06713	0.03713	0.05961	0.21834	0.16414
ICT Investment	0.34431***	0.05081	0.07388	0.05433	-0.01427	0.04229
FDI	0.11383***	0.02512	0.22214***	0.02373	-0.07890**	0.04023
Enterprises	0.00683	0.03493	0.06687**	0.03084	0.21700***	0.04725
T2			0.17986*	0.09604	0.26094***	0.05343
T3			0.22798***	0.09669	0.36348***	0.05650
T4			0.43102***	0.09845	0.64232***	0.06519
T5			0.55685***	0.10227	0.79025***	0.08091
T6			0.71157***	0.10901	0.95040***	0.10217
T7			0.91109***	0.11152	1.14208***	0.11447
T8			1.10893***	0.11480	1.39374***	0.12870
T9			1.07599***	0.11216	1.39447***	0.14366
T10			1.25014***	0.11356	1.54445***	0.15722
ID2					-0.18536	0.16917
ID3					-0.85479***	0.15326
ID4					-0.78021***	0.18879
ID5					-0.91176***	0.20107

Table 4. (Continued)

Parameters	Model I		Model II		Model III	
	Coefficients	Std.Dev.	Coefficients		Coefficients	Std.Dev.
ID7					-0.48317***	0.13314
ID8					-0.83688***	0.13541
ID9					-1.38633***	0.17807
ID10					-0.20545	0.21576
ID11					-0.24757	0.22649
ID12					-0.55388***	0.20861
ID13					-0.72364***	0.22065
ID14					0.84060***	0.21520
ID15					0.74698***	0.20173
ID16					-0.47778**	0.20245
ID17					0.55023***	0.20843
ID18					0.51908***	0.19298
ID19					0.10666	0.16464
ID20					-0.16620	0.24258
ID21					0.14462	0.24487
ID22					0.15029	0.25915
ID23					-0.45781*	0.25170
ID24					-0.41806**	0.16544
ID25					0.54290***	0.19788
ID26					-0.46657**	0.19923
ID27					-0.3778*	0.21446
ID28					-0.4489**	0.20402
ID29					-0.4751***	0.18227
ID30					-1.0532***	0.18196
ID31					-0.1654	0.17669
ID32					-0.6802***	0.22267
ID33					-0.2656	0.23737
ID34					-0.8027***	0.25806
ID35					-0.2790*	0.16748
ID36					1.0927***	0.21242
ID37					-0.0535	0.21492
ID38					0.6705***	0.22775
ID39					-0.0091	0.18926
ID40					0.6615***	0.24314
ID41					-0.9850***	0.30334
ID42					-0.9788***	0.30004
ID43					-0.5769	0.37446
ID44					-0.7331***	0.19213
ID45					-0.6793***	0.18305
ID46					0.1635	0.21914
ID47					-1.0940***	0.37041
ID48					-0.8022***	0.29535
ID49					-0.5391***	0.18231
ID50					-0.9154***	0.24540
ID51					-1.1163***	0.25686
ID52					-1.9678***	0.30724
Adj R-Sq	0.8267		0.8706		0.9626	
F Value	486.72		245.58		205.90	
Pr>F	0.0001		0.0001		0.0001	
Root MSE	0.55139		0.47652		0.25605	

Significant level: * 10%, **5%, ***1%.

When looking at Model II, we estimate the one-way error component model accounting for time effects but ignoring park effects. In this model, the significant variables including the number of workers, FDI inflow and number of enterprises alter. The coefficient associated with the number of workers now reduces to 0.80857. In addition, the coefficients of time dummies for all years except for 1995 are statistically significant. Also in Table 4, it can be found that the coefficients of time dummies increases from 0.22798 in 1996 to 1.25014 in 2003. It means with time elapsing, value added increases.

In the LSDV model accounting for both park and time effects, the parameter estimate results show that FDI inflow is no longer significant while the coefficients of number of workers and number of enterprises are still significant. The changed significance level of FDI is due to collinearity between park effects and FDI. With regard to the above two models, the coefficient of number of workers decreases to 0.53827. But interestingly, coefficients of time dummies for all years are statistically significant. The time effect coefficient is 0.26094 in 1995 and it increases to 1.54445 in 2003. Among all the parks, the coefficients of 34 park dummies are statistically significant while 38 coefficients of park dummies have a negative sign. The sign and sizes are to be interpreted in relation with the park number 1 used as a reference park.

In summary, in every model the coefficient of number of workers is statistically significant. This subsequently leads to the conclusion that the number of workers is assured to contribute positively to the value added of a park.

Compared to the LSDV model, accounting for both park and time effects, the model of one-way error component accounting for only time effects but ignoring park effects reflects basically the regression of value added with regard to its main determinant variables. Since there is no obvious interaction between the value added and parks, it seems that Model II is relatively better here.

7.2 Various Elasticities

As we pointed out in Section 6, based on the estimation results of model II we can compute the rate of technical change, returns to scale and TFP growth rates.

It is shown in the regression of value added with respect to the time dummies that the coefficients of time dummies are significant and they increase from 0.22798 in 1996 to 1.25014 in 2003 (see in Table 4). Because time can be seen as RTC (Rate of Technical Change), the biggest elasticity of 1.25014 for time dummies in 2003 indicates that the rate of technological change or shift in the production function over time contributes more and more to the value added.

In the case of RTS, it is sum of the input elasticities, i.e. the coefficients of the number of workers, capital stock, ICT investment, FDI inflow and the number of enterprises. Based on the each elasticity (see in Table 4), we get the sum of 1.2086, which is bigger than 1. This is interpreted as RTS is not always constant and increasing. The fact that the elasticity of 1.2501 for time dummies is greater than zero and combined with increasing returns to scale confirms the increasing contribution to the output value than other factors.

Recalling the TFP growth function (6), given the results on RTC and RTS we can easily compute the parametric measure of the TFP growth.

7.3 Determinants of TFP Growth

Once we have obtained the estimates of TFP growth for each observation of the data, we can identify the determinants of TFP growth rate. Here we identify the variables of investment, foreign direct investment, government expenditure, percentage of the labor force with a university degree, openness and a time trend to serve as determinants of TFP growth of the parks. Table 5 gives us the result of the regression of TFP growth on its determinants to estimate their impacts on economic growth of parks.

Table 5. Determinants of TFP Growth

Formulation:

$$TFP = \alpha_0 + \alpha_1 \log INV_{it} + \alpha_2 \log FDI_{it} + \alpha_3 \log GOV_{it} + \alpha_4 PCNT_{it} + \alpha_5 \log OPEN_{it} + \alpha_6 TRN_{it} + \varepsilon_{it}$$

Variables	Estimate	Std Error	T-value	Pr>|t|
Intercept	8.12070	12.26482	0.66	0.5082
ICT Investment	1.89926	1.43558	1.32	0.1864
Investment Expenditure	-3.15996	2.24997	-1.56	0.1183
FDI	1.51886*	0.85971	1.77	0.0779
Government Expenditure	-0.19959	2.07546	-0.10	0.9234
Percent of Educated persons	-0.11611	0.10025	-1.16	0.2473
Openness	-0.40263	0.91712	-0.44	0.6608
Time Trend	0.50601*	0.30163	1.68	0.0940
Adj R-Sq	0.0047			
F Value	1.34			
Pr>F	0.2273			
Root MSE	12.74138			

Significant level: * 10%, **5%, ***1%.

Unfortunately, coefficients of all factors are statistically insignificant.[1] The adjusted R^2 of this regression is low, just 0.0047. The coefficients of ICT investment, FDI and time trend are positive, while the coefficients of investment expenditure, government expenditure, percent of educated persons and openness are negative. It seems that only ICT investment, FDI and time trend promote the TFP growth. The coefficient of ICT investment is 1.8993 dominating the other coefficients. It is desirable that ICT investment influence TFP growth intensively.

[1] One main reason for insignificant coefficients is that the dependet variable is measured as growth in TFP. Unlike the level of TFP, it is rather difficult to find determinants of growth rate.

7.4. Variations in Elasticities and TFP Growth Rates

Table 6 reports the correlation coefficient among the growth variables, number of enterprises, number of workers, output value, total income, exports, TFP growth and corresponding for Solow residual. For instance, growth in income and value added (dinc-dval) is (0.90039) and Solow residual and growth in value added (solow-dval) is (0.87193). These are found to be highly correlated and their effects might be difficult to separate. The correlation coefficients are higher among the variable couples such as value added and growth in number of enterprises (dval-dent), income and enterprises (dinc-dent), TFP growth and growth in number of workers (TFP-dwor), growth in export and valued added (dexp-dval), growth in export and income (dexp-dinc) and Solow residual and income growth (solow-dinc). The lowest correlation is between the growth total income and year. Moreover, the signs of growth rates of the number of workers, output value, total income and exports correlated over time are all negative. This means that over time, these growth rates all decrease.

Table 6. Correlation matrix between growth variables, N=510 observations, Prob>|r| under H0: Rho=0

	Year	Dent	Dwor	dval	dinc	dexp	TFP	Solow
Year	1.0000							
Dent	0.0475	1.0000						
	0.2835							
Dwor	-0.0677	0.4266	1.0000					
	0.1265	0.0001						
Dval	-0.0280	0.5698	0.4406	1.0000				
	0.5272	0.0001	0.0001					
Dinc	-0.0047	0.5341	0.4882	0.9003	1.0000			
	0.9143	0.0001	0.0001	0.0001				
Dexp	-0.1203	0.3708	0.3550	0.5792	0.5654	1.0000		
	0.0065	0.0001	0.0001	0.0001	0.0001			
TFP	0.0640	0.3989	0.7338	0.4648	0.4105	0.3654	1.0000	
	0.1485	0.0001	0.0001	0.0001	0.0001	0.0001		
Solow	0.0090	0.3861	-0.0429	0.8719	0.7411	0.4540	0.1044	1.0000
	0.8380	0.0001	0.3332	0.0001	0.0001	0.0001	0.0184	

Glossary of variables:

Dent growth of number of enterprises;
Dwor growth of number of workers;
Dval growth of value added;
Dinc growth of total income;
Dexp growth of total export;
TFP total factor productivity releasing the restrictive assumption of constant returns to scale;
Solow total factor productivity growth assuming constant return to scale.

Table 7: Sample Means

Table 7A: Means of key indicators by Year

Year	Mict	Mcap	Minv	Mfdi	Mgov	Mpcnt	Mopen	Mreform	Ment	Mwor	Mval
1994	126903	71450	30364	8235627	9487	6.228	0.483	38.751	232	15587	6588579
1995	104101	73617	32396	8487037	11062	7.743	0.430	38.863	250	20336	10141331
1996	141390	78515	34195	8939237	12155	8.117	0.369	33.223	267	25086	13388885
1997	152504	87514	36204	9909387	14047	8.071	0.368	30.568	266	28563	19105422
1998	220059	100571	42878	9580189	15876	8.044	0.337	33.380	313	33774	27471256
1999	298689	115449	46290	8961842	17744	8.159	0.344	55.556	339	42916	39145266
2000	356849	126698	49747	8733493	21172	8.633	0.391	52.005	404	45475	51689008
2001	392500	140174	55295	9941677	25480	9.478	0.379	50.958	471	53451	77015743
2002	312371	156526	64603	11374770	29492	12.097	0.418	50.056	549	67460	83143963
2003	297611	170809	83700	10331478	33538	16.415	0.486	49.046	638	76196	107521101
Sample Mean	240297	112132	47567	9449473	19005	9.298	0.401	43.241	372	40884	43521055
Std.Dev.	204595	84694	36419	12098564	15536	6.917	0.480	18.760	925	42021	71535875
Year	Minc	Mexp	Mdent	Mdwor	Mdval	Mdinc	Mdexp	Mrtc	Mrts	Mtfp	Msolow
1994	7337554	108569	0.000	0.000	0.000	0.000	0.000	0.000	1.209	0.000	0.000
1995	11052202	195777	23.757	61.568	78.626	78.850	304.312	17.986	1.209	29.477	33.046
1996	14511384	280371	11.387	26.624	31.353	31.914	41.153	4.813	1.209	10.657	8.172
1997	21010282	460475	19.294	34.000	73.657	71.604	138.595	20.304	1.209	27.569	44.840
1998	30993188	577831	21.064	23.547	40.908	43.188	72.908	12.583	1.209	17.600	21.008
1999	44742393	830165	11.489	28.759	44.766	51.370	99.999	15.472	1.209	20.637	24.278
2000	60032216	12650788	20.230	12.358	36.362	36.348	98.778	19.952	1.209	22.635	25.719
2001	65133756	15226708	21.296	19.539	51.294	17.907	33.939	19.784	1.209	24.644	32.018
2002	98682081	217631	13.419	28.278	21.283	55.518	-83.013	-3.294	1.209	2.091	-0.075
2003	131254989	334751	15.164	15.391	32.696	34.777	48.079	17.414	1.209	20.055	22.222
Sample Mean	48475004	579332	15.710	25.007	41.094	42.148	75.475	12.501	1.209	17.536	21.123

Table 7B. Means of key indicators by Park

Park	Ment	Mwor	Mval	Minc	Mexp	Mdent	Mdwor	Mdval	Mdinc	Mdexp	Mtfp	Msolow
Anshan	157	31986	14283224	15148946	386794	18.9	30.8	68.8	86.8	61.4	18.7	44.0
Baoding	103	28816	15307207	15166119	1150325	11.5	10.1	23.8	26.5	21.5	15.6	11.5
Baoji	77	25048	10958577	10645391	336063	23.0	93.7	42.4	47.2	109.8	30.2	-27.8
Beijing	5725	226033	263635331	368469572	27506879	15.5	17.9	32.8	33.0	29.0	15.9	19.5
Changchu	513	68964	69096318	70748095	2108930	9.2	17.6	43.5	43.4	58.5	15.9	30.1
Changsha	408	42902	33927639	42326094	1568678	14.1	24.9	38.4	41.9	25.9	17.7	17.9
Changzhou	170	29032	25366676	25472849	3407664	30.8	27.6	51.4	46.6	66.5	18.3	28.2
Chengdu	228	58685	23982553	25853432	1147145	12.1	26.2	23.0	27.8	139.5	17.3	4.2
Chongqing	351	52263	35509413	38154607	751927	9.3	19.9	39.6	40.9	22.7	16.2	25.1
Dalian	756	65258	34179681	40579129	5499014	8.3	25.3	33.7	38.4	53.6	17.7	13.2
Daqing	159	19704	15139758	15967329	65601	7.0	27.9	43.1	35.5	307.4	17.4	23.5
Foshan	33	14171	32622830	32308783	4064727	25.5	40.5	53.3	53.8	46.0	20.2	22.7
Fuzhou	105	19492	23566683	22476765	3155875	8.1	15.1	29.2	33.3	29.7	16.4	13.9
Guangzhou	557	33057	40272515	53628058	4855860	12.1	27.2	42.8	38.1	219.8	17.8	21.9
Guilin	154	24915	10967965	11037662	672200	14.0	20.5	35.4	37.1	39.8	16.2	20.7
Guiyang	68	25457	9648058	9304853	281740	2.1	11.3	31.6	32.4	31.3	14.8	22.5
Hainan	50	6352	9799055	9738616	263218	53.0	53.2	171.5	150.5	459.8	22.0	133.7
Hangzhou	267	20782	40716967	46484387	2981900	9.6	24.8	54.8	57.7	42.0	18.0	33.1
Harbin	291	62169	32961817	36760777	3601847	-1.8	23.6	26.0	28.0	7.7	16.6	9.8
Hefei	143	34681	30223970	29674743	1255981	6.7	12.2	30.2	31.4	15.2	15.0	20.4
Huizhou	52	21810	42760950	44592986	10738012	9.4	18.1	31.5	32.0	36.0	16.2	16.7
Jilin	286	57608	54032166	53301743	1044654	23.9	20.0	46.2	43.8	25.6	16.5	30.4
Jinan	259	45740	35649427	38167913	1160562	1.8	20.6	35.3	33.6	4.7	16.7	18.6
Kunming	106	19176	11864320	13907654	1035126	7.3	15.4	26.5	26.5	91.5	16.0	12.5
Lanzhou	296	20757	14400714	15842075	221735	6.3	13.0	36.6	33.6	19.1	15.6	24.4
Luoyang	200	34590	13884149	15841712	1198816	7.7	14.9	26.8	30.8	-8.3	15.4	15.3
Mianyang	64	30809	29331148	24905834	726216	7.8	43.9	39.2	35.0	104.4	20.2	8.7
Nanchang	108	25634	17258057	19377068	448954	8.1	27.4	34.8	33.8	103.9	18.9	9.3
Nanjing	168	43338	113074228	115962534	8282137	21.5	22.2	41.2	40.2	65.8	17.3	22.1
Nanning	170	15396	9728232	11885504	210158	12.2	27.0	43.2	49.3	57.0	17.3	24.3
Qingdao	100	41511	72114772	76247463	6605042	27.2	32.7	37.2	30.7	15.2	19.1	11.0
Shanghai	365	75601	231396377	254542946	43493136	11.5	9.9	36.3	36.3	39.7	15.0	26.4
Shenyang	912	53244	44691984	63077364	3889922	17.7	6.9	24.3	34.4	62.1	14.7	15.6

Table 7B. Means of key indicators by Park (Continued)

Park	Ment	Mwor	Mval	Minc	Mexp	Mdent	Mdwor	Mdval	Mdinc	Mdexp	Mtfp	Msolow
Shenzhen	109	42074	109706640	106018455	27379949	45.4	39.9	44.4	43.6	26.3	20.4	13.1
Shijiazhuang	366	35693	22827438	28517812	4514150	4.8	11.2	26.3	30.9	38.5	15.7	13.6
Suzhou	236	59338	103620177	99743795	35075017	13.2	16.5	38.4	41.4	42.2	16.2	23.6
Taiyuan	266	41238	23297740	25718761	833225	15.0	21.1	42.3	43.7	40.2	16.9	25.0
Tianjing	1560	88920	80911786	88476713	17368759	7.8	14.2	27.0	28.8	23.9	15.4	15.3
Urumqi	116	8015	2667096	3717609	276538	-1.5	8.5	25.7	25.9	1.6	13.8	20.7
Weifang	63	17623	17464677	18329095	619656	33.0	32.0	36.4	34.9	58.9	19.1	10.4
Weihai	81	27254	20522041	19874677	5092082	20.9	23.1	32.9	45.5	42.5	17.4	13.4
Wuhan	404	65076	55961404	64689151	2598549	19.2	20.2	33.6	33.0	26.3	16.8	16.6
Wuxi	180	38114	83542875	96493451	25541084	46.8	46.9	80.3	86.0	585.3	21.8	43.3
Xiamen	55	15202	26391958	27049742	7324073	11.7	27.7	57.2	52.6	55.2	18.6	33.2
Xian	1406	80557	59292719	76391819	2208260	10.6	19.0	36.5	35.8	53.4	16.5	20.8
Xiangfan	58	37891	18200627	19878726	246212	10.1	12.4	37.9	47.0	38.4	15.3	26.7
Zhengzhou	207	27275	21382793	23574178	1637472	12.3	19.3	27.1	35.6	13.2	16.2	12.4
Zhongshan	217	44888	38688649	36911883	13543933	37.9	50.1	35.1	37.3	76.9	22.0	-2.6
Zhuhai	103	19173	27851585	27247729	4626710	38.3	44.4	56.1	62.7	120.4	21.0	22.2
Zhuzhou	98	19541	12436619	13424257	1046610	9.6	34.9	54.8	44.4	193.4	19.3	27.8
Zibo	97	42251	27454246	28568382	1410369	15.0	11.0	29.0	30.2	8.8	15.3	18.0

Table 7C. Means of key indicators by Province

Province	Mict	Mcap	Minv	Mfdi	Mgov	Mpcnt	Mopen	Mreform	Ment	Mwor
Anhui	137532	48068	25888	1242474	9785	5.3	0.1	44.6	143	34681
Beijing	277448	155441	43507	7572138	12423	41.2	0.8	52.5	5725	226033
Fujian	170893	56916	26705	10093086	12719	7.7	0.5	21.8	80	17347
Gansu	101420	44143	14899	224001	5671	6.3	0.1	64.8	296	20757
Guangdong	594035	153522	97104	36052640	42523	7.3	1.6	20.3	178	29196
Guangxi	82086	29606	14229	1522622	9874	4.7	0.1	49.3	162	20156
Guizhou	75814	18705	11159	134763	4976	3.5	0.1	71.4	68	25457
Hainan	40471	20237	6679	2140233	1903	5.0	0.3	52.9	50	6352
Hebei	187732	138955	50980	3506447	15635	7.4	0.1	41.8	235	32254

Heilongjiang	158139	58072	20545	1160548	11287	9.7	0.1	61.7	225	40936
Henan	171565	90945	38935	1562692	18168	5.3	0.1	43.6	204	30933
Hubei	201870	79875	39745	3162625	12578	10.0	0.1	45.7	231	51484
Hunan	162725	44771	24793	1963324	14012	7.0	0.1	48.6	253	31222
Jiangsu	373875	247260	97091	24716117	30853	10.2	0.4	26.3	188	42455
Jiangxi	113006	45818	20008	2230539	9442	6.5	0.1	61.0	108	25634
Jilin	111715	51996	18044	1103723	7884	12.1	0.2	61.7	399	63286
Liaoning	231118	144502	39210	6402184	19214	13.6	0.4	47.7	609	50163
Shaanxi	126022	66722	20483	1191820	7376	11.6	0.1	63.4	836	60898
Shandong	269509	180063	71923	9563521	31364	7.2	0.3	35.0	120	34876
Shanghai	301464	359609	87862	16991496	17140	28.4	0.9	39.5	365	75601
Shanxi	100772	57073	17380	660802	8287	7.2	0.1	55.1	77	25048
Sichuan	234349	74521	39554	1706480	15247	5.3	0.1	50.6	214	47252
Tianjin	83604	75340	21929	6558709	7508	22.9	0.8	30.9	1560	88920
Xinjiang	75558	34517	14362	84658	5983	7.4	0.1	69.7	116	8015
Yunnan	101373	32477	16471	284308	7709	4.5	0.1	70.4	106	19176
Zhejiang	297558	124048	69979	5941352	20627	7.5	0.4	20.5	267	20782
Province	Mval	Minc	Mexp	Mdent	Mdwor	Mdval	Mdinc	Mdexp	Mtfp	Msolow
Anhui	30223970	29674743	1255981	6.7	12.2	30.2	31.4	15.2	15.0	20.4
Beijing	263635331	368469572	27506879	15.5	17.9	32.8	33.0	29.0	15.9	19.5
Fujian	24979321	24763254	5239974	9.9	21.4	43.2	42.9	42.5	17.5	23.5
Gansu	14400714	15842075	221735	6.3	13.0	36.6	33.6	19.1	15.6	24.4
Guangdong	48650528	50117982	10868198	28.1	36.7	43.9	44.6	87.5	19.6	15.7
Guangxi	10348098	11461583	441179	13.1	23.8	39.3	43.2	48.4	16.7	22.5
Guizhou	9648058	9304853	281740	2.1	11.3	31.6	32.4	31.3	14.8	22.5
Hainan	9799055	9738616	263218	53.0	53.2	171.5	150.5	459.8	22.0	133.7
Hebei	19067322	21841966	2832237	8.1	10.7	25.1	28.7	30.0	15.7	12.6
Heilongjiang	24050787	26364053	1833724	2.6	25.8	34.5	31.8	157.6	17.0	16.6
Henan	17633471	19707945	1418144	10.0	17.1	27.0	33.2	2.5	15.8	13.8
Hubei	37081015	42283939	1422380	14.6	16.3	35.8	40.0	32.3	16.1	21.7
Hunan	25682129	27875175	1307644	11.9	29.9	46.6	43.1	109.7	18.5	22.9
Jiangsu	81400989	84418157	18076476	28.1	28.3	52.8	53.6	190.0	18.4	29.3
Jiangxi	17258057	19377068	448954	8.1	27.4	34.8	33.8	103.9	18.9	9.3
Jilin	61564242	62024919	1576792	16.5	18.8	44.9	43.6	42.0	16.2	30.2
Liaoning	31051629	39601813	3258577	15.0	21.0	42.3	53.2	59.1	17.0	24.3
Shaanxi	41295229	51055290	1520742	12.8	20.1	39.4	39.7	46.8	16.7	22.9
Shandong	34641033	36237506	2977542	19.6	23.9	34.2	35.0	26.0	17.5	14.3

Table 7C. Means of key indicators by Province (Continued)

Province	Mict	Mcap	Minv	Mfdi	Mgov	Mpcnt	Mopen	Mreform	Ment	Mwor
Shanghai	231396377	254542946	43493136	11.5	9.9	36.3	36.3	39.7	15.0	26.4
Shanxi	10958577	10645391	336063	23.0	93.7	42.4	47.2	109.8	30.2	-27.8
Sichuan	29607705	29637958	875096	9.7	30.0	33.9	34.6	88.9	17.9	12.7
Tianjin	80911786	88476713	17368759	7.8	14.2	27.0	28.8	23.9	15.4	15.3
Xinjiang	2667096	3717609	276538	-1.5	8.5	25.7	25.9	1.6	13.8	20.7
Yunnan	11864320	13907654	1035126	7.3	15.4	26.5	26.5	91.5	16.0	12.5
zhejiang	40716967	46484387	2981900	9.6	24.8	54.8	57.7	42.0	18.0	33.1

Glossary of variables:

Mict mean of ICT Investment
Mcap mean of Capital Stock
Minv mean of Investment Expenditure
Mfdi mean of Foreign Direct Investment Inflow
Mgov mean of Government Expenditure
Mpcnt mean of Percent Educated Person
Mopen mean of Openness
Mreform mean of Reform
Ment mean of Enterprises of Science Parks
Mwor mean of Workers of Science Parks
Mval mean of Value-added of Science Parks
Minc mean of Total Income of Science Parks
Mexp mean of Total Export of Science Parks
Mdent mean of growth of number of enterprises
Mdwor mean of growth of number of workers
Mdval mean of growth of value added
Mdinc mean of growth of total income
Mdexp mean of growth of total export
Mrtc mean of rate of technical change
Mrts mean of return to scale
Mtfp mean of total factor productivity
Msolow mean of Solow total factor productivity

Table 7 shows the means of all variables computed by year, park and province. In Table 7A, almost all means increase over time during the period of this study. The mean of output value of science parks has sharply enlarged to 18 times as it was 65.8 billion yuans in 1994 and jumped to 1075.2 billion yuans in 2003. Correspondingly, the number of enterprises grew from 232 to three times that. Also the percent of educated people increased rapidly from 6.228 to 16.415 due to the rapid development of higher education. Following the globalization and progress in the information and communication technology, ICT investment changed dramatically from 1.2 billion yuans in 1994 to 2.9 billion yuans in 2003. At the same time, the speed of growth for all main variables, such as number of workers and total income, showed a steadily declining trend.

In Table 7B we see the diversity among those parks. The biggest park is Beijing Zhongguancun with the number of enterprises reaching 5725 while the smallest one is Foshan which has just 33 enterprises. Also every year Zhongguancun park produces 2636 billion yuans in output, greater than the second one of Shanghai producing 323 billion yuans. Beijing park is No.1 in total income reaching 3684 billion yuans, while Shanghai park is the highest in exports, at 43.4 billion US dollars. Hainan park is the one which grows fastest with an annual growth rate of 53% in number of enterprises, 53.2% in number of workers, 171.5% in output, 150.5% in total income and 459.8% in exports. So we come to the conclusion that there is great and increasing diversity in those Science Parks in China.

Similar tendencies are found when the means are accounted across the provincial locations (see Table 7C). Beijing and Shanghai top the list in mean of total output and income while Guizhou, Hainan and Xinjiang are ranked at the lowest mean values. Guangdong, Jiangsu, Shanghai and Fujian attract most FDI for the reason of geographical and historical advantages. Yet the East Coastal provinces such as Shanghai, Jiangsu, Shandong, Beijing and Guangdong attract the most capital stock. A clear gap exists between the East provinces and the West provinces in attracting FDI.

8. THE SCIENCE PARK POLICY

Results show that Science Parks are productive and have rapid growth. It is an indication of a successful policy and development strategy implemented by parks and provinces in China. There is significant heterogeneity, which is not necessarily a reflection of failure of some parks, rather a reflection of differences in initial conditions and the attractiveness of parks to investors and access to productive resources. Based on the analysis of the empirical results presented above, we suggest the following policies:

Firstly, as Chinese parks show a strong tendency to produce more and more output value over time, it will be assured to gain more by investing in technology and related R&D, although China can still enjoy the advantage of a large labor force. Simultaneously, improvement in the size and quality of human resources will benefit the gross output of parks.

Secondly, because it is evident that the rate of technological change is the main contributor to the TFP growth, more attention should be paid to the share of technology progress rather than other factors and a simple expansion in scale will achieve the desired level of economic growth.

Thirdly, information technology as an active applied technology should be strongly promoted to improve the productivity of parks and economic growth in general. Actually Beijing's Zhongguancun park operates based on this radical technology policy and is in support of this viewpoint. It benefits most from this farsighted development strategy.

Finally, there is great diversity among these 51 parks in both their capacity and growth speeds. From the national perspective, efficient aggregation is needed to promote the gross developing level of these science parks. With respect to the gap between East and West provinces, according to the above studies different methods should be adopted to achieve the different policy targets.

9. Conclusions

In the 21st century, competitiveness will strongly be linked with the technology field rather than other traditional production factors. The countries which achieve technology power will deeply influence the different aspects of development and relations such as trade and security. So every country tries to strengthen their status in the international technology domain. Science Parks, as organizations managed by specialized professionals, whose main aim is to increase the wealth of its community by promoting the culture of innovation and the competitiveness of its associated businesses and knowledge-based institutions are getting a more and more important position in international competitiveness.

In this paper we have tried to describe the general situation of science parks in China and lead to some thoughts to further methods and policies to develop those parks. Although science parks have not existed for a long time in China, due to the intensively competitive environment, Chinese technology strategies including science parks need to be enhanced to cope with the country's rapid economic development.

This study aimed to analyze the growth and performance of 51 science parks in China during 1994 to 2003. After the declaration of the definition and introduction of the background, by using panel data methodology a production function was estimated accounting for parks, provinces and time heterogeneity. We estimate total factor productivity, return to scale and rate of technological change and evaluate their level and variations by provinces, parks and over time. Based on the results obtained we suggest policy recommendations to enhance the parks' performance and their contribution to overall Chinese economic growth.

References

Bakouros Y. L., D. C. Mardas and C. N. Varsakelis (2002), Science park, a high tech fantasy?: an analysis of the science parks of Greece, *Technovation* 22, 123–128.

Bigliardi B., A. I. Dormio, A. Nosella and G. Petroni (2005), Assessing science parks' performances: directions from selected Italian case studies, *Technovation* 25, 1–17.

Chen C-J. and C-C. Huang (2004), A multiple criteria evaluation of high-tech industries for the science-based industrial park in Taiwan, *Information and Management* 41, 839–851.

Chen K.F. and T. Lau (2005), Assessing technology incubator programs in the science park: the good, the bad and the ugly, *Technovation* 25, 1215–1228.

Chen C-J., H-L. Wu and B-W. Lin (2006), Evaluating the development of high-tech industries: Taiwan's science park, *Technological Forecasting and Social Change* 37(4), 452-465.

Durao D., M. Sarmento, V. Varela and L. Maltez (2005), Virtual and real-estate science and technology parks: a case study of Taguspark, *Technovation* 25, 237–244.

Fukugawa N. (2006), Science parks in Japan and their value-added contributions to new technology-based firms, *International Journal of Industrial Organization* 24(2), 381-400.

Hansson F., K. Husted and J. Vestergaard (2005), Second generation science parks: from structural holes jockeys to social capital catalysts of the knowledge society, *Technovation* 25, 1039–1049.

Kihlgren A. (2003), Promotion of innovation activity in Russia through the creation of science parks: the case of St. Petersburg (1992–1998), *Technovation* 23, 65–76.

Koh F. C. C., T. H. W. Koh and F. T. Tschang (2005), An analytical framework for science parks and technology districts with an application to Singapore, *Journal of Business Venturing* 20, 217–239.

Lai H-C. and J. Z. Shyu (2005), A comparison of innovation capacity at science parks across the Taiwan Strait: the case of Zhangjiang High-Tech Park and Hsinchu Science-based Industrial Park, Technovation 25, 805–813.

Lee W-H. and W-T. Yang (2000), The cradle of Taiwan high technology industry development - Hsinchu Science Park (HSP), Technovation, Industrial Viewpoint, 20, 55–59.

Lindelöf P. and H. Löfsten (2002), Growth, management and financing of new technology-based firms - assessing value-added contributions of firms located on and off Science Parks, Omega 30, 143- 154.

Link A. N. and J. T. Scott (2003), U.S. science parks: the diffusion of an innovation and its effects on the academic missions of universities, *International Journal of Industrial Organization* 21, 1323–1356.

Löfsten H. and P. Lindelöf (2002), Science Parks and the growth of new technology-based firms—academic-industry links, innovation and markets, Research Policy, 31, 859–876.

Löfsten H. and P. Lindelöf (2003), Determinants for an entrepreneurial milieu: Science Parks and business policy in growing firms, *Technovation* 23, 51–64.

Löfsten H. And P. Lindelöf (2005), R&D networks and product innovation patterns - academic and non-academic new technology-based firms on Science Parks, *Technovation* 25, 1025–1037.

Phana P. H., D. S. Siegel and M. Wright (2005), Science parks and incubators: observations, synthesis and future research, *Journal of Business Venturing* 20, 165–182.

Siegel D. S., P. Westhead and M. Wright (2003), Assessing the impact of university science parks on research productivity: exploratory firm-level evidence from the United Kingdom, *International Journal of Industrial Organization* 21, 1357–1369.

In: Recent Developments in the Chinese Economy ISBN: 1-60021-449-5
Editor: Almas Heshmati, pp. 83-134 © 2007 Nova Science Publishers, Inc.

Chapter 4

PRODUCTIVITY GROWTH IN CHINESE ECONOMY AND INDUSTRIES

Yi Feng[♣]
Techno-Economics and Policy Program
College of Engineering, Seoul National University

ABSTRACT

Productivity is commonly defined as the ratio of a volume measure of output to a volume measure of input use. With the increasing recognition that productivity growth is the key to sustained economic expansion, measuring productivity accurately is becoming important to economists and policy makers as well for putting forth better policy recommendations and making the right decisions (Owyong, 1998). The pace of economic change in China has been extremely rapid since the start of economic reforms 27 years ago. Economic growth has averaged 9.5% over the past two decades and is very likely to continue at that pace for some time. Such an increase in output represents one of the most sustained and rapid economic transformations seen in the world economy in the past 50 years (OECD, 2005). So far the industries have been the main drivers of national economic growth, attracting a huge number of investments, expanding international trade and meeting domestic demand. However, there has been an increasing concern related to upgrading technologies, improving economic efficiencies, lowering resource use, reducing environmental pollution, and fully developing human resources, etc. In fact, the Chinese government has formulated and implemented a series of general programs for scientific and technological research and development, aiming at improving China's competitiveness in science and technology in the 21st century (China, 2004). To measure the degree of the technology innovation efforts indirectly at national aggregate and industry level is an essential issue. Therefore, it is of necessity and significance to conduct an empirical research for Chinese productivity growth, since not very much has been done in this field in the case of China. This study begins with a comprehensive literature investigation on productivity growth theory and China-related empirical

[♣] Feng Yi, Director of Nuclear Safety Division, Department of System Engineering, China Atomic Energy Authority, Tel: 86-10-8858-1293(O), e-mail: fysnu@yahoo.com.cn, No.8A, Fucheng Road, Haidian District, Beijing, P.R. China 100037

research evidence. Then it focuses on empirical measurements of Chinese economic productivity growth at the national aggregate level in the midterm (1978-2004) and industrial-level (36 sectors during the period 1998-2003) in the short term. A trans-logarithm model is used to estimate the production function using a panel data approach. Finally, some empirical conclusions are drawn concerning the determinants of Chinese aggregate economic growth post 1978, the productivity change rate of Chinese industrial sectors and the productivity differences across industrial sectors from 1998 to 2003, etc.

Key words: China, productivity growth, national aggregate, industry-level, and panel data

1. INTRODUCTION

Productivity is commonly defined as a ratio of a volume measure of output to a volume measure of input use. The objectives of productivity measurement include: technology, efficiency, real cost savings, benchmarking production process and living standards (OECD 2001, pp. 11-12). Measures of productivity growth constitute core indicators for the analysis of economic growth, which have been applied intensively and extensively in the developed community. With the increasing recognition that productivity growth is the key to sustained economic expansion, measuring productivity accurately is becoming important to economists and policy makers as well for putting forth better policy recommendations and making the right decisions (Owyong, 1998).

The pace of economic change in China has been extremely rapid since the start of economic reforms just 27 years ago. Economic growth has averaged 9.5% over the past two decades and it seems likely to continue at that pace for some time. Such an increase in output represents one of the most sustained and rapid economic transformations seen in the world economy in the past 50 years (OECD, 2005). Many industries have become completely integrated into the world supply chain and, given the current trend, China could become the largest exporter in the world by the beginning of the next decade (OECD, 2005). China is the world's most populous and the biggest developing country with her rational pursuits of economic growth not only in quantity but also in quality. The process of industrialization and urbanization has been promoted by institutional innovation and market power in parallel with a system conversion from a planned economy into a socialist market economy. China's active participation of global industry specialization, regional integration and labor division has obviously enhanced her industrial growth. So far the industries have been the main drivers of the national economic growth attracting a huge amount of investment, expanding international trade and meeting the needs of domestic consumers. However, there has been an increasing concern related to upgrading technologies, improving economic efficiencies, lowering resource consumption, reducing environmental pollution, and fully developing human resources, etc. In fact, the Chinese government has formulated and implemented a series of general programs for scientific and technological research and development, aimed at improving China's competitiveness in science and technology in the 21st century (China 2004). These programs cover the Key Technology R&D Program, 863 and 973 Programs, the Spark Program and the Torch Program. In 2003 China decided on a "New Path toward Industrialization" strategy for the sake of promoting industrial restructuring, upgrading and incessancy. Measuring the degree of the industrial technology innovation efforts indirectly at national aggregate and industrial level is an essential issue to economists, policy makers as well as investors. Therefore, it is of necessity and significance to conduct an empirical research for Chinese productivity growth with updated data and techniques, since not very much has been done in this field in the case of China.

This study begins with a comprehensive review of the literature investigating productivity growth theory and China-related empirical research evidence. Then it focuses on empirical measurements of Chinese economic productivity growth at the national aggregate level in the midterm during 1978-2004 and at the industrial-level in the short term (36 sectors during 1998-2003). The model assuming a T-L (trans-logarithm) production function is estimated by a fixed effect panel data approach.

This study demonstrates that in the midterm, the Chinese economy enjoys a rapid and a sustaining growth with some cyclical fluctuations during the period 1978-2004 with an average of 8.96% of annual real GDP growth rate. The mean of annual growth rate of Chinese real capital stock varies from 9.17% (with depreciation rate δ=5%) to 9.29% (δ=9%). The average annual growth rate of labor working hours is 2.38%. The capital stock partial elasticity (elk) is increasing from 0.91 to 0.96 while the labor partial elasticity (ela) is increasing from 0.71 to 0.88. Thus, the increasing RTS varies from 1.62 (1978) to 1.83 (2004). The mean of Chinese TFP growth rate is from 6.41% (δ=5%) to 6.62% (δ=9%) during the period 1979-2004. Empirically, it implies that in the midterm, both factor inputs and TFP growth are the main determinants of Chinese economic growth post 1978. In addition to these, the main sources of Chinese TFP growth are technical efficiency change of scale economy due to both the combination and gradual saving of capital and labor. The negative pure technical change empirically implies insufficient innovation in Chinese aggregate economy during the period under study. It suggests that economic growth is still mainly relying on quantitative expansion but not quality improvement by technology innovation.

As for an industrial level analysis during the period 1998-2003, it should be noted that the traditional infrastructures, heavy, chemical and textile sectors are the dominant sources of value added among the 36 Chinese industrial sectors. The 36 sectors as a whole enjoy 12.75% per year value added increase. 26 among the 36 sectors have experienced growth rates in double figures. The main contributors of rapid growth are infrastructure sectors, such as medical and pharmaceutical products, ordinary machinery, but especially ICT. In looking at capital stock by industrial sectors, the infrastructure sectors accounts for the majority of the total stock. The industrial sectors as a whole enjoy 8.61% per year of capital stock increase. In the case of labor input by industrial sectors, Textile, Basic materials, Transportation equipments, Ordinary machinery, Equipments for special purposes and Electric supply take on more labor. However, the 36 Chinese industrial sectors as a whole witness 0.40% per year of employee reduction during the period in contrast with the growth of value added and capital stock. It reflects the reform effect in forms of improving efficiency with employee reduction, and the tendency of fewer job openings with capital intensity industrial sectors' development and labor surplus.

The returns to scale (RTS) of the 36 sectors as a whole is 0.50, which means a decreasing return to scale during the whole period of this study. However, among the 36 sectors, there are 8 sectors with increasing RTS. The industrial sectors as a whole enjoy 10.45% per year of TFP growth during 1998-2003. It implies that in the short term, both the combination of factors inputs and technology progress are the main determinants of Chinese industrial growth during 1998-2003. The decomposition of Chinese industrial TFP growth shows that the exogenous rate of technical change (TC) is 11.07% per year and the technical efficiency change (TEC) is –0.62% per year during 1998-2003. So the industrial productivity growth attributes much to the exogenous technical change. It shows that the innovation promotion efforts made by the Chinese government and inflow of FDI have led to some partial returns in the industrial sectors during 1998-2003. However, the lower TEC rate means that there is an urgent need and great room to reallocate the industrial factor resources during the period.

The contribution of this study compared with previous studies relies on: focusing on the Chinese national aggregate in the midterm and the industrial sectors in the short term, utilization of updated data set and application of state of the arts regression techniques.

The study is organized as follows: Section 2 focuses on reviewing productivity growth theory and empirical research evidence. Section 3 and 4 conduct empirical studies by modeling Chinese productivity growth at national aggregate and industrial-level respectively and give policy implications. Section 5 presents brief conclusions.

2. Review of the Literature

2.1. Review of Productivity Growth Theory

Productivity is commonly defined as a ratio of a volume measure of output to a volume measure of input use. The objectives of productivity measurement include: technology (tracing technical change), efficiency (allocation efficiency), real cost savings (capacity utilization and learning-by-doing), benchmarking production process (identification of inefficiencies), and living standards (a key element towards assessing standards)(OECD 2001, pp. 11-12). Multifactor production measurement helps disentangle the direct growth contributions of labor, capital, intermediate inputs and technology.

The economic theory of productivity measurement goes back to the work of Tinbergen (1942) and independently, to Solow (1957) (OECD 2001, pp. 11-12). They formulated productivity measures in a production function context and linked them to the analysis of economic growth. The field has since developed considerably, particularly following major contributions by Dale Jorgenson, Zvi Griliches and Erwin Diewert. Today, the production theoretical approach to productivity measurement offers a consistent and well-founded approach that integrates the theory of the firm, index number theory and national accounts. However, the growth accounting framework has to rely on several simplifying assumptions. These in particular include: Production processes can be represented by production or transformation functions at various levels of the economy. Production functions relate maximum producible output to sets of available inputs. Producers behave efficiently, i.e. they minimize costs and/or maximize revenues. Markets are competitive, and market participants are price-takers who can only adjust quantities but not act individually on market prices.

Three factors or components of economic growth are of prime importance in any society: capital accumulation (including new investments in land, physical equipment and human resources through improvements in health, education, and job skills), growth in population and eventual growth in the labor force, technological progress (Todaro, 0000, p.79).

There have been three waves in the evolution of mainstream macroeconomic growth theory in the past half-century (Ruttan, 2001). The first was stimulated by the work of Harrod (1939) and Domar (1946, 1947). The second wave began in the 1950s with the development by Solow (1956, 1957) and Swan (1956) for a neoclassical model of economic growth. The third wave initiated by Romer (1986) and Lucas (1988) in the mid-1980s. In addition to these developments within the neoclassical models of growth, another traditional perspective is associated with Schumpeter's economic theory (Conceicao, Gibson and Heitor, 2001).

In the Harrod-Domar view, instability in economic growth was the result of failure to equate a "warranted" and a "natural" rate of growth (Ruttan, 2001). The warranted rate of growth is dependent on the savings rate and on a given capital requirement per unit of output. The natural rate is the maximum long-run sustainable rate of growth. It is determined by the rate of growth of the labor force and the rate of growth of output per worker. In models of structural-change, the Lewis two-sector model explains self-sustaining structural transformation process in surplus-labor.

The modern study of economic growth and long-run productivity growth dates from the 1950s when Solow, Swan, Abramovitz (Abramovitz, 1953) and Jorgenson (1963) identified the basic inputs of a growing economy as labor, capital and technology. Solow (1957) concluded that technological change, not labor and capital, was responsible for most economic growth even if it was measured indirectly as an exogenous residual. Solow and Swan's theoretical framework for the analysis of economic growth served as the basis for the development, by Edward Denison (1962), of a growth-accounting framework that attributed economic growth to a number of sources, including increases in the education of the labor force, the contribution of capital, the shift of resources from low productivity endeavors to the mainstream of the modern economy and gains from knowledge and economies of scale.

The economics literature of the 1980s on endogenous growth was initially motivated by the apparent inconsistency between the implications of the neoclassical theory and the accounting for post-1973 productivity slowdown. A key feature of many of these models is their emphasis on knowledge as the driving force of productivity growth. Romer (1987) contributed to the issue of growth accounting by arguing that the direct attribution of labor and capital productivity is misleading, as technological progress exhibits both a direct and an indirect effect, through its influence on labor productivity, on economic growth. Hence the important issue in analyzing growth is not so much of the factors of capital and labor, but technological progress. The three elements, decreasing returns in the production of new knowledge, externalities associated with new knowledge, and increasing returns in the production of output ensure that a competitive equilibrium will exist, even in the presence of externalities. The endogenous growth models explicitly introduce imperfect competition as well as increasing returns and admit, by preventing the marginal product of capital from falling, the possibility of differences in country growth rates and lack of convergence of per capita incomes.

In the Lucas (1988) alternative to the neoclassical model, human capital serves as the engine of economic growth. Lucas employed a two-sector model in which human capital is produced by a single input as the schooling or the learning-by-doing, and in which final output is produced by both human and physical capital. As his work continues to mature, Romer has turned to the contribution of ideas as the primary source of economic growth (Romer, 1993, 1997). The most important implication of the Romer-Lucas-inspired endogenous growth literature for economic development has been the endogenization of human capital formation. Thus, at least in the model, the incentive to enhance the quality of human and physical capital may permanently raise the long-run rate of growth in per capita income.

For Schumpeter, businessmen and firms are not passive elements merely adjusting the prices to the idiosyncrasies of the market. He argued that the expectations of profits would not only lead to price setting, but would also drive the "entrepreneur" to innovate following the process of creative destruction (Conceicao et al., 2000, p.3). Therefore, innovation appears at the forefront of economic progress, driving prosperity. In his final work (Schumpeter 1942), he acknowledged that some large corporations could sustain a market advantage by an institutionalization of the effort to innovate through the establishment of large R and D facilities.

Instead of directly measuring the effect of human capital on productivity, Griliches (1995, p. 52) attempted to measure its indirect effect, by quantifying R&D productivity growth and related spillovers. Coe and Helpman (1995) tested the idea that productivity of a country depends on the stock of past-accumulated R&D of the country as well as on that of its trading partners (domestic and international).

The public sector is also reported to have a major influence on economic growth. While public investment has a positive effect, public consumption correlates negatively with changes in GDP (Barro, 1990). In addition to these, trade policy is regarded as having some ties with growth (Angus Maddison, 1987 and De Long and Summers in 1993).

A great importance has been attached to multi-faceted determinants or sources of productivity. Based on a review of the cross-country growth literature, Harris (1999) identifies three proximate drivers (the Big Three) of productivity growth: investment in machinery and equipment; investment in education, training and human capital; and openness to trade and investment. In addition, he notes that once one moves from the proximate determinants to the indirect linkage, productivity growth can be influenced by a large number of factors. His compendium of potential indirect productivity determinants includes innovation (both product and process), diffusion of technology (national and international), spatial agglomeration (e.g., Silicon Valley), external economies of scale at the industrial level, government consumption (negative), management practices, public infrastructure (positive), income inequality (negative), high taxes (negative), small firms (negative), labor market flexibility (positive), exchange rate stability (positive) and low inflation (positive).

Sharpe (1998) identifies the following seven determinants of productivity growth: (a) the rate of technical progress, determined by the rate of developing new product and process innovations and the pace of diffusing those innovations; (b) Investment in physical capital such as machinery and equipment and structures. It is estimated that 80 percent of technical change is embodied in new capital equipment, particularly machinery; (c) The quality of the workforce, including average educational, training and experience levels; (d) The size and quality of the natural resource base; (e) Industrial structure and inter-sector shifts; (f) The macroeconomic environment or aggregate demand conditions defined by the size of the output gap and relationship between actual and potential output growth.; (g) The microeconomic policy environment, broadly defined as the policies that affect behavior at the firm level, including trade policy, tax policy, industrial policy, competition policy, and policies on privatization, intellectual property, regulation and foreign ownership. He also feels that there is still considerable uncertainty about the drivers of productivity. The relative and absolute contributions made by the different determinants may vary over time and across space. Many of the factors in productivity growth are interrelated and may act in synergy.

Both theoretical and empirical work of the last ten years tried to model the remaining, unexplained share of technological change after human capital by a policy variable dealing with the role of politics, institutions, knowledge and innovation. Durlauf, Johnson and Temple (2004) identified 42 "growth theories" using a total of 102 variables.

Stefan Bergheim (2005) identified the sources of long-term economic growth for 34 economies with the help of Formel-G (Foresight Model for Evaluating Long-term Growth), which included population growth, the investment ratio, and human capital and trade openness as major drivers of GDP growth.

Bottazzi and Peri (2005) estimated the dynamic relationship between employment in R&D and generation of knowledge as measured by patent applications for new idea generating across OECD countries. They found that a country's stock of knowledge, its R&D resources and the stock of international knowledge move together in the long run.

Despite the interest these theories have sparked within theoretical macroeconomics, Mankiw (1995), in an assessment of growth theory, has claimed that we should go back to the pure Solownian formulation, which conforms much better to the empirical facts.

2.2. Empirical Evidences on Chinese Productivity Growth

There are a great number of papers on productivity growth, especially, relating to the topical issue of the East Asian economy after the 1990's. Felipe (1997) notes this literature, mainly focusing on four stands, such as cross-country regression analysis to explain differences in growth rates across nations, the debate on the role of public policy, the role of high investment rates and export orientation, decomposition growth into factor accumulation and productivity gains.

A. At the National Aggregate Level

Chow (1993) and Hu and Khan (1996) have estimated aggregate total factor productivity increases in the Chinese economy for the periods 1953–85 and 1953–94, respectively. These authors stress the role of the high rates of fixed capital accumulation in explaining output growth. Chow (1993, p.841) concludes from his estimated Cobb-Douglas production functions that technological change was absent in the growth of the Chinese economy from 1952 to 1980. Hu and Khan introduce a new data set based on official Chinese sources, select a translog production function, and find out that (1996, p.12): for the years 1953–94 as a whole, real capital grew at 6.8 percent, labor grew at 2.6 percent and total factor productivity growth was 2.1 percent. While the average TFP growth amounted to about 1.1 percent during 1953–78, it rose sharply to 3.9 percent during 1979–94 when China was making progress in market-oriented reforms. The opening up to foreign trade and investment, the gradual removal of price control, the rise of rural township and village enterprises, and the expansion of new private business brought competitive forces into the Chinese economy and helped to make the economy more efficient during the reform period.

Borensztein and Ostry (1996) conclude that the growth rate of TFP, which was negative before reform, rose to 3.8% per year in the post-reform period, accounting for more than one-third of the total increase in output, while the role of capital accumulation was only secondary.

Krugman (1994) argues that China will face a limit on growth sooner or later, since it depends heavily on a massive increase in input with only small improvement in productivity, as in the case of East Asian economies. Moreover, Young (2000) claims that the productivity performance of China's non-agricultural sector during the reform period, while respectable, is not outstanding. More specifically, he finds that systematic understatement of inflation by enterprises accounts for 2.5 percentage points of growth per annum in the nonagricultural sector during the reform period (1978–1998). The usual suspects—rising participation rates, improvements in educational attainment, and the transfer of labor out of agriculture—account for most of the remainder. As such, it is possible to recast the recent growth experience of China from the extraordinary to the mundane.

Dahlman (1994), Hobday (1995), Nelson and Pack (1998) and Kim (1998) insist that the critical source of growth in East Asia has been productivity growth resulting from the learning, entrepreneurship and innovation that those economies in the region have gone through, which has made not only adoption of foreign technologies but also development of indigenous technologies possible.

Hu (1998) summarized the process of China's economy development as "down and rise" within two centuries with citing Maddison's analysis. China was economically strong, with relatively high per-capita income in 1820. However, during the process of global industrialization, China fell far behind: By the middle of the 20th century, it had become one of the poorest countries. From the early 1950s to the late 1970s, despite starting the process of industrialization and having an economic development rate increasing relatively quickly, China's economic growth rate was lower than the world average rate. Therefore, China's per-capita GDP, relative to the average world level, declined slightly. However, since 1978, reform and openness policies have improved China's economic growth rate substantially (TFP from –0.78% during1952-1978 to 2.23% during 1978-1995), China is catching up with the average economic development in the rest of the world.

Wu (1999) applied a stochastic frontier technique to regional statistics and examined productivity growth in China's reforming economy during the period 1981—1995. It found that the pattern of TFP growth resembled a J-shaped curve: productivity growth declined sharply in the initial years of the reform and recovered gradually over time. In addition, it found that China's economic growth in the 1980s was mainly due to efficiency improvement and growth in inputs. This has however changed in the 1990s. Technological progress has now become an important factor propelling China's economic growth.

Caruso (2002) has analyzed the pro-cyclical behavior of Chinese TFP. It shows that measured Solow residuals are correlated to the growth rate of real imports per worker and to other macroeconomic variables that fluctuate at cyclical frequencies. The magnitude of the trend shift in TFP after the start of economic reforms in 1978 is found to be robust to the introduction of cyclical factor utilization and other systematic influences on productivity. Labor hoarding still has an important role at cyclical frequencies. The propagation mechanisms of macroeconomic shocks to output are also evaluated on the basis of a seven-variable VAR system. The empirical results indicate that the growing openness of the economy has contributed to sustaining the observed long run productivity increases and has raised spatial inequality. One main argument is given that those favorable TFP patterns are likely to represent a source of economic growth in the future because of a large technological gap with the industrialized countries and the underlying trends in human capital.

Wang and Yao (2003) construct a measure of China's human capital stock over 1952–1999 using a simple growth-accounting framework. They find that the accumulation of human capital (measured by the average years of schooling in population aged 15-64) was quite rapid and it significantly contributed (29.8%) to growth and welfare. After incorporating human capital, the growth of TFP for the entire period of 1953-1999 is 0.02%, near zero, with physical accumulation accounting for 51% of growth. TFP still played a positive role in GDP growth in the reform period (1978-1999, 2.41%), while it was negative in the pre-reform period (1953-1977, -1.39%). However, these results are robust changes in labor shares in GDP and in depreciation rates. A high priority should be given to human capital accumulation and productivity growth, if China is to sustain its growth and welfare improvement in the next decade.

B. At the Industry-level

Liao and Holmes (2002) applied a stochastic production frontier to sector-level data within manufacturing to examine TFP growth for eight East Asian economies during 1963-1998, using both single and cross identity regression. The analysis focuses on the trend of technological progress (TP) and technical efficiency change (TEC), and the role of productivity change in economic growth. The results reveal that although input factor accumulation is still the main source for East Asia economies' growth, TFP growth is accounting for an increasing and important proportion of output growth, among which the improved TEC plays a crucial role in productivity growth. The single country regression shows that as for China the average TFP growth is 7.55% (TEC is 0, and TP is 7.55%), probably due to its technology imports since it has opened up.

Wang and Szirmai (2003) conducted an empirical study of productivity growth and R&D at sector level in China's high-tech manufacturing industries. Using a version of perpetual inventory method (PIM), estimates were made for the physical capital stock and the R&D stock by sector. The study found that the R&D stock of the electronic industry plays a special role for the whole of the high-tech sector and a significant positive influence of R&D in electronics on productivity growth in other high-tech industries with the help of a production function basing on endogenous growth theory.

Huang, Zhang and Zhao (2005) conducted research on the underlying reasons for developing countries' growth export competitiveness based on the database of more than 150 thousand Chinese manufacturing firms. They found that the processing trade played an important role in the rising of China's export competitiveness, especially in the high technology sectors. They concluded that in Chinese manufacturing sectors in general, lowering the unit labor cost did not help increase export intensity, but promoting foreign direct investment and a firm's competition significantly boosted the export growth. The R&D and innovation effort made by Chinese manufacturing firms had hardly any relation with their export performance, even in the high-tech manufacturing firms.

3. Empirical Analysis of Productivity Growth at the Aggregate National Level

In this section, a dynamic trans-log production model is applied in order to identify the sources of economic growth in China during the period 1978—2004. There are several different aspects compared to the previous research: a) Adoption of generalized T-L aggregate production model with trend for Chinese aggregate TFP regression analysis; b) Updating all data up to 2004; c) Decomposition of TFP into several components to trace the trajectory of Chinese growth post 1978; d) Calculating TFP with six comprehensive capital depreciation rates and income share weighted hours-worked as labor input proxy.

3.1 Model and Method

Following the previous research, especially, Jorgenson, Gollop and Fraumeni (1980, 1986, 1987), the author would like to measure the Chinese national aggregate economic productivity growth during the period of 1978-2004 by using a generalized T-L aggregate production function with time trend written as (1):

$$\begin{aligned} \ln Y_t &= \alpha_0 + \alpha_K \ln K_t + \alpha_L \ln L_t + \alpha_T t \\ &\quad + 1/2\left\{\beta_{KK}(\ln K_t)^2 + \beta_{LL}(\ln L_t)^2 + \beta_{TT}t^2\right\} \\ &\quad + \beta_{KL}(\ln K_t)(\ln L_t) + \beta_{KT}(\ln K_t)\bullet t + \beta_{LT}(\ln L_t)\bullet t + \varepsilon_t \end{aligned} \tag{1}$$

Where output (Y_t) is a function of the logarithms of capital stock (K_t), labor (L_t) and trend (t). A time trend is introduced to capture the level of technology, which is the key driver to steady increases in output per capita, and increases in the standard of living in the long run (Blanchard, 2000). ε_t is a random error term assumed to be independent and identically distributed with zero mean and constant variance σ^2 and independent of the explanatory variables, K_t, L_t and t.

In a Cobb-Douglas production function, it is often assumed that production exhibits constant returns to scale. This implies that a proportional change in all inputs will result in a proportional change in output. However, in practice due to imperfect markets and irrational behavior, management characteristics and changing production technology and environment, it is hard to justify the assumption of constant returns to scale to hold for a long period of time. Thus, in this case it is reasonable to allow for variable returns to scale and test it against constant returns to scale assumption.

Since parameter of a generalized production function arc not directly interpretable, inputs elasticity is to be calculated. Differentiating equation (1) with respect to inputs $\ln K_t$ and $\ln L_t$, we obtain input elasticity at each point of the data defined as (2) and (3):

$$EK_t = \partial \ln Y_t / \partial \ln K_t = \alpha_K + \beta_{KK} \ln K_t + \beta_{KL}(\ln L_t) + \beta_{KT}\bullet t \tag{2}$$

$$EL_t = \partial \ln Y_t / \partial \ln L_t = \alpha_L + \beta_{LL} \ln L_t + \beta_{KL}(\ln K_t) + \beta_{LT} \cdot t \quad (3)$$

And return to scale (RTS) is calculated as the sum of the input (X) elasticity as (4):

$$RTS_t = \sum_j EX_j = \sum_j \partial \ln Y_t / \partial \ln X_t^j \quad (4)$$

where the subscript j indicates inputs (K_t, L_t). In a similar way the rate of exogenous technical change (TC), or shift in the production function over time is obtained as the derivative of output with respect to time like (5):

$$TC_t = \partial \ln Y_t / \partial t = \alpha_T + \beta_{TT} \cdot t + \beta_{KT}(\ln K_t) + \beta_{LT}(\ln L_t) \quad (5)$$

It should be noted that in equation (5) the input elasticity, RTS and TC are all time variant due to inclusion of the square and interaction terms. A positive (or negative) first order input coefficient (α_T <0 or α_T >0) suggests that the input has positive (or negative) effects on output, while a negative (or positive) second order or square term coefficient (β_{TT} <0 or β_{TT} >0) suggests that impact changes at a decreasing (or increasing) rate. The rate of TC might be further decomposed into neutral (pure trend items) and non-neutral input components (interaction between time and inputs). The interaction terms ($\beta_{KT}(\ln K_t), \beta_{LT}(\ln L_t)$) help to indicate specific input using TC change (β_{KT} >0, β_{LT} >0) or a specific input saving TC change (β_{KT} <0, β_{LT} <0) (Baltagi and Griffin, 1988).

The potential technology efficiency change (TEC) or the (non-constant returns to) scale effects due to reallocation of resources is obtained from the relations (6):

$$TEC_t = (RTS_t - 1) \cdot \sum_{j=1}^{k} \Psi_j \dot{\mathbf{x}}_{jt} \quad (6)$$

Where $\dot{\mathbf{x}}_{jt}$ is the annual growth rate of input items, considering the data at discrete points in time, $\dot{\mathbf{x}}_{jt}$ can be approximately expressed as; $dX_t = \ln X_t - \ln X_{t-1}$.

Thus, the estimate of parametric total factor productivity growth is obtained from the rate of technological change (TC) and technology efficiency change (TEC) of scale effects as (7):

$$TFP_t = TC_t + TEC_t = TC_t + (RTS_t - 1) \cdot \sum_{j=1}^{k} \Psi_j \dot{\mathbf{x}}_{jt} \quad (7)$$

3.2. The Data

The main data source in this section is Chinese Statistics Yearbook 1996 to 2004. The data is annual time series and it covers the period 1978 to 2004 with 27 observations. There are 4 variables in this research: output (Y_t) is real GDP as dependent variable, and other independent variables, such as aggregate capital stock value (K_t), worked hours of employees on job (L_t) and trend (t). 1995 is regarded as the base year.

A. Real GDP (Y_t)

The nominal GDP series and GDP indices with comparable price to preceding year (1978-2004) are extracted from the Chinese Statistics Yearbook 1996 to 2004. An implicit GDP deflator series could be calculated following the method of Zhang (2003). Based on the year 1995, the current values of GDP series have been transformed into real value GDP series with constant prices. *Table 1* shows the process of the calculation.

Table 1. Chinese Nominal GDP, Implicit GDP deflator and Real GDP (1978—2004)

Year	Nominal **GDP** (100 million Yuan)	GDP indices With Comparable Price	GDP Indices With Current Price	Implicit GDP Deflator	Total Deflator Basing on 1995	Real GDP (100 million Yuan)
1978	3624.1	111.7	113.19	101.33	30.77	11779.58
1979	4038.2	107.6	111.43	103.56	31.86	12674.40
1980	4517.8	107.8	111.88	103.79	33.07	13662.59
1981	4862.4	105.2	107.63	102.31	33.83	14372.72
1982	5294.7	109.1	108.89	99.81	33.77	15680.74
1983	5934.5	110.9	112.08	101.06	34.13	17390.52
1984	7171.0	115.2	120.84	104.90	35.80	20033.19
1985	8964.4	113.5	125.01	110.14	39.43	22737.50
1986	10202.2	108.8	113.81	104.61	41.24	24737.95
1987	11962.5	111.6	117.25	105.06	43.33	27608.52
1988	14928.3	111.3	124.79	112.12	48.58	30728.90
1989	16909.2	104.1	113.27	108.81	52.86	31988.62
1990	18547.9	103.8	109.69	105.67	55.86	33204.54
1991	21617.8	109.2	116.55	106.73	59.62	36259.73
1992	26638.1	114.2	123.22	107.90	64.33	41409.62
1993	34634.4	113.5	130.02	114.56	73.69	46999.30
1994	46759.4	112.6	135.01	119.90	88.36	52920.64
1995	58478.1	110.5	125.06	113.18	100.00	58478.1
1996	67884.6	109.6	116.09	105.92	105.92	64089.52
1997	74462.6	108.8	109.69	100.82	106.79	69729.38
1998	78345.2	107.8	105.21	97.60	104.22	75171.24
1999	82067.5	107.1	104.75	97.81	101.94	80509.29
2000	89468.1	108.0	109.02	100.94	102.90	86948.20
2001	97314.8	107.5	108.77	101.18	104.11	93469.64
2002	105172.3	108.3	108.04	99.76	103.86	101259.77
2003	117251.9	109.1	111.49	102.19	106.14	110469.99
2004	136515	109.5	116.43	106.33	112.86	120963.41

B. Capital Stock (K_t) and Investment Expenditure

The capital stock aggregate data is not available in Chinese statistics, which is a problem to all economists who want to study the Chinese economy. However; there are some provincial data after 1982 available, which is not sufficient to be aggregated to national coverage. Some capital stock series have been computed. Thus, the capital stock series might be a potential source for varying results produced by different authors at present.

In this section, the Chinese real stock of the aggregate economy is calculated by applying the standard perpetual inventory method (PIM) as shown in (8) to construct the capital stock series under six uniform annual comprehensive depreciation rates, such as 4%, 5%, 6%, 7%, 8% and 9%, with the stock in 1952 as the base.

$$K_{i,t+1} = I_{i,t+1} + (1-\delta)K_{i,t} \tag{8}$$

Where $K_{i,t+1}$ and $I_{i,t+1}$ are respectively capital stock and capital formation/investment of unit (province, industry or country) i at period t, and δ is comprehensive depreciation rate.

An initial level of capital stock in 1952 price is given as 175 billion by Yuan Chow (1993), Hu and Khan (1997), which is utilized as an initial benchmark of capital stock following Wang and Yao (2002).

The fixed asset formation/investment series at current prices are available in the expenditure GDP structure table of the yearbook 2004. However, the corresponding investment price indices are partly available only from 1991 to 2004. So the investment price indices from 1978 to 1990 have been established in the light of urban residence consumption price indices and retail goods price indices at the same period. The real investment series are calculated based on the year of 1995 (see *Table2*).

The depreciation rate should be an estimation of the aggregate depreciation rate across different capital components of physical machinery and building. Wang and Yao (2002) conducted a sensitivity analysis of capital stock accumulations with 5%, 10% and 15% as depreciation rates. They found that the rate of real capital stock growth during the reform period is rather robust to different depreciation rates. Liao and Holmes (2002) used a depreciation rate of 4% in their measurement. Li (2003) used national aggregate, national sources of finance, provincial aggregate and financial data to construct a capital stock series with a depreciation rate of 4%. Guo Li Hong (2001) has reviewed the situation of state-owned enterprises' comprehensive depreciation rates as 4.3% in 1982, 7.2% in 1994, 3.8% in 1996, 4.1% in 1997 and 4.7% in 1999. In this section, six uniform comprehensive depreciation rates of 4%, 5%, 6%, 7%, 8% and 9% are chosen. Thus, several capital stock series have been calculated as shown in Table 3.

C. Quantity and Quality of Labor Input (L_t)

Following OECD Manual of Measuring Productivity, the total hours worked are utilized to reflect the quantity of labor input in Chinese national aggregate. Liu and Yoon (2000) felt that working hours could be ignored in China because of workers being employed full time. However, there should be some error due to the 48 hours per week being replaced by 44 hours in 1994 and 40 hours after 1995, which has been considered for adjustment of labor hours worked.

In the meantime, the number of employees should be selected suitably, which is another problem in Chinese aggregate economic analysis. The labor force population aged 15-64 and total employees as a simple sum of the urban and the rural labor force are popularly applied in much research with obvious shortcomings.

Table 2. Chinese Nominal Fixed Asset Formation and Real Investment Series (1978—2004)

Year	Fixed Asset Formation With current price (100 million Yuan)	Investment Price Indices*	Total Investment Price indices Basing on 1995	Real Investment Series (100 million Yuan)
1978	1073.9	100.7	25.096	4279.15
1979	1151.2	101.9	25.586	4499.43
1980	1318.0	106.7	27.313	4825.63
1981	1253.0	102.4	27.982	4477.94
1982	1493.2	101.9	28.527	5234.29
1983	1709.0	101.7	29.027	5887.72
1984	2125.6	102.7	29.825	7126.97
1985	2641.0	108.7	32.420	8146.33
1986	3098.0	106.0	34.365	9015.08
1987	374.2	107.0	36.770	10176.72
1988	4624.0	118.5	43.573	10612.16
1989	4339.0	116.3	50.675	8562.40
1990	4732.0	105.6	53.513	8842.74
1991	5940.0	109.5	58.597	10137.12
1992	8317.0	115.3	67.562	12310.21
1993	12980.0	126.6	85.533	15175.39
1994	16856.3	110.4	94.429	17850.82
1995	20300.5	105.9	100.000	20300.50
1996	23336.1	104.0	104.000	22438.56
1997	25154.2	101.7	105.768	23782.43
1998	27630.8	99.8	105.557	26176.32
1999	29475.5	99.6	105.134	28036.06
2000	32623.8	101.1	106.291	30692.99
2001	36813.3	100.4	106.716	34496.55
2002	41918.3	100.2	106.929	39201.88
2003	51248.3	102.2	109.282	46895.57
2004	70073.0	105.6	115.402	60721.03

Note: * The investment price indices from 1978 to 1990 are not available and established in the light of the urban residence consumption price indices and retail goods price indices at the same period.

For instance, the labor participation rate and the strong features of the Chinese dual labor market are ignored in these proxies of labor input. The Chinese rural labor surplus and urban unemployment has been intensively discussed by some researchers, such as Rawski (1999, 2001), Solinger (2002), Caifang, Duyang and Gaoshuwen (2004), Xiongzuyuan and Yuedong (2004), John and Xue (2004), etc. So far in Chinese official statistics, only urban registered unemployment rate is available, which might not cover the laid-off workers in the large scale restructuring plants and might hint at a strong assumption that there is no unemployment in rural areas.

Table 3. Chinese Capital Stock Series with Constant Price (Basing on 1995 with 6 different depreciation rates) (1978—2004)*

Year	K4	K5	K6	K7	K8	K9
1978	35077.20	32627.70	30475.20	28574.80	26889.10	25386.90
1979	38173.55	35495.74	33146.08	31073.96	29237.40	27601.49
1980	41472.24	38546.58	35982.94	33724.41	31724.04	29942.98
1981	44291.29	41097.19	38301.90	35841.64	33664.05	31726.05
1982	47753.92	44276.62	41238.08	38567.01	36205.22	34104.99
1983	51731.49	47950.51	44651.51	41755.04	39196.52	36923.27
1984	56789.20	52679.95	49099.39	45959.16	43187.77	40727.14
1985	62663.96	58192.29	54299.76	50888.35	47879.08	45208.03
1986	69172.48	64297.75	60056.85	56341.24	53063.83	50154.38
1987	76582.30	71259.58	66630.16	62574.08	58995.44	55817.21
1988	84131.17	78308.76	73244.51	68806.05	64887.97	61405.82
1989	89328.32	82955.73	77412.24	72552.03	68259.33	64441.70
1990	94597.93	87650.68	81610.25	76316.13	71641.33	67484.69
1991	100951.10	93405.27	86850.75	81111.12	76047.14	71548.18
1992	109223.30	101045.20	93949.92	87743.55	82273.58	77419.06
1993	120029.70	111168.30	103488.30	96776.88	90867.08	85626.73
1994	133079.40	123460.70	115129.80	107853.30	101448.50	95771.14
1995	148056.70	137588.20	128522.50	120604.10	113633.10	107452.20
1996	164573.00	153147.40	143249.70	134600.40	126981.10	120220.10
1997	181772.50	169272.40	158437.20	148960.80	140605.00	133182.70
1998	200677.90	186985.10	175107.30	164709.80	155532.90	147372.60
1999	220686.90	205671.90	192636.90	181216.20	171126.40	162145.10
2000	242552.40	226081.30	211771.70	199224.10	188129.20	178245.10
2001	267346.80	249273.80	233561.90	219774.90	207575.40	196699.60
2002	295854.90	2760120	258750.10	243592.60	230171.30	218198.50
2003	330916.20	309107.00	290120.70	273436.70	258653.20	245456.20
2004	378400.60	354372.60	333434.50	315017.10	298681.90	284086.20

Notes: *

The table is calculated basing on data of *Chinese Statistical Yearbook 1996—2004*.

K4, K5, K6, K7, K8 and K9 are comparable price capital stocks (100 million Yuan) corresponding to depreciation rates as 4%, 5%, 6%, 7%, 8% and 9% respectively. The benchmark of capital stock in 1952 is 175 billion Yuan at 1952 prices estimated by Chow (1993) and Hu and Khan (1997).

Following the results of Xiongzuyuan and Yuedong (2004), and John and Xue (2004), the author applies the land-labor ratio adjusted surplus labor for the Chinese rural employees and the estimated urban unemployment with the revised rate by the household survey data and the population census data on the basis of the urban registered unemployment rate. The adjusted urban and rural total employees are given in *Table 4*.

Table 4. Adjusted Chinese Rural and Urban Employee Numbers (1978—2004)

Year	Total Rural Employee (10,000)	Rural Surplus Labor (10,0000)*	Adjusted Rural Labor	Total Urban Employee	Urban Unemployed Number	Registered Rate	Adjusted Rate**	Adjusted Unemployed Number	Urban Surplus Number	Adjusted Urban Employee
1978	30638.00	9889.4	20748.6	9514	530.0	5.3	6.6	669.0	139.0	9375.0
1979	31004.50	10440.6	20563.9	10019	567.6	5.4	6.7	713.7	146.1	9873.4
1980	31836.00	11124.0	20712.0	10525	541.5	4.9	6.8	751.5	209.9	10315.0
1981	32629.25	11550.4	21078.9	11095	439.5	3.8	4.2	485.8	46.2	11049.5
1982	33628.50	12035.8	21592.7	11666	379.4	3.2	4.2	498.0	118.5	11547.9
1983	34198.75	12411.4	21787.3	12237	271.4	2.3	3.1	365.8	94.4	12142.9
1984	35674.38	12957.3	22717.1	12522	235.7	1.9	2.7	334.9	99.2	12423.4
1985	37065.00	13485.7	23579.3	12808	238.5	1.8	2.6	344.5	106.0	12702.0
1986	31004.50	14363.1	16641.4	13293	264.4	2.0	3.0	396.6	132.2	13160.8
1987	31836.00	15294.4	16541.6	13783	276.6	2.0	3.1	428.7	152.1	13630.9
1988	32629.25	16269.8	16359.5	14267	296.2	2.0	3.2	473.9	177.7	14089.3
1989	33628.50	17103.3	16525.2	14390	377.9	2.6	4.2	610.5	232.5	14157.5
1990	47708.00	20642.0	27066.0	17041	383.2	2.5	4.1	628.5	245.2	16795.8
1991	48026.00	19991.8	28034.2	17465	352.2	2.3	4.0	612.5	260.3	17204.7
1992	48291.00	19297.9	28993.1	17861	363.9	2.3	4.2	672.4	308.5	17552.5
1993	48546.00	18584.7	29961.4	18262	420.1	2.6	5.0	816.0	395.8	17866.1
1994	48802.00	17851.3	30950.7	18653	476.4	2.8	5.6	961.3	484.9	18168.1
1995	49025.00	17091.1	31933.9	19040	519.6	2.9	6.1	1101.9	582.3	18457.7
1996	49028.00	17062.4	31965.6	19922	552.8	3.0	8.1	1501.8	948.9	18973.0
1997	49039.00	17048.7	31990.4	20781	576.8	3.1	8.8	1637.4	1060.5	19720.4
1998	49021.00	17003.7	32017.3	21616	571.0	3.1	9.1	1676.2	1105.1	20510.8
1999	48982.00	16938.9	32043.1	22412	575.0	3.1	9.4	1752.8	1177.8	21234.2
2000	48934.00	16853.5	32080.5	23151	595.0	3.1	9.9	1909.8	1314.7	21836.2
2001	49085.00	17401.9	31683.1	23940	681.0	3.6	11.0	2080.8	1399.8	22540.2
2002	48960.00	17815.6	31144.4	24780	770.0	4.0	11.7	2261.9	1491.8	23288.1
2003	48793.00	18228.4	30564.6	25639	800.0	4.3	11.2	2083.7	1283.7	24355.3
2004	48914.00	18717.3	30196.7	26498	830.0	4.2	12.2	2411.0	1580.9	24917.1

Notes:

*Following the results of Xiongzuyuan and Yuedong (2004)[1]

**Following the result of John and Xue (2004)[2] and Xiongzuyuan and Yuedong (2004)[3]

[1] Xiongzuyuan and Yuedong (2004), A simple measurement of Chinese unemployment rate. Statistical Research No.7, 2004.

As for the quality of labor input, following OECD Manual of Measuring Productivity, labor compensation sharing factors have been weighted based on the equation (9) in order to reflect the dual labor market reality of China.

$$\ln(Labor)_t = \alpha_u \ln(urbanLabor)_t + \alpha_r \ln(ruralLabor)_t \qquad (9)$$

Where α_u and α_r are urban and rural labor compensation factors respectively. The annual per capital net income of rural households and the annual per capita disposable incomes of city residents are applied to represent the sharing factors (see *Table 5*).

Table 5. Chinese Labor Compensation and the Sharing Factors in Urban and Rural Areas (1978—2004)*

Year	Annual Per capita Net Income of Rural Households	Annual Per Capita Disposable Incomes of City Residents	Rural Labor Compensation Sharing Factor	Urban Labor Compensation Sharing Factor
1978	133.6	343.4	0.28	0.720
1979	160.2	405.0	0.28	0.720
1980	191.3	477.6	0.29	0.710
1981	223.4	500.4	0.31	0.690
1982	270.1	535.3	0.33	0.665
1983	309.8	564.6	0.35	0.650
1984	355.3	652.1	0.35	0.647
1985	397.6	739.1	0.35	0.650
1986	423.8	900.9	0.32	0.680
1987	462.6	1002.1	0.31	0.684
1988	544.9	1180.2	0.31	0.684
1989	601.5	1373.9	0.30	0.695
1990	686.3	1510.2	0.31	0.690
1991	708.6	1700.6	0.29	0.710
1992	784.0	2026.6	0.27	0.721
1993	921.6	2577.4	0.26	0.740
1994	1221.0	3496.2	0.25	0.741
1995	1577.7	4283.0	0.26	0.731
1996	1926.1	4838.9	0.28	0.715
1997	2090.1	5160.3	0.28	0.712
1998	2162.0	5425.1	0.28	0.715
1999	2210.3	5854.0	0.27	0.730
2000	2253.4	6280.0	0.26	0.740
2001	2366.4	6859.6	0.25	0.743
2002	2475.6	7702.8	0.24	0.760
2003	2622.2	8472.2	0.23	0.764
2004	2936.0	9422.0	0.23	0.762

*The table is calculated basing on data of *Chinese Statistical Yearbook 1996—2004*.

[2] John and Xue (2004), How High Is Urban Unemployment in China?

[3] Xiongzuyuan and Yuedong (2004), A simple measurement of Chinese unemployment rate. Statistical Research No.7, 2004.

D. Time Trend (T)

The samples are from 1978 to 2004. So the trend value is taking values from 1 to 27, which reflects the broad sense of technology.

3.3. Regressions and Testing Procedures

There are 27 observations and 9 parameters in the general model (1). There are 6 specific models considering the capital stock series with 6 different depreciation rates and one labor input. A series of regressions have been conducted with variable selection, namely OLS method in a stepwise method. An obvious first order autocorrelation is found in the models' test. In this regard, a model correcting for first order autoregressive disturbance is brought into the analysis of model (1) as (10).

$$\varepsilon_t = \rho\varepsilon_{t-1} + v_t \tag{10}$$

The estimation involves the iterative Prais and Winstern algorithm transformation of the data and the GLS estimation in a repeated two-step estimation procedure.

All coefficients are statistically significant at less than 2.5% level of significance with an exception of the 4% depreciation rate capital stock model (K4 model). According to the regression results, some interaction items are not statistically significant and have been removed finally. Only neutral (pure trend terms) technology change with first order has been found, that could not be regarded as a full dynamic analysis here.

The regression results are shown in *Table 6.*

Table 6. The Regression Results of Chinese Aggregate Production Functions

Model	Variable	Coefficient	Standard Error	T-value
K4	T	0.138551	7.82E-02	1.771
K4	Lk4La	6.59E-02	1.05E-03	62.963
K4	Lk4T	-1.08E-02	5.74E-03	-1.881
K4	Rho	0.672002	0.145233	4.627
K5	T	-1.03E-02	4.34E-03	-2.383
K5	LK5La	6.82E-02	4.64E-04	147.005
K5	Rho	0.729670	0.134104	5.441
K6	T	-1.12E-02	4.36E-03	-2.575
K6	LK6La	6.86E-01	4.69E-04	146.397
K6	rho	0.733892	0.133214	5.509
K7	T	-1.21E-02	4.38E-03	-2.763
K7	LK7La	6.91E-02	4.74E-04	145.828
K7	rho	0.738036	0.132331	5.577
K8	T	-1.30E-02	4.40E-03	-2.946
K8	LK8La	6.95E-02	4.79E-04	145.284
K8	Rho	0.742122	0.131449	5.646
K9	T	-1.38E-02	4.41E-03	-3.121
K9	LK9La	6.99E-02	4.83E-04	144.751
K9	Rho	0.746176	0.130563	5.715

Table 7-8 shows the summary of all input data in this analysis. *Table 9* presents the descriptive statistics of the data. *Table10* reports the change rates of all variables used.

Table 7. Chinese Real GDP, Capital Stock (with 6 different depreciations), Total Hours-worked in Urban and Rural, the Income Sharing (1978—2004)*

YEAR	Y	K4	K5	K6	K7	K8	K9	LU	WU	LR	WR
1978	11779	35077	32627	30475	28574	26889	25386	450000	0.72	995931	0.280
1979	12674	38173	35495	33146	31074	29237	27601	473923	0.716	987067	0.283
1980	13662	41472	38546	35982	33724.	31724	29943	495122	0.714	994176	0.286
1981	14372	44291	41097	38301	35841	33664	31726	530375	0.691	1.01E+06	0.309
1982	15680	47753	44276	41238	38567	36205	34105	554301	0.665	1.04E+06	0.335
1983	17390	51731	47950	44651	41755	39196	36923	582857	0.646	1.05E+06	0.354
1984	20033	56789	52679	49099	45959	43187	40727	596322	0.647	1.09E+06	0.353
1985	22737	62664	58192	54299	50888	47879	45208	609696	0.650	1.13E+06	0.350
1986	24738	69172	64297	60056	56341	53063	50154	631718	0.680	798789	0.320
1987	27608	76582	71259	66630	62574	58995	55817	654282	0.684	793997	0.316
1988	30728	84131	78308	73244	68806	64888	61405	676285	0.684	785255	0.316
1989	31988	89328	82955	77412	72552	68259	64441	679557	0.696	793210	0.305
1990	33204	94597	87650	81610	76316	71641	67484	806196	0.688	1.30E+06	0.313
1991	36259	100951	93405	86850	81111	76047	71548	825825	0.706	1.35E+06	0.294
1992	41409	109223	101045	93949	87743	82273	77419	842519	0.721	1.39E+06	0.279
1993	46999	120030	111168	103488	96776	90867	85626	857575	0.737	1.44E+06	0.263
1994	52920	133079	123461	115130	107853	101449	95771	799396	0.741	1.36E+06	0.259
1995	58478	148057	137588	128523	120604	113633	107452	738308	0.731	1.28E+06	0.269
1996	64089	164573	153147	143250	134600	126981	120220	758921	0.715	1.28E+06	0.285
1997	69729	181773	169272	158437	148961	140605	133183	788817	0.711	1.28E+06	0.288
1998	75171	200678	186985	175107	164710	155533	147373	820434	0.715	1.28E+06	0.285
1999	80509	220687	205672	192637	181216	171126	162145	849367	0.726	1.28E+06	0.274
2000	86948	242552	226081	211772	199224	188129	178245	873450	0.736	1.28E+06	0.264
2001	93469	267347	249274	233562	219775	207575	196700	901607	0.744	1.27E+06	0.257
2002	101260	295855	276012	258750	243593	230171	218199	931525	0.757	1.25E+06	0.243
2003	110470	330916	309107	290121	273437	258653	245456	974211	0.764	1.22E+06	0.236
2004	120963	378401	354373	333435	315017	298682	284086	996682	0.762	1.21E+06	0.238

Notes: *

The table is calculated basing on data of Chinese Statistical Yearbook 1996—2004.

K4, K5, K6, K7, K8 and K9 are comparable price capital stocks (100 million Yuan) corresponding to depreciation rates as 4%, 5%, 6%, 7%, 8% and 9% respectively. The benchmark of capital stock in 1952 is 175 billion Yuan at 1952 prices estimated by Chow (1993) and Hu and Khan (1997).

Table 8. The Logarithm Values of Input Data

YEAR	LY	LK4	LK5	LK6	LK7	LK8	LK9	LLU	LLR	LA*
1978	9.37412	10.4653	10.3929	10.3247	10.2603	10.1995	10.1420	13.0170	13.8114	13.2395
1979	9.44734	10.5499	10.4772	10.4087	10.3441	10.2832	10.2256	13.0688	13.8025	13.2768
1980	9.52242	10.6328	10.5596	10.4908	10.4260	10.3648	10.3071	13.1126	13.8097	13.3119
1981	9.57309	10.6985	10.6237	10.5533	10.4869	10.4242	10.3649	13.1813	13.8272	13.3807
1982	9.66019	10.7738	10.6982	10.6271	10.5602	10.497	10.4372	13.2255	13.8513	13.4353
1983	9.76368	10.8538	10.7779	10.7066	10.6396	10.5763	10.5166	13.2757	13.8603	13.4828
1984	9.90515	10.9471	10.8720	10.8016	10.7355	10.6733	10.6146	13.2985	13.9021	13.5114
1985	10.0318	11.0455	10.9715	10.9023	10.8374	10.7764	10.7190	13.3207	13.9393	13.5371
1986	10.1161	11.1444	11.0713	11.0030	10.9392	10.8793	10.8229	13.3562	13.5909	13.4313
1987	10.2259	11.2461	11.1741	11.1069	11.0441	10.9852	10.9298	13.3913	13.5848	13.4524
1988	10.3330	11.3401	11.2684	11.2016	11.1390	11.0804	11.0253	13.4244	13.5738	13.4716
1989	10.3731	11.4001	11.3261	11.2569	11.1921	11.1311	11.0735	13.4292	13.5838	13.4763
1990	10.4104	11.4574	11.3811	11.3097	11.2426	11.1794	11.1197	13.6001	14.0772	13.7492
1991	10.4985	11.5224	11.4447	11.3719	11.3036	11.2391	11.1781	13.6241	14.1124	13.7677
1992	10.6313	11.6011	11.5233	11.4505	11.3822	11.3178	11.2570	13.6442	14.1460	13.7841
1993	10.7579	11.6955	11.6188	11.5472	11.4802	11.4172	11.3578	13.6619	14.1789	13.7980
1994	10.8765	11.7987	11.7237	11.6538	11.5885	11.5273	11.4697	13.5916	14.1243	13.7295
1995	10.9764	11.9054	11.8320	11.7639	11.7003	11.6407	11.5848	13.5121	14.0603	13.6597
1996	11.0680	12.0111	11.9392	11.8723	11.8101	11.7518	11.6971	13.5397	14.0613	13.6882
1997	11.1524	12.1105	12.0393	11.9731	11.9114	11.8537	11.7995	13.5783	14.0621	13.7178
1998	11.2275	12.2095	12.1388	12.0732	12.0119	11.9546	11.9007	13.6176	14.0629	13.7445
1999	11.2961	12.3045	12.2340	12.1686	12.1074	12.0502	11.9962	13.6522	14.0637	13.7650
2000	11.3731	12.3990	12.3286	12.2633	12.2022	12.1449	12.0909	13.6802	14.0649	13.7818
2001	11.4454	12.4963	12.4263	12.3612	12.3004	12.2432	12.1894	13.7119	14.0524	13.7993
2002	11.5254	12.5976	12.5282	12.4636	12.4033	12.3466	12.2932	13.7446	14.0353	13.8153
2003	11.6125	12.7096	12.6414	12.5781	12.5188	12.4632	12.4109	13.7894	14.0165	13.8431
2004	11.7032	12.8437	12.7781	12.7172	12.6604	12.6071	12.557	13.8122	14.0044	13.8578

Note: *La is income weighted labor input considering the dual economy of China.

The calculated input elasticity of capital stock (elk) and labor hours worked (ela), returns to scale (RTS), the rate of technical change (TC), the rate of technical efficiency change (TEC), and the total factor productivity (TFP) growth are reported in *Table 11-16.*

Table 9. Data Descriptive Statistics of the Logarithm Value of Input Data

Descriptive Statistics					
All results based on non-missing observations.					
Variable	Mean	Std. Dev.	Minimum	Maximum	Cases
LY	10.5511315	0.73306219	9.3741245	11.7032433	27
LK4	11.5836955	0.71320615	10.4653066	12.8437087	27
LK5	11.5107580	0.71505134	10.3929169	12.7781042	27
LK6	11.4426309	0.71708420	10.3246685	12.7172017	27
LK7	11.3787968	0.71919895	10.2602805	12.6603822	27
LK8	11.3187998	0.72132345	10.1994763	12.6071344	27
LK9	11.2622403	0.72341107	10.1419886	12.5570330	27
LA	13.6114085	0.19164966	13.2395069	13.8578454	27
T	14.0000000	7.93725393	1.0000000	27.0000000	27
All observations in current sample					

Table 10. Percentage Change Rate (D) of Chinese Real GDP, Real Capital Stock (with 6 different depreciations), Income Weighted Total Hours-worked (1979—2004)

YEAR	DLY	DLK4	DLK5	DLK6	DLK7	DLK8	DLK9	DLA
1979	7.32	8.46	8.43	8.40	8.38	8.37	8.36	3.73
1980	7.51	8.29	8.25	8.21	8.19	8.16	8.14	3.52
1981	5.07	6.58	6.41	6.25	6.09	5.94	5.78	6.88
1982	8.71	7.53	7.45	7.39	7.33	7.28	7.23	5.47
1983	10.35	8.00	7.97	7.95	7.94	7.94	7.94	4.75
1984	14.15	9.33	9.41	9.50	9.59	9.70	9.81	2.86
1985	12.66	9.84	9.95	10.07	10.19	10.31	10.44	2.57
1986	8.43	9.88	9.98	10.08	10.18	10.28	10.38	-10.58
1987	10.98	10.18	10.28	10.39	10.49	10.60	10.70	2.12
1988	10.71	9.40	9.43	9.46	9.49	9.52	9.54	1.91
1989	4.02	5.99	5.76	5.53	5.30	5.07	4.83	0.47
1990	3.73	5.73	5.51	5.28	5.06	4.84	4.61	27.29
1991	8.80	6.50	6.36	6.22	6.09	5.97	5.85	1.86
1992	13.28	7.88	7.86	7.86	7.86	7.87	7.89	1.64
1993	12.66	9.43	9.55	9.67	9.80	9.93	10.08	1.39
1994	11.87	10.32	10.49	10.66	10.84	11.02	11.20	-6.85
1995	9.99	10.66	10.83	11.00	11.17	11.34	11.51	-6.98
1996	9.16	10.58	10.71	10.85	10.98	11.11	11.23	2.85
1997	8.43	9.94	10.01	10.08	10.14	10.19	10.24	2.96
1998	7.51	9.89	9.95	10.00	10.05	10.09	10.12	2.67
1999	6.86	9.50	9.53	9.54	9.55	9.55	9.55	2.05
2000	7.69	9.45	9.46	9.47	9.47	9.47	9.47	1.68
2001	7.23	9.73	9.77	9.79	9.82	9.84	9.85	1.75
2002	8.01	10.13	10.19	10.24	10.29	10.33	10.37	1.60
2003	8.71	11.20	11.32	11.44	11.56	11.67	11.77	2.78
2004	9.07	13.41	13.67	13.91	14.16	14.39	14.62	1.48
MEAN	8.96	9.15	9.17	9.20	9.23	9.26	9.29	2.38

3.4 Analysis of the Results

A. Summary Statistics of the data

Following the summary statistics of the data in the 27 years' Reform and Opening Period, it is easy for us to observe the following facts:

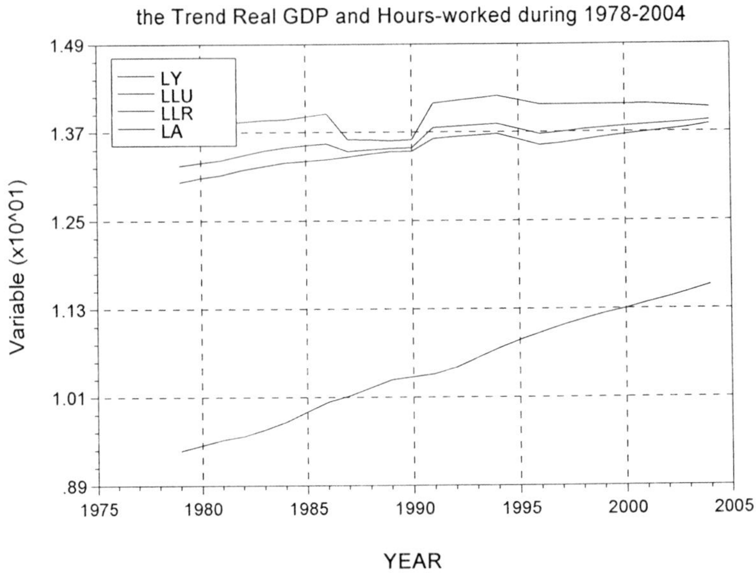

Figure 1. The Trend of Chinese Real GDP and Hours-worked During 1978-2004.

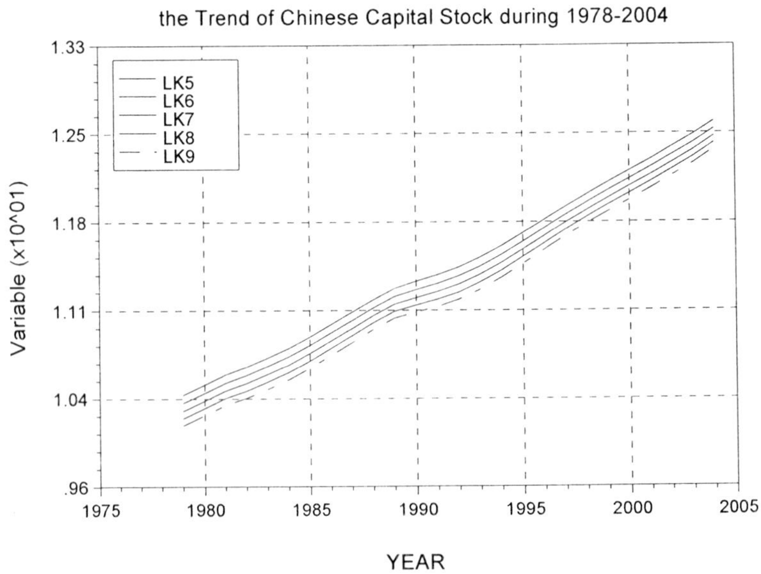

Figure 2. The Trend of Chinese Capital Stock During 1978-2004.

The general trend of Chinese real GDP, capital stock and labor working hours is increasing during the period.

Figure 3. The Growth Rate of Chinese Real GDP During 1979-2004.

B. About Real Gdp

The average growth rate of Chinese real GDP is 8.96% per year (S.D.=0.0265) from 1979-2004 with 14.15% per year as one peak in 1984 (introduction of urban economic system reform) and 13.28% per year as another peak in 1992 (declaration of market economy and extending the opening to the outside). Three declining periods happened in 1981 (the hesitating period of the reform) by 5.07% per year, in 1990 (the consequences of pricing system reform and political riot) by 3.73% per year, and in 1999 (the Asian financial crisis in 1997 and the flooding in 1998) by 6.86% per year. From 1979 to 1989, the average real GDP growth rate is 9.08% per year. In the period of 1990 to 1999, the average growth rate of real GDP is 9.24% per year and it slows down slightly from 2000 to 2004 averaged at 8.14% per year. The year 2001 witnesses a speeding up cycle of positive trend in growth until now (the end of 2005).

C. About Real Capital Stock

As for the average annual growth rate of Chinese real capital stock, it is 9.15% (S.D.=0.0173 with depreciation rate δ=4%), 9.17% (S.D.=0.0185 with δ=5%) 9.20% (S.D.=0.0196 with δ=6%), 9.23% (S.D.=0.0208 with δ= 7%), 9.26% (S.D.=0.0219 with δ=8%), and 9.29% (S.D.=0.0229 with δ=9%) respectively, which are higher than that of real GDP. In 1987, 1995 and 2004 the economy experienced three peak values by 10.44%, 11.09% and 14.03% respectively, while in 1981 experienced slowdown periods of 6.17%, in 1990 of 5.17%, and in 2000 of 9.47% as sample averages.

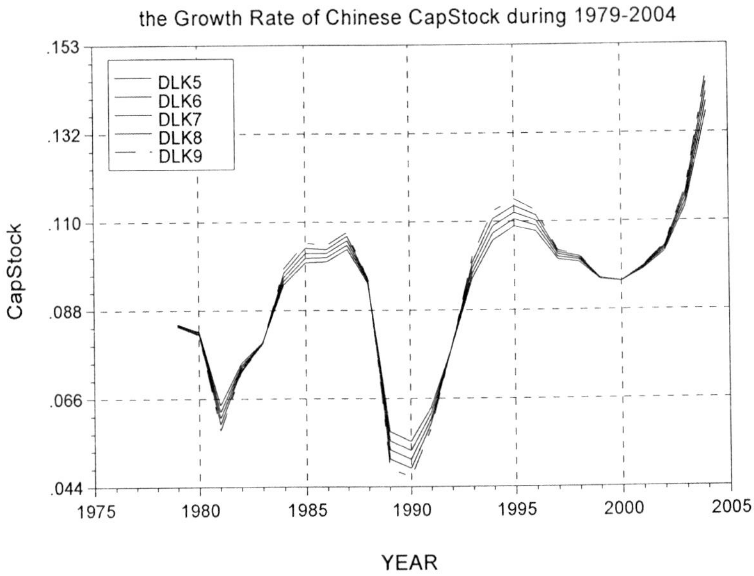

Figure 4. The Growth Rate of Chinese Capital Stock During 1979-2004.

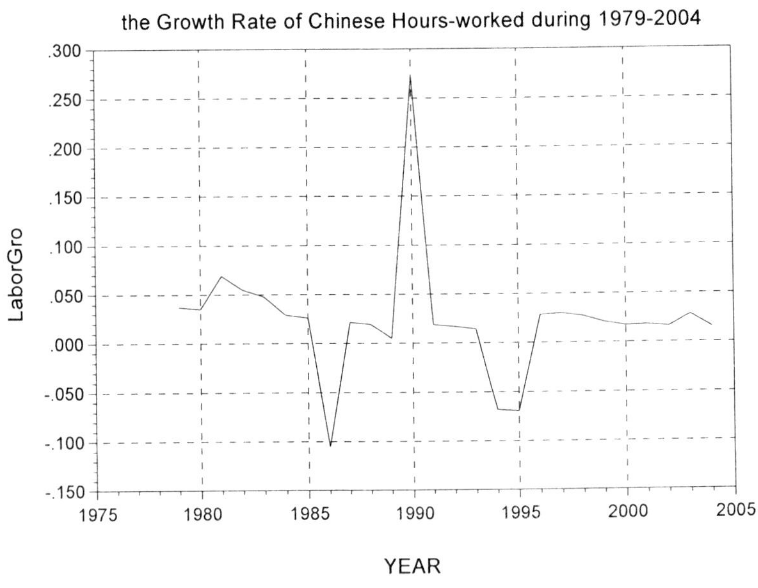

Figure 5. The Growth Rate of Chinese Hours-worked During 1979-2004.

D. About Labor Working Hours

The average annual growth rate of labor working hours during the study period is 2.38% (SD 0.01635). In 1985 (state owned enterprise reform) and 1995 (working hours per week reduction reform) experienced two lowest values as –10.58% and –6.98% respectively. In 1990 (urban labor market opening) experienced a peak of 27.29%. The average annual growth rate of working hours is 2.15% from 1979 to 1989, 2.89% from 1990 to 1999, and 1.86% from 2000 to 2004.

E. About Capital Elasticity

Based on the regression results, the capital partial elasticity (elk) of output shows an increasing trend during 1978-2004 with a decline in 1987, rising up again in 1991 and a slight decline in 1996. The elk fluctuates from 0.91 (in 1978 samples average) to 0.96 (in 2004 samples average). The average of elk during the study period depending on the choice of different depreciation rates is 0.93 (with δ=5%), 0.93 (δ=6%), 0.94 (δ=7%), 0.95 (δ=8%), and 0.95 (δ=9%).

Table 11. The Capital Stock Elasticity of Chinese Real GDP (with 5 different depreciation rates) (1978—2004)

YEAR	ELK5	ELK6	ELK7	ELK8	ELK9
1978	0.90	0.91	0.91	0.92	0.93
1979	0.90	0.91	0.92	0.92	0.93
1980	0.91	0.91	0.92	0.93	0.93
1981	0.91	0.92	0.92	0.93	0.94
1982	0.92	0.92	0.93	0.93	0.94
1983	0.92	0.93	0.93	0.94	0.94
1984	0.92	0.93	0.93	0.94	0.95
1985	0.92	0.93	0.94	0.94	0.95
1986	0.92	0.92	0.93	0.93	0.94
1987	0.92	0.92	0.93	0.94	0.94
1988	0.92	0.92	0.93	0.94	0.94
1989	0.92	0.92	0.93	0.94	0.94
1990	0.94	0.94	0.95	0.96	0.96
1991	0.94	0.94	0.95	0.96	0.96
1992	0.94	0.95	0.95	0.96	0.96
1993	0.94	0.95	0.95	0.96	0.97
1994	0.94	0.94	0.95	0.95	0.96
1995	0.93	0.94	0.94	0.95	0.96
1996	0.93	0.94	0.95	0.95	0.96
1997	0.93	0.94	0.95	0.95	0.96
1998	0.94	0.94	0.95	0.96	0.96
1999	0.94	0.94	0.95	0.96	0.96
2000	0.94	0.95	0.95	0.96	0.96
2001	0.94	0.95	0.95	0.96	0.97
2002	0.94	0.95	0.95	0.96	0.97
2003	0.94	0.95	0.96	0.96	0.97
2004	0.94	0.95	0.96	0.96	0.97
MEAN	0.93	0.93	0.94	0.95	0.95

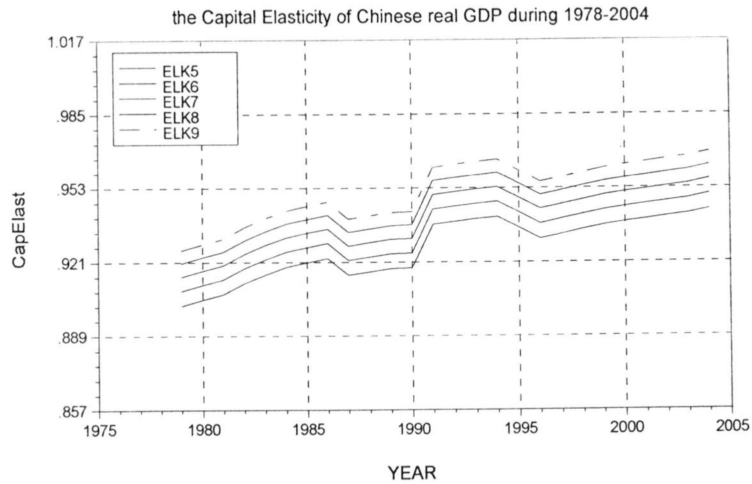

Figure 6. The Capital Elasticity of Chinese Real GDP During 1978-2004.

F. About Labor Elasticity

The labor partial elasticity (ela) of output also shows an increasing trend during 1978-2004. The ela fluctuates from 0.71 (in 1978 samples average) to 0.88 (in 2004 samples average). The average of ela during the study period depending on the choice of different depreciation rates is 0.79 (with δ=5%), 0.79 (δ=6%), 0.79 (δ=7%), 0.79 (δ=8%), and 0.79 (δ=9%).

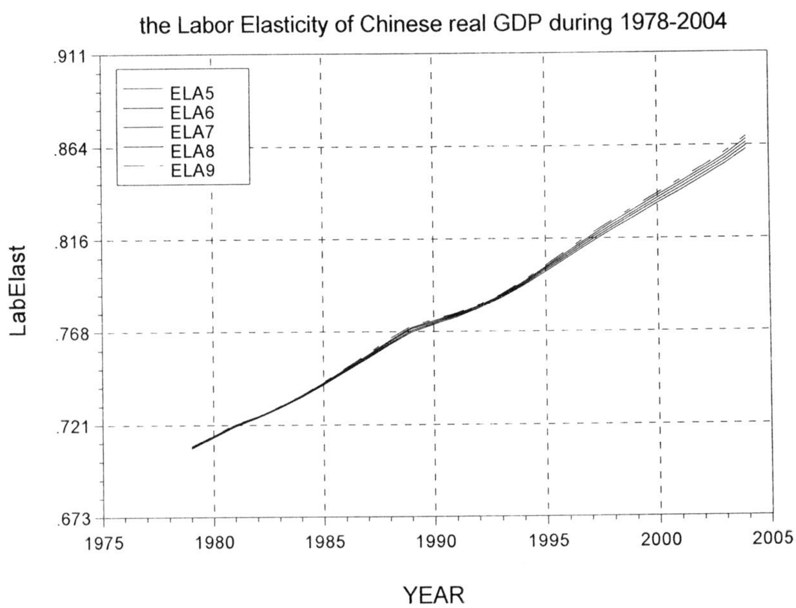

Figure 7. The Labor Elasticity of Chinese Real GDP During 1978-2004.

Table 12. The Labor Elasticity of Chinese Real GDP (with 5 different depreciation rates) (1978—2004)

YEAR	ELA5	ELA6	ELA7	ELA8	ELA9
1978	0.71	0.71	0.71	0.71	0.71
1979	0.71	0.71	0.71	0.71	0.72
1980	0.72	0.72	0.72	0.72	0.72
1981	0.72	0.72	0.72	0.72	0.72
1982	0.73	0.73	0.73	0.73	0.73
1983	0.73	0.73	0.74	0.74	0.74
1984	0.74	0.74	0.74	0.74	0.74
1985	0.75	0.75	0.75	0.75	0.75
1986	0.75	0.76	0.76	0.76	0.76
1987	0.76	0.76	0.76	0.76	0.76
1988	0.77	0.77	0.77	0.77	0.77
1989	0.77	0.77	0.77	0.77	0.77
1990	0.78	0.78	0.78	0.78	0.78
1991	0.78	0.78	0.78	0.78	0.78
1992	0.79	0.79	0.79	0.79	0.79
1993	0.79	0.79	0.79	0.79	0.79
1994	0.80	0.80	0.80	0.80	0.80
1995	0.81	0.81	0.81	0.81	0.81
1996	0.81	0.81	0.82	0.82	0.82
1997	0.82	0.82	0.82	0.82	0.83
1998	0.83	0.83	0.83	0.83	0.83
1999	0.83	0.84	0.84	0.84	0.84
2000	0.84	0.84	0.84	0.84	0.85
2001	0.85	0.85	0.85	0.85	0.85
2002	0.85	0.86	0.86	0.86	0.86
2003	0.86	0.86	0.86	0.87	0.87
2004	0.87	0.87	0.87	0.88	0.88
MEAN	0.78	0.79	0.79	0.79	0.79

Table 13. Percentage rate of the Pure Technical Change Rate (with 5 different depreciation rates) (1978—2004)

YEAR	TC5	TC6	TC7	TC8	TC9
1978	-1.03	-1.12	-1.21	-1.30	-1.38
1979	-1.03	-1.12	-1.21	-1.30	-1.38
1980	-1.03	-1.12	-1.21	-1.30	-1.38
1981	-1.03	-1.12	-1.21	-1.30	-1.38
1982	-1.03	-1.12	-1.21	-1.30	-1.38
1983	-1.03	-1.12	-1.21	-1.30	-1.38
1984	-1.03	-1.12	-1.21	-1.30	-1.38
1985	-1.03	-1.12	-1.21	-1.30	-1.38
1986	-1.03	-1.12	-1.21	-1.30	-1.38
1987	-1.03	-1.12	-1.21	-1.30	-1.38
1988	-1.03	-1.12	-1.21	-1.30	-1.38
1989	-1.03	-1.12	-1.21	-1.30	-1.38
1990	-1.03	-1.12	-1.21	-1.30	-1.38
1991	-1.03	-1.12	-1.21	-1.30	-1.38
1992	-1.03	-1.12	-1.21	-1.30	-1.38
1993	-1.03	-1.12	-1.21	-1.30	-1.38
1994	-1.03	-1.12	-1.21	-1.30	-1.38
1995	-1.03	-1.12	-1.21	-1.30	-1.38
1996	-1.03	-1.12	-1.21	-1.30	-1.38
1997	-1.03	-1.12	-1.21	-1.30	-1.38
1998	-1.03	-1.12	-1.21	-1.30	-1.38
1999	-1.03	-1.12	-1.21	-1.30	-1.38
2000	-1.03	-1.12	-1.21	-1.30	-1.38
2001	-1.03	-1.12	-1.21	-1.30	-1.38
2002	-1.03	-1.12	-1.21	-1.30	-1.38
2003	-1.03	-1.12	-1.21	-1.30	-1.38
2004	-1.03	-1.12	-1.21	-1.30	-1.38
MEAN	-1.03	-1.12	-1.21	-1.30	-1.38

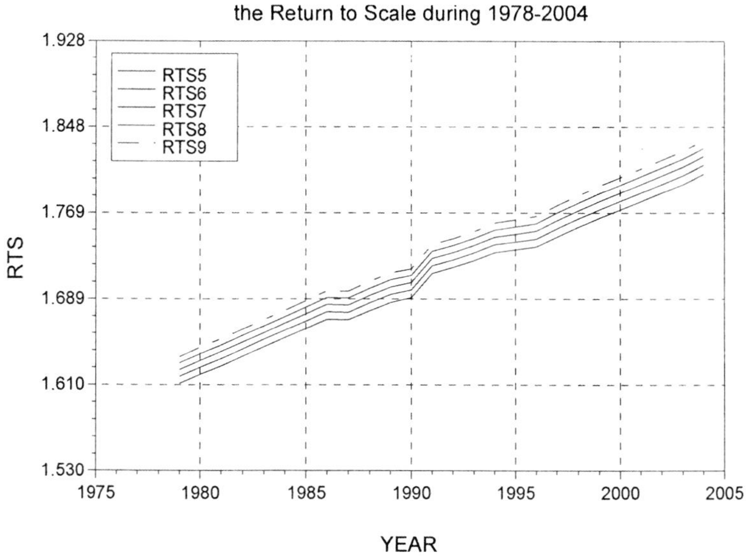

Figure 8. The Returns to Scale of Chinese Aggregate Economy During 1978-2004.

Table 14. The Return to Scale (with 5 different depreciation rates) (1978—2004)

YEAR	RTS5	RTS6	RTS7	RTS8	RTS9
1978	1.61	1.62	1.62	1.63	1.64
1979	1.62	1.63	1.63	1.64	1.64
1980	1.63	1.63	1.64	1.65	1.65
1981	1.64	1.64	1.65	1.66	1.66
1982	1.64	1.65	1.66	1.66	1.67
1983	1.65	1.66	1.67	1.67	1.68
1984	1.66	1.67	1.68	1.68	1.69
1985	1.67	1.68	1.68	1.69	1.70
1986	1.67	1.68	1.68	1.69	1.70
1987	1.68	1.69	1.69	1.70	1.71
1988	1.69	1.69	1.70	1.71	1.71
1989	1.69	1.70	1.70	1.71	1.72
1990	1.71	1.72	1.73	1.73	1.74
1991	1.72	1.73	1.73	1.74	1.74
1992	1.72	1.73	1.74	1.75	1.75
1993	1.73	1.74	1.75	1.75	1.76
1994	1.73	1.74	1.75	1.76	1.76
1995	1.74	1.74	1.75	1.76	1.77
1996	1.75	1.75	1.76	1.77	1.78
1997	1.76	1.76	1.77	1.78	1.78
1998	1.76	1.77	1.78	1.79	1.79
1999	1.77	1.78	1.79	1.79	1.80
2000	1.78	1.79	1.80	1.80	1.81
2001	1.79	1.80	1.80	1.81	1.82
2002	1.80	1.80	1.81	1.82	1.83
2003	1.80	1.81	1.82	1.83	1.84
2004	1.82	1.82	1.83	1.84	1.85
MEAN	1.71	1.72	1.73	1.73	1.74

G. About RTS

The values of returns to scale (RTS) shows an increasing trend during 1978-2004 and is bigger than one suggesting increasing returns to scale during the entire period. The RTS varies from 1.62 (in 1978 samples average) to 1.83 (in 2004 samples average). The mean of RTS during the studying period depending on chosen depreciation rate is 1.71 (with δ=5%), 1.72 (δ=6%), 1.73 (δ=7%), 1.73 (δ=8%), and 1.74 (δ=9%).

H. TFP Growth Rate During1979-2004

Corresponding to the trend of input factors during the study period, the TFP growth rate of Chinese fluctuates between –0.22% and 17.65% (per year, with δ=5%), –0.20% and 17.64% (δ=6%), –0.17% and 17.61% (δ=7%), -0.14% and 17.58% (δ=8%), and, -0.11% and 17.53% (δ=9%). The mean of TFP growth rate within the 26 years depending on the depreciation rate chosen is 6.41% (δ=5%), 6.47% (δ=6%), 6.52% (δ=7%), and 6.57% (δ=8%) and 6.62% (δ=9%).

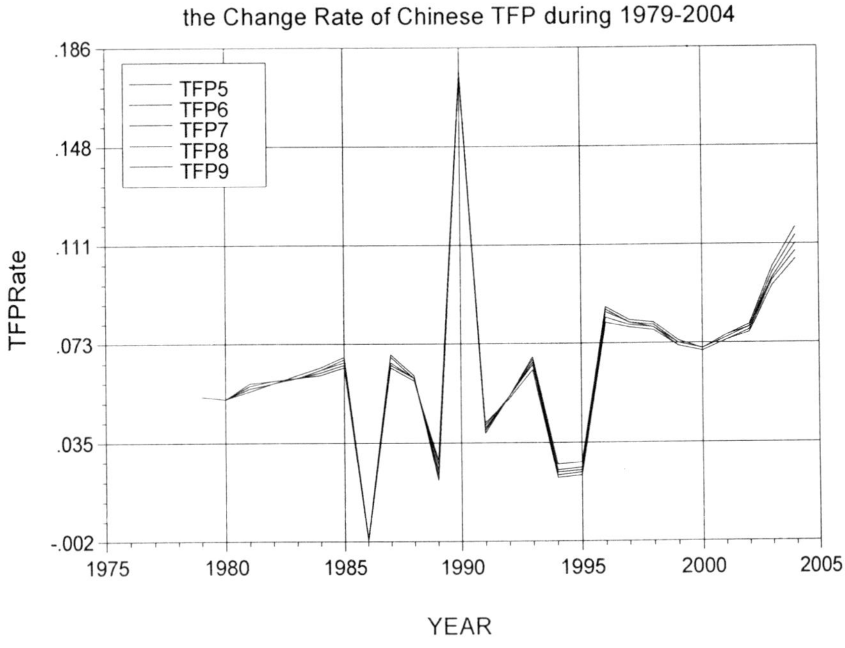

Figure 10. The Change Rate of Chinese TFP growth During 1979-2004.

Table 15. Percentage rate Technical Efficiency Change (with 5 different depreciation rates) (1979—2004)

YEAR	TEC5	TEC6	TEC7	TEC8	TEC9
1979	6.35	6.44	6.53	6.62	6.70
1980	6.26	6.35	6.43	6.51	6.58
1981	6.86	6.87	6.87	6.86	6.85
1982	6.95	7.01	7.08	7.14	7.20
1983	7.05	7.14	7.24	7.34	7.43
1984	7.12	7.29	7.46	7.64	7.82
1985	7.43	7.62	7.82	8.02	8.21
1986	0.82	0.93	1.04	1.15	1.27
1987	7.48	7.67	7.86	8.05	8.23
1988	6.94	7.08	7.21	7.34	7.46
1989	3.91	3.82	3.73	3.63	3.52
1990	18.69	18.76	18.82	18.87	18.91
1991	5.32	5.31	5.30	5.29	5.27
1992	6.28	6.38	6.48	6.58	6.68
1993	7.37	7.58	7.79	8.00	8.22
1994	3.22	3.42	3.63	3.84	4.05
1995	3.32	3.52	3.73	3.93	4.13
1996	9.18	9.42	9.66	9.90	10.13
1997	8.89	9.08	9.26	9.44	9.61
1998	8.80	8.98	9.15	9.32	9.48
1999	8.21	8.36	8.49	8.62	8.75
2000	8.02	8.16	8.29	8.41	8.53
2001	8.39	8.55	8.70	8.85	8.98
2002	8.71	8.89	9.07	9.24	9.41
2003	10.51	10.77	11.03	11.28	11.53
2004	11.56	11.95	12.34	12.72	13.10
MEAN	7.45	7.59	7.73	7.87	8.00

Table 16. Percentage rate of Total Factor Productivity Change Rates of Chinese Economy (with 5 different depreciation rates) (1979—2004)

YEAR	TFP5	TFP6	TFP7	TFP8	TFP9
1979	5.32	5.32	5.32	5.32	5.32
1980	5.23	5.22	5.22	5.21	5.21
1981	5.83	5.74	5.66	5.57	5.48
1982	5.92	5.89	5.87	5.85	5.83
1983	6.01	6.02	6.03	6.04	6.06
1984	6.09	6.17	6.25	6.34	6.44
1985	6.40	6.50	6.61	6.72	6.84
1986	-0.22	-0.20	-0.17	-0.14	-0.11
1987	6.44	6.54	6.65	6.75	6.85
1988	5.91	5.95	6.00	6.04	6.08
1989	2.87	2.70	2.52	2.34	2.15
1990	17.65	17.64	17.61	17.58	17.53
1991	4.28	4.19	4.09	3.99	3.89
1992	5.24	5.25	5.26	5.28	5.30
1993	6.34	6.45	6.58	6.71	6.84
1994	2.19	2.30	2.42	2.54	2.67
1995	2.29	2.40	2.52	2.63	2.75
1996	8.14	8.30	8.45	8.60	8.75
1997	7.85	7.96	8.05	8.15	8.23
1998	7.76	7.86	7.94	8.02	8.10
1999	7.17	7.23	7.28	7.33	7.37
2000	6.98	7.03	7.08	7.12	7.15
2001	7.35	7.42	7.49	7.55	7.61
2002	7.67	7.77	7.86	7.95	8.03
2003	9.47	9.65	9.82	9.99	10.15
2004	10.53	10.83	11.13	11.43	11.72
MEAN	6.41	6.47	6.52	6.57	6.62

I. Decomposition of TFP

The exogenous rate of technical change (TC) is negative during 1978-2004. The mean rate of TC is for different depreciate rates: –1.04 (% per year, with δ=5%), -1.12 (δ=6%), -1.21 (δ=7%), -1.30 (δ=8%) and –1.38 (δ=9%).

However, the mean rate of technical efficiency change (TEC) during 1979-2004 for different depreciation rates is: 7.45 (% per year, with δ=5%), 7.59 (δ=6%), 7.73 (δ=7%), 7.87 (δ=8%) and 8.00 (δ=9%). Thus, the contribution of scale effect is positive out-weighting the negative exogenous rate of technical change in the midterm period.

3.5. Policy Implication of the results for Chinese Aggregate Economy

Based on the analysis of the Chinese economy productivity growth discussed above, some policy implications could be discussed as follows:

Firstly, the descriptive statistics of the data suggest that, the Chinese economy enjoyed a rapid and sustainable growth with some cyclical fluctuations during the period of 1978-2004 with on average, an annual real GDP growth rate of 8.96% and 8.14% from 2000 to 2004. As an important input factor, the mean of annual growth rate of Chinese real capital stock calculated with PIM varies from 9.15% (with depreciation rate δ=5%) to 9.29% (δ=9%) due to continuous and stable fixed asset investment. The average annual growth rate of labor working hours as another input factor is 2.38% with stable labor supply after having considered the labor surplus in rural China, the modified unemployment in urban China and the income sharing weighted factors in the dual economy.

Secondly, the regression results show that the combination of capital stock and labor force is positively correlated to the real GDP growth and the trend is negatively correlated to the output. The capital stock partial elasticity (elk) is increasing from 0.91 (in 1978) to 0.96 (in 2004). The labor partial elasticity (ela) is also increasing from 0.71 (in 1978) to 0.88 (in 2004). Thus, the increasing RTS varies from 1.62 (in 1978) to 1.83 (in 2004). The mean of Chinese TFP growth rate is from 6.41% (δ=5%) to 6.62% (δ=9%) during 1979-2004. It suggest that both factor inputs and TFP growth are the main determinants of Chinese economic growth post 1978.

In addition to these, the main sources of Chinese TFP growth are technical efficiency change of scale economy due to the combination and gradual saving of capital and labor. The negative pure technical change indicates insufficient innovation in Chinese aggregate economy during the study period. This implies that in general the economic growth is still mainly relying on quantitative expansion but also quality improvement through technology innovation.

Further, it should be noted that to enhance the overall efficiency of capital circulation relying on market mechanism and to improve the quality of a large labor force, especially the surplus labor force, via intensive training and education could be a rational choice of the public policy for further growth. In the meantime, technology innovation should be enforced with increased R&D expenditure, technology introduction and effective diffusion over the country, which will create much opportunity for the accumulated investment as well as loosening the present restrictions on natural resources and environment.

4. Empirical Analysis of Productivity Growth at the Industrial Sector Level

This section focuses on Chinese industry level productivity growth in the short term during 1997-2003 with two-way fixed effects panel data models to capture the sources of the industrial growth. The differences compared to the previous research are as follows: a) Adoption of panel data methodology to analyse 36 Chinese industrial sectors for 7 years; b) Using updated capital stock series; and c) Getting much information about TFP growth for different industrial sectors.

4.1. Model and Method

Following the method of Kumbhakar, Heshmati and Hjalmarsson (1999), the author would like to apply a panel data two-way fixed effects error component model as in (11) to conduct a production function approach analysis.

$$\ln Y_{it} = \alpha_0 + \sum_{j=1}^{k} \beta_j \ln \mathbf{x}_{jit} + \mu_i + \lambda_t + \varepsilon_{it} \tag{11}$$

Here Y_{it} is value added of sector i in year t, x_{jit} represents K_{it} and L_{it}, which are capital stock of sector i in year t and total employment of sector i in year t respectively, λ_t is a vector of dummy variables reflecting unobserved time effects and μ_i is another vector of dummy variables reflecting unobserved sector effects, and ε_{it} is random error term. Under the assumptions of cost minimization, we could can derive the input elasticity as in (12).

$$EX_{it} = \partial \ln Y_{it} / \partial \ln X_{it} \tag{12}$$

and RTS as in (13)

$$RTS_{it} = \sum EX_{it} \tag{13}$$

Technical change (TC) will be derived as in (14)

$$TC_{it} = \partial \ln Y_{it} / \partial t \tag{14}$$

while technical efficiency change (TEC) is obtained as in (15)

$$TEC_{it} = (RTS_{it} - 1) \cdot \sum_{j=1}^{k} \beta_j \ln \dot{\mathbf{x}}_{jit} \tag{15}$$

And finallt the rate of TFP growth is computed as in (16)

$$TFP_{it} = TC_{it} + TEC_{it} = TC_{it} + (RTS_{it} - 1) \cdot \sum_{j=1}^{k} \beta_j \ln \dot{\mathbf{x}}_{jit} \tag{16}$$

4.2. The Data

36. Specific Industrial Sectors Studied

The industrial sectors studied here include mining and quarrying (denoted by I1 to I5), manufacturing (denoted by I6 to I33), and electric power and gas water production (denoted by I34 to I36). Table 17 shows the detailed names of the 36 specific sectors, which is based on the Chinese industrial sector classification standard of GB/T 4754-2002. All data used in this study is obtained from the Chinese Yearbook of Statistics 1996 to 2004 and the capital stock series of these industrial sectors are calculated by Wangling (2004), which is not available in the Chinese Yearbook of Statistics.

Table 17. 36 specific industrial sectors of China

Sector Numbers	Code of GB/T 4754-2002*	Name of Sectors
I1	B6	Coal mining and dressing
I2	B5	Petroleum and natural gas extraction
I3	B4	Ferrous metal mining and dressing
I4	B3	Nonferrous metals mining and dressing
I5	B2	Nonmetal minerals mining and dressing
I6	C30	Food processing
I7	C29	Food production
I8	C28	Beverage production
I9	C27	Tobacco processing
I10	C26	Textile industry
I11	C25	Garments and other fiber products
I12	C24	Leather furs down and related products
I13	C23	Timber processing bamboo cane palm fiber and straw products
I14	C22	Furniture manufacturing
I15	C21	Papermaking and paper products
I16	C20	Printing and record medium reproduction
I17	C19	Cultural educational and sports articles
I18	C18	Petroleum processing and coking
I19	C17	Raw chemical materials and chemical products
I20	C16	Medical and pharmaceutical products
I21	C15	Chemical fiber
I22	C14	Rubber products
I23	C13	Plastic products
I24	C12	Nonmetal mineral products
I25	C11	Smelting and pressing of ferrous metals
I26	C10	Smelting and pressing of nonferrous metals
I27	C9	Metal products
I28	C8	Ordinary machinery
I29	C7	Equipment for special purposes
I30	C6	Transportation equipment
I31	C5	Electric equipment and machinery
I32	C4	Electronic and telecommunications equipment
I33	C3	Instruments meters cultural and office machinery
I34	D3	Production and supply of electric power steam and hot water
I35	D2	Production and supply of gas
I36	D1	Production and supply of tap water

Note: * The Chinese Industrial Sector Classification Standard GB/T 4754-2002

A. Value-Added of the Industries

The real value-added growth of industrial sectors is regarded as a proxy of economic growth of these sectors. All nominal value-added data have been extracted from the mentioned yearbooks. With the help of "Ex-factory price indices of industrial products by sector (1997-2003)", constant price deflators have been calculated with the base year of 1998 and real value-added data have been made available for the analysis.

B. Labor Inputs

The number of employees working in each industrial sector has been utilized to measure labor input. The data is from the same sources mentioned above.

C. Capital Stock Series

In the Chinese Yearbook of Statistics 1996 to 2004, there are only original values of fixed assets and the net value of fixed assets by sectors. Wangling (2004) calculated the sector specific capital stock series as follows: Firstly, by estimating the base year capital stock following the method of incremental capital and its output ratio by Timmer (1999) in the developing economy with capital used at full capacity. Secondly, by dividing the base year capital stock into two groups including buildings and machines in accordance with the Huangyongfeng (2002) approach. Thirdly, by getting investment series of buildings and machines and the capital stock series by PIM with the method proposed by Wu and Xu (2002).

4.3. Regressions and Testing Procedures

Least square regressions ignoring the unobserved time and sector effects called pooled model and using pooled data was estimated. Then fixed effects and random effects models incorporating sector effect, time effect, and sector and time effects have been estimated respectively. The Hausman test has been conduced, showing that the process is a fixed effect instead of a random effect model. We have tested and corrected for heteroscedasticity. F-tests have been conducted for the model comparison purpses. Table 18 shows the basic descriptive statistics of the data used in the analysis. Table 19 and Table 20 show the average values and average change rate of sector value added, capital stock and employment respectively in 36 industrial sectors during 1998-2003. Table 21 shows the results of two-way fixed effects model estimation. Table 22 shows different input elasticities, sector heterogeneity and RTS. Table 23 gives the TFP growth rate of 36 industrial sectors during 1998-2003.

Table 18. Data description for Chinese industrial sector analysis

All results based on non-missing observations.

Variable	Mean	Std. Dev.	Minimum	Maximum	Cases
LY	6.1594424	1.0677490	2.2929892	8.3140321	252
LK	6.6303864	1.0906621	4.0734613	10.0756759	252
LA	4.4549271	0.8927100	2.6390573	6.3902406	252
T	4.0000000	2.0039801	1.0000000	7.0000000	252
I	18.5000000	10.4089679	1.0000000	36.0000000	252
Year	2000.0000	2.0039801	1997.0000	2003.00000	252

All observations in current sample

Table 19. The average values of value added, capital stock and employment in Chinese 36 specific industrial sectors during 1998-2003

Sector Numbers (Chinese SIC code)	Name of Sectors	Value Added (100 million Yuan) (Sharing Ratio %)	No.	Capital stock (100 million Yuan) (Sharing Ratio %)	No.	Employee (10 thousand Person) (Sharing Ratio %)	No.
I1 (B6)	Coal mining and dressing	718.91		2049.93 (3.71%)	6	377.94 (8.42%)	1
I2 (B5)	Petroleum and natural gas extraction	1311.09 (4.64%)	8	3492.84 (6.06%)	3	85.28	
I3 (B4)	Ferrous metal mining and dressing	80.15		107.22		17.40	
I4 (B3)	Nonferrous metals mining and dressing	143.73		204.08		36.23	
I5 (B2)	Nonmetal minerals mining and dressing	132.75		365.79		35.94	
I6 (C30)	Food processing	1024.98		574.77		126.11	
I7 (C29)	Food production	487.23		602.68		73.18	
I8 (C28)	Beverage production	686.99		1424.98		84.00	
I9 (C27)	Tobacco processing	1189.58 (4.21%)	10	910.74		25.87	
I10 (C26)	Textile industry	1417.00 (5.01%)	7	1882.11 (3.27%)	8	358.86 (8.42%)	2
I11 (C25)	Garments and other fiber products	677.04		651.33		151.53	
I12 (C24)	Leather furs down and related products	397.10		278.81		75.73	
I13 (C23)	Timber processing bamboo cane palm fiber and straw products	182.13		245.00		37.14	
I14 (C22)	Furniture manufacturing	116.80		137.24		21.40	
I15 (C21)	Papermaking and paper products	494.39		1306.37		76.33	
I16 (C20)	Printing and record medium reproduction	252.68		395.05		58.24	
I17 (C19)	Cultural educational and sports articles	195.56		242.67		38.19	

Table 19. (Continued)

I18 (C18)	Petroleum processing and coking	591.08		1848.32 (3.21%)	9	60.45	
I19 (C17)	Raw chemical materials and chemical products	1689.04 (5.98%)	4	3900.20 (6.77%)	2	266.39 (6.25%)	4
I20 (C16)	Medical and pharmaceutical products	728.05		958.32		88.57	
I21 (C15)	Chemical fiber	261.07		632.69		32.87	
I22 (C14)	Rubber products	268.06		464.35		47.04	
I23 (C13)	Plastic products	552.76		844.35		76.15	
I24 (C12)	Nonmetal mineral products	1277.68 (4.52%)	9	1486.75		268.20 (6.30%)	3
I25 (C11)	Smelting and pressing of ferrous metals	1581.10 (5.59%)	5	2963.63 (5.14%)	4	228.15 (5.36%)	7
I26 (C10)	Smelting and pressing of nonferrous metals	570.58		977.66		84.43	
I27 (C9)	Metal products	766.73		794.52		111.37	
I28 (C8)	Ordinary machinery	1098.34		848.21		236.58 (5.55%)	6
I29 (C7)	Equipment for special purposes	733.06		364.31		170.89 (4.01%)	9
I30 (C6)	Transportation equipment	1894.48 (6.70%)	3	1779.35 (3.09%)	10	260.30 (6.11%)	5
I31 (C5)	Electric equipment and Machinery	1482.70 (5.25%)	6	1081.31		169.19 (3.97%)	10
I32 (C4)	Electronic and telecommunications equipment	2268.80 (8.03%)	2	2156.24 (3.74%)	5	162.74	
I33 (C3)	Instruments meters cultural and office machinery	278.04		244.03		51.16	
I34 (D3)	Production and supply of electric power steam and hot water	2524.70 (8.93%)	1	19286.65 (33.46%)	1	222.07 (5.21%)	8
I35 (D2)	Production and supply of gas	29.71		145.22		18.12	
I36 (D1)	Production and supply of tap water	151.01		1912.51 (3.32%)	7	45.55	

Table 20. The average change rates of value added, capital stock and employment in Chinese 36 specific industrial sectors

Sector Numbers (Chinese SIC code)	Name of Sectors	Value Added (% per year)	No.	Capital stock (% per year)	No.	Employee (% per year)	No.
I1 (B6)	Coal mining and dressing	5.80		10.26	10	-4.49	
I2 (B5)	Petroleum and natural gas extraction	4.22		23.94	1	-7.79	
I3 (B4)	Ferrous metal mining and Dressing	16.10	9	1.03		5.24	7
I4 (B3)	Nonferrous metals mining and dressing	5.72		1.52		-4.44	
I5 (B2)	Nonmetal minerals mining and dressing	-0.65		3.96		-2.81	
I6 (C30)	Food processing	11.81		4.35		-0.75	
I7 (C29)	Food production	11.94		9.59		-2.01	
I8 (C28)	Beverage production	7.26		3.49		-5.39	
I9 (C27)	Tobacco processing	12.11		4.96		-7.36	
I10 (C26)	Textile industry	10.61		3.97		-2.96	
I11 (C25)	Garments and other fiber products	12.55		3.65		9.66	3
I12 (C24)	Leather furs down and related products	12.64		4.40		11.1	2
I13 (C23)	Timber processing bamboo cane palm fiber and straw products	8.77		9.77		-0.81	
I14 (C22)	Furniture manufacturing	13.34		11.40	7	6.15	5
I15 (C21)	Papermaking and paper products	13.99		8.96		-1.41	
I16 (C20)	Printing and record medium reproduction	11.99		11.03	8	-6.92	
I17 (C19)	Cultural educational and sports articles	14.02		5.61		15.20	1
I18 (C18)	Petroleum processing and coking	4.77		21.89	3	-3.59	
I19 (C17)	Raw chemical materials and chemical products	14.31		7.59		-3.84	
I20 (C16)	Medical and pharmaceutical products	17.38	8	9.65		2.22	9
I21 (C15)	Chemical fiber	7.89		0.75		-6.32	
I22 (C14)	Rubber products	11.64		4.12		-1.72	
I23 (C13)	Plastic products	14.78	10	8.31		5.56	6
I24 (C12)	Nonmetal mineral products	9.26		7.91		0.39	
I25 (C11)	Smelting and pressing of ferrous metals	17.79	7	13.39	6	-3.78	
I26 (C10)	Smelting and pressing of nonferrous metals	18.65	5	10.11		1.40	10
I27 (C9)	Metal products	13.66		5.08		-0.27	
I28 (C8)	Ordinary machinery	14.71		8.97		-5.86	
I29 (C7)	Equipment for special purposes	13.39		5.41		-4.81	

Table 20. (Continued)

I30 (C6)	Transportation equipment	20.78	4	14.04	5	-1.74	
I31 (C5)	Electric equipment and machinery	18.21	6	10.45	9	2.59	8
I32 (C4)	Electronic and telecommunications equipment	25.66	1	17.83	4	8.42	4
I33 (C3)	Instruments meters cultural and office machinery	21.43	3	3.66		-1.56	
I34 (D3)	Production and supply of electric power steam and hot water	11.17		9.36		1.34	
I35 (D2)	Production and supply of gas	24.73	2	23.29	2	-4.31	
I36 (D1)	Production and supply of tap water	6.61		6.34		1.22	

Table 21. Regression Results of two way fixed effect models for Chinese industries

Least Squares with Group Dummy Variables and Period Effects
Ordinary least squares regression Weighting variable = none
Dep. var. = LY Mean=6.159442430, S.D.= 1.067749045
Model size: Observations = 252, Parameters =43, Deg. Fr.=209
Residuals: Sum of squares= 3.318775399, Std. Dev.= 0.12601
Fit: R-squared= 0.988402, Adjusted R-squared = 0.98607
Model test: F [42, 209] = 424.10, Prob value = 0.00000
Diagnostic: Log-L = 187.9865, Restricted (b=0) Log-L = -373.5908
LogAmemiyaPrCrt.= -3.985, Akaike Info. Crt.= -1.151
Estd. Autocorrelation of e(i,t) 0.346143

Variable	Coefficient	Standard Error	t-ratio	P[|T|>t]	Mean of X
LKA	0.045368813	0.00722016	6.284	0.0000	30.1795
Constant	4.790233048	0.21804572	21.969	0.0000	

Group effects include
Time effects include
Test results suggest that both effects should be included in the mode specification

Table 22. Mean capital elasticity, mean labor elasticity and mean RTS of Chinese 36 specific industrial sectors

Sector Numbers (Chinese SIC code)	Name of Sectors	Capital Elasticity Mean	Labor Elasticity Mean	Sector Heterogeneity Dummy Coefficient (mean=0)	Return To Scale (Whole Sector Mean As Benchmark)
I1 (B6)	Coal mining and dressing	0.27	0.35	Insignificant	0.61
I2 (B5)	Petroleum and natural gas extraction	0.20	0.37	0.75	1.32
I3 (B4)	Ferrous metal mining and dressing	0.13	0.21	-1.12	-0.78
I4 (B3)	Nonferrous metals mining and dressing	0.16	0.24	-0.73	-0.32
I5 (B2)	Nonmetal minerals mining and dressing	0.16	0.27	-0.84	-0.41
I6 (C30)	Food processing	0.22	0.29	0.70	1.17
I7 (C29)	Food production	0.19	0.29	Insignificant	0.48
I8 (C28)	Beverage production	0.20	0.33	0.23	0.76
I9 (C27)	Tobacco processing	0.15	0.31	1.20	1.66
I10 (C26)	Textile industry	0.27	0.34	Insignificant	0.61
I11 (C25)	Garments and other fiber products	0.23	0.29	0.18	0.70
I12 (C24)	Leather furs down and related products	0.19	0.26	Insignificant	0.45
I13 (C23)	Timber processing bamboo cane palm fiber and straw products	0.16	0.25	-0.54	-0.13
I14 (C22)	Furniture manufacturing	0.14	0.22	-0.79	-0.44
I15 (C21)	Papermaking and paper products	0.20	0.33	Insignificant	0.52
I16 (C20)	Printing & record medium reproduction	0.18	0.27	-0.43	0.02
I17 (C19)	Cultural educational and sports articles	0.16	0.25	-0.49	-0.08
I18 (C18)	Petroleum processing and coking	0.19	0.34	0.20	0.73
I19 (C17)	Raw chemical materials and chemical products	0.25	0.38	Insignificant	0.63
I20 (C16)	Medical and pharmaceutical products	0.20	0.31	0.28	0.79
I21 (C15)	Chemical fiber	0.16	0.29	-0.31	0.14
I22 (C14)	Rubber products	0.17	0.28	-0.35	0.10
I23 (C13)	Plastic products	0.19	0.31	Insignificant	0.50
I24 (C12)	Nonmetal mineral products	0.25	0.33	0.46	1.04
I25 (C11)	Smelting and pressing of ferrous metals	0.25	0.36	0.49	1.10
I26 (C10)	Smelting and pressing of nonferrous metals	0.20	0.31	Insignificant	0.51
I27 (C9)	Metal products	0.21	0.30	0.32	0.84
I28 (C8)	Ordinary machinery	0.25	0.31	0.43	0.99
I29 (C7)	Equipment for special purposes	0.23	0.27	0.33	0.84
I30 (C6)	Transportation equipment	0.25	0.34	0.72	1.31
I31 (C5)	Electric equipment and machinery	0.23	0.32	0.76	1.31
I32 (C4)	Electronic and telecommunications equipment	0.23	0.35	0.99	1.56
I33 (C3)	Instruments meters cultural and office machinery	0.18	0.25	-0.31	0.11
I34 (D3)	Production and supply of electric power steam and hot water	0.25	0.45	Insignificant	0.69
I35 (D2)	Production and supply of gas	0.13	0.22	-2.24	-1.88
I36 (D1)	Production and supply of tap water	0.17	0.34	-1.11	-0.60

Table 23. TFP average change rate of Chinese 36 specific industrial sectors

Sector Numbers (Chinese SIC code)	Name of Sectors	TFP rate (% per year) The Whole Sector Mean as Benchmark the year of 1998 as Base year	No.
I1 (B6)	Coal mining and dressing	10.61	
I2 (B5)	Petroleum and natural gas extraction	11.74	6
I3 (B4)	Ferrous metal mining and dressing	8.81	-5
I4 (B3)	Nonferrous metals mining and dressing	12.12	4
I5 (B2)	Nonmetal minerals mining and dressing	11.18	
I6 (C30)	Food processing	11.31	9
I7 (C29)	Food production	10.43	
I8 (C28)	Beverage production	11.33	7
I9 (C27)	Tobacco processing	10.08	-10
I10 (C26)	Textile industry	11.11	
I11 (C25)	Garments and other fiber products	10.14	
I12 (C24)	Leather furs down and related products	9.21	-6
I13 (C23)	Timber processing bamboo cane palm fiber & straw products	9.37	-7
I14 (C22)	Furniture manufacturing	6.68	-3
I15 (C21)	Papermaking and paper products	10.48	
I16 (C20)	Printing and record medium reproduction	10.77	
I17 (C19)	Cultural educational and sports articles	6.13	-2
I18 (C18)	Petroleum processing and coking	10.23	
I19 (C17)	Raw chemical materials and chemical products	10.89	
I20 (C16)	Medical and pharmaceutical products	10.57	
I21 (C15)	Chemical fiber	12.53	2
I22 (C14)	Rubber products	10.85	
I23 (C13)	Plastic products	9.53	-8
I24 (C12)	Nonmetal mineral products	11.31	8
I25 (C11)	Smelting and pressing of ferrous metals	11.30	10
I26 (C10)	Smelting and pressing of nonferrous metals	9.88	-9
I27 (C9)	Metal products	11.00	
I28 (C8)	Ordinary machinery	11.13	
I29 (C7)	Equipment for special purposes	11.10	
I30 (C6)	Transportation equipment	12.08	5
I31 (C5)	Electric equipment and machinery	12.26	3
I32 (C4)	Electronic and telecommunications equipment	15.32	1
I33 (C3)	Instruments meters cultural and office machinery	10.85	
I34 (D3)	Production and supply of electric power steam and hot water	10.18	
I35 (D2)	Production and supply of gas	5.17	-1
I36 (D1)	Production and supply of tap water	8.66	-4

4.4. Analysis of the Results

A. Descriptive analysis of the data

It should be noted that some facts might be found via observation of the data as follows:

B. About Value Added

The top 10 big value added producing sectors based on the mean value during 1998-2003 among the 36 specific sectors are as follows (see Table 19): Production and supply of electric power steam and hot water (I34, 8.93% of the total), Electronic and telecommunications equipment (sector code and share = I32, 8.03%), Transportation equipment (I30, 6.70%),

Raw chemical materials and chemical products (I19, 5.98%), Smelting and pressing of ferrous metals (I25, 5.59%), Electric equipment and machinery (I31, 5.25%), Textile industry (I10, 5.01%), Petroleum and natural gas extraction (I2, 4.64%), Nonmetal mineral products (I24, 4.52%), and Tobacco processing (I9, 4.21%). The sum of shares of the top 10 sectors is about 58.86% of the total value added.

The whole Chinese industrial sectors enjoyed on average 12.75% per year of value added increase during 1998-2003.

As for the average change rates of value added (see Table 20), 35 sectors have been experiencing growth of value added during 1998-2003. All sectors studied enjoyed an increasing value-added during the study period. 26 sectors among the 36 sectors experienced on average growth rates in double figures. The top 10 fast growing sectors are as follows: Electronic and telecommunications equipment (code and growth rate = I32, 25.66% per year), Production and supply of gas (I35, 24.73% per year), Instruments meters cultural and office machinery (I33, 21.73% per year), Transportation equipment (I30, 20.78% per year), Smelting and pressing of nonferrous metals (I26, 18.65% per year), Electric equipment and machinery (I31, 18.21% per year), Smelting and pressing of ferrous metals (I25, 17.79% per year), Medical and pharmaceutical products (I20, 17.38% per year), Ferrous metal mining and dressing (I3, 16.10% per year), and Ordinary machinery (I28,14.71% per year).

C. About Capital Stock

The top 10 industrial sectors with the highest capital stock based on the mean value during 1998-2003 among the 36 sectors are as follows: Production and supply of electric power steam and hot water (sector code and share = I34, 33.46% of the total), Raw chemical materials and chemical products (I19, 6.77%), Petroleum and natural gas extraction (I2, 6.06%), Smelting and pressing of ferrous metals (I25, 5.14%), Electronic and telecommunications equipment (I32, 3.74%), Coal mining and dressing (I1, 3.71%), Production and supply of tap water (I36, 3.32%), Petroleum processing and coking (I18, 3.21%), Textile industry (I10, 3.27%), and Transportation equipment (I30, 3.09%). The sum share of the top 10 sectors is about 71.77% of the total capital stock.

As a whole, the Chinese industrial sectors enjoyed on average 8.61% per year of capital stock increase during 1998-2003.

As for the average change rates of capital stock, the top 10 fast growing sectors are as follows: Petroleum and natural gas extraction (code and growth rat = I2, 23.94% per year), Production and supply of gas (I35, 23.29% per year), Petroleum processing and coking (I18, 21.89% per year), Electronic and telecommunications equipment (I32, 17.83% per year), Transportation equipment (I30, 14.04% per year), Smelting and pressing of ferrous metals (I25, 13.39% per year), Furniture manufacturing (I14, 11.40% per year), Printing and record medium reproduction (I16, 11.03% per year), Electric equipment and machinery (I31, 10.45% per year), and Coal mining and dressing (I1, 10.26% per year).

D. About Labor Input

The top 10 major industrial sectors the with highest labor input (employment creation) based on the mean values during 1998-2003 among the 36 sectors are as follows: Textile industry (code and share = I10, 8.42% of the total employee), Coal mining and dressing (I1, 8.42%), Nonmetal mineral products (I24, 6.30%), Raw chemical materials and chemical products (I19, 6.25%), Transportation equipment (I30, 6.11%), Ordinary machinery (I28,

5.55%), Smelting and pressing of ferrous metals (I25, 5.36%), Production and supply of electric power steam and hot water (I34, 5.21%), Equipment for special purposes (I29, 4.01%), and Electric equipment and machinery (I31, 3.97%). These 10 sectors account for 59.6 % of the total employment on average.

As a whole, the Chinese industrial sectors enjoy on average 0.40% per year of employee reduction during 1998-2003.

As for the average change rates of employment, 23 sectors have been experiencing reduction in employment, and the other 13 sectors have increased their employment. The top 10 successful sectors for job openings are as follows: Cultural educational and sports articles (code and increase = I17, 15.20% per year), Leather, furs, down and related products (I12, 11.10% per year), Garments and other fiber products (I11, 9.66% per year), Electronic and telecommunications equipment (I32, 8.42% per year), Furniture manufacturing (I14, 6.15% per year), Plastic products (I23, 5.56% per year), Ferrous metal mining and dressing (I3, 5.24% per year), Electric equipment and machinery (I31, 2.59% per year), Medical and pharmaceutical products (I20, 2.22% per year), and Smelting and pressing of nonferrous metals (I26, 1.40% per year).

E. Capital, Labor Elasticity, Sector Heterogeneity Coefficient and RTS

The mean capital elasticity of the Chinese industrial sectors as a whole is 0.20. The mean labor elasticity is 0.30. The RTS on the average is 0.50, which means decreasing return to scale during the period of study in the short-term period.

The sector heterogeneity coefficient reflects the degree of differences among the sectors compared to the mean of the whole sectors. There are 9 insignificant coefficients among the 36 unobservable sector coefficients or effects.

The RTS of different sectors is also available in Table 22. There are 8 sectors among the 36 sectors with increasing returns to scale as follows: Petroleum and natural gas extraction (code and scale effect = I2, RTS=1.32), Food processing (I6, RTS=1.17), Tobacco processing (I9, RTS=1.66), Nonmetal mineral products (I24, RTS=1.04), Smelting and pressing of ferrous metals (I25, RTS=1.10), Transportation equipment (I30, RTS=1.31), Electric equipment and machinery (I31, RTS=1.31), and Electronic and telecommunications equipment (I32, RTS=1.56).

F. TFP Growth Rate of Industrial Sectors During1998-2003

As a whole, the Chinese industrial sectors enjoyed on the average 10.45% annual TFP growth rate during 1998-2003 using 1998 as the base year.

TFP growth rates of the 36 industrial sectors have been computed. Figure 11-18 show the trend of these TFP changes during 1998-2003 respectively.

On average, the top 10 sectors with the fastest technological progress during the period are as follows: Electronic and telecommunications equipment (cose and annual growth rate = I32, 15.32%per year), Chemical fiber (I21, 12.53% per year), Electric equipment and machinery (I31, 12.26% per year), Nonferrous metals mining and dressing (I4, 12.12% per year), Transportation equipment (I30, 12.08% per year), Petroleum and natural gas extraction (I2, 11.74% per year), Beverage production (I8, 11.33% per year), Nonmetal mineral products (I24, 11.311% per year), Food processing (I6, 11.31% per year), and Nonmetal minerals mining and dressing (I5, 11.18% per year).

On average, the 10 sectors with the relatively slowest technological progress during the period are as follows: Production and supply of gas (code and growth rate = I35, 5.17% per year), Cultural educational and sports articles (I17, 6.13% per year), Furniture manufacturing (I14, 6.68% per year), Production and supply of tap water (I36, 8.66% per year), Ferrous metal mining and dressing (I3, 8.81% per year), Leather, furs, down and related products (I12, 9.21% per year), Timber processing, bamboo, cane, palm fiber and straw products (I13, 9.37% per year), Plastic products (I23, 9.53% per year), Smelting and pressing of nonferrous metals (I26, 9.88% per year), and Tobacco processing (I9, 10.08% per year).

G. Decomposition of TFP of Industrial Sectors During 1998-2003

Table 24. Average TC and TEC rates of Chinese industrial sectors

Sector Numbers (Chinese SIC code)	Name of Sectors	TC Rate (% Per year) (Basing On The year of 1998)	TEC Rate (% Per year)
I1 (B6)	Coal mining and dressing	11.07	-0.46
I2 (B5)	Petroleum and natural gas extraction	11.07	-0.67
I3 (B4)	Ferrous metal mining and dressing	11.07	-2.26
I4 (B3)	Nonferrous metals mining and dressing	11.07	1.05
I5 (B2)	Nonmetal minerals mining and dressing	11.07	0.11
I6 (C30)	Food processing	11.07	0.24
I7 (C29)	Food production	11.07	-0.64
I8 (C28)	Beverage production	11.07	0.26
I9 (C27)	Tobacco processing	11.07	-0.99
I10 (C26)	Textile industry	11.07	0.04
I11(C25)	Garments and other fiber products	11.07	-0.94
I12 (C24)	Leather furs down and related products	11.07	-1.86
I13 (C23)	Timber processing bamboo cane palm fiber and straw products	11.07	-1.70
I14 (C22)	Furniture manufacturing	11.07	-4.39
I15 (C21)	Papermaking and paper products	11.07	-0.59
I16 (C20)	Printing and record medium reproduction	11.07	-0.30
I17 (C19)	Cultural educational and sports articles	11.07	-4.94
I18 (C18)	Petroleum processing and coking	11.07	-0.85
I19 (C17)	Raw chemical materials and chemical products	11.07	-0.18
I20 (C16)	Medical and pharmaceutical products	11.07	-0.50
I21 (C15)	Chemical fiber	11.07	1.46
I22 (C14)	Rubber products	11.07	-0.22
I23 (C13)	Plastic products	11.07	-1.54
I24 (C12)	Nonmetal mineral products	11.07	0.24
I25 (C11)	Smelting and pressing of ferrous metals	11.07	0.23
I26 (C10)	Smelting and pressing of nonferrous metals	11.07	-1.19
I27 (C9)	Metal products	11.07	-0.07
I28 (C8)	Ordinary machinery	11.07	0.06
I29 (C7)	Equipment for special purposes	11.07	0.03
I30 (C6)	Transportation equipment	11.07	1.01
I31 (C5)	Electric equipment and machinery	11.07	1.19
I32 (C4)	Electronic and telecommunications equipment	11.07	4.25
I33 (C3)	Instruments meters cultural and office machinery	11.07	-0.22
I34 (D3)	Production and supply of electric power steam and hot water	11.07	-0.89
I35 (D2)	Production and supply of gas	11.07	-5.90
I36 (D1)	Production and supply of tap water	11.07	-2.41

The exogenous rate of technical change on average (TC) is 11.07% per year during 1998-2003. And the mean rate of technical efficiency change (TEC) of different industrial sectors during 1998-2003 is available in the Table 24. The technical efficiency change (TEC) of the whole industry is –0.617% per year during 1998-2003. The main contribution to TFP is from the pure rate of technical chage, TC.

4.5 Policy Implication for Chinese Industrial Sectors

In light of the analysis of the Chinese industrial sector productivity growth described above, some policy implications could be discussed as follows:

Firstly, in terms of value added by industrial sector among the 36 industrial sectors during 1998-2003, traditional infrastructure, heavy, chemical and textile sectors are in the dominant position. The 10 biggest value added producing sectors are: Production and supply of electric power steam and hot water, Electronic and telecommunications equipment, Transportation equipment, Raw chemical materials and chemical products, Smelting and pressing of ferrous metals, Electric equipment and machinery, Textile industry, Petroleum and natural gas extraction, Nonmetal mineral products, and Tobacco processing.. Their share of the total value added is about 58.86%. The 36 sectors as a whole enjoy 12.75% per year value added increase during 1998-2003. 26 sectors have experienced two figure growth rates. The main contributors to the fast growth rates are infrastructure sector (especially, ICT), medical and pharmaceutical products, and ordinary machinery. The 10 fastest growing sectors are: Electronic and telecommunications equipment, Production and supply of gas, Instruments meters cultural and office machinery, Transportation equipment, Smelting and pressing of nonferrous metals, Electric equipment and machinery, Smelting and pressing of ferrous metals, Medical and pharmaceutical products, Ferrous metal mining and dressing, and Ordinary machinery.

Secondly, in terms of capital stock by industrial sector during 1998-2003, Production and supply of electric power steam and hot water share is one third of the total stock of fixed assets. The infrastructure sector accounts for the majority of the capital stock. The 10 sectors with the highest capital stock are as follows: Production and supply of electric power steam and hot water, Raw chemical materials and chemical products, Petroleum and natural gas extraction, Smelting and pressing of ferrous metals, Electronic and telecommunications equipment, Coal mining and dressing, Production and supply of tap water, Petroleum processing and coking, Textile industry, and Transportation equipment. Together they account for about 71.77% of the total capital stock.. The 36 industrial sectors as a whole enjoyed 8.61% per year of capital stock increase during 1998-2003. The infrastructure, Furniture manufacturing, and Printing and record medium reproduction experienced a fast process of fixed asset formation during the period. The top 10 fast growing sectors with more than two figure growth rates are: Petroleum and natural gas extraction, Production and supply of gas, Petroleum processing and coking, Electronic and telecommunications equipment, Transportation equipment, Smelting and pressing of ferrous metals, Furniture manufacturing, Printing and record medium reproduction, Electric equipment and machinery, and Coal mining and dressing.

Thirdly, in terms of labor input by industrial sector during 1998-2003, Textiles, Basic materials, Transportation equipment, Ordinary machinery, Equipment for special purposes, and Electric supply take on more labor. The 10 sectors with the highest share of employment are as follows: Textile industry, Coal mining and dressing, Nonmetal mineral products, Raw chemical materials and chemical products, Transportation equipment, Ordinary machinery, Smelting and pressing of ferrous metals, Production and supply of electric power steam and hot water, Equipment for special purposes, Electric equipment and machinery. Together their share is 59.60 % of the total employment in the industy. However, the 36 Chinese industrial sectors as a whole witness 0.40% per year of employment reduction during 1998-2003 in contrast to the value added and capital stock. 23 sectors have experienced a reduction of employment, and the remaining 13 sectors have created more job opportunities. It reflects the reality of the reform of improving efficiency with employment reduction during that period and the challenge of employment, which means job openings will decrease with the advancement of capital intensive production technology in the industrial sectors under the circumstances of having a labor surplus in China. The 10 fastest growing industrial sectors for job openings are: Cultural educational and sports articles, Leather, furs, down and related products, Garments and other fiber products, Electronic and telecommunications equipment, Furniture manufacturing, Plastic products, Ferrous metal mining and dressing, Electric equipment and machinery, Medical and pharmaceutical products, and Smelting and pressing of nonferrous metals.

Fourthly, the regression results show that the combination of capital stock and labor is positively correlated to value-added for the whole industrial sector. The mean capital elasticity 0.20 while the mean labor elasticity is 0.30. The RTS as a whole is 0.50, which means decreasing return to scale during the the period of this study. However, there are 8 sectors with increasing RTS including: Petroleum and natural gas extraction, Food processing (I6), Tobacco processing, Nonmetal mineral products, Smelting and pressing of ferrous metals, Transportation equipment, Electric equipment and machinery, and Electronic and telecommunications equipment.

Fifthly, the Chinese industrial sectors as a whole enjoy on average 10.45% annual TFP growth rate during 1998-2003. It is an obvious result of technological progress due to partially intensive investment programs. It indicates that both the combination of factors and technology progress are the main determinants of Chinese industrial growth during 1998-2003. The top 10 sectors with fastest technological progress during the study period are: Electronic and telecommunications equipment (15.32% per year), Chemical fiber (12.53%), Electric equipment and machinery (12.26%), Nonferrous metals mining and dressing (12.12%), Transportation equipment (12.08%), Petroleum and natural gas extraction (11.74%), Beverage production (1.33%), Nonmetal mineral products (11.31%), Food processing (11.31%), and Nonmetal minerals mining and dressing (11.18%). The 10 industrial sectors with relatively slower technological progress during the study period are: Production and supply of gas (5.17% per year), Cultural educational and sports articles (6.13%), Furniture manufacturing (6.68%), Production and supply of tap water (8.66%), Ferrous metal mining and dressing (8.81%), Leather furs down and related products (9.21%), Timber processing, bamboo, cane, palm fiber and straw products (9.37%), Plastic products (9.53%), Smelting and pressing of nonferrous metals (9.88%), and Tobacco processing (10.08%).

Finally, the decomposition of Chinese industrial TFP growth shows that the exogenous rate of technical change (TC) is 11.07% per year and the technical efficiency change (TEC) is –0.617% per year during 1998-2003. Therefore, the industrial productivity growth attributes much to the exogenous rate technical change. It shows that the innovation promotion efforts made by the Chinese government led to some partial positive returns in the industrial sectors during 1998-2003. However, the low level of TEC means that there is an urgent need and great room to reallocate the industrial factor resources.

5. Conclusions

With the increasing recognition that productivity growth is the key to sustained economic expansion, measuring productivity accurately is becoming important to economists and policy makers as well as putting forth better policy recommendations and making the right decisions (Owyong, 1998). This study has conducted indirect measurements of the Chinese technological innovation and productivity efforts at national aggregate in the midterm and industrial sector level in the short-term in order to verify the sustainability of Chinese economic growth. It begins with a comprehensive review of productivity growth theory and China-related empirical research evidence. Then it focuses on a TFP calculation of Chinese economic growth at national aggregate in the midterm (1978-2004, with 6 different depreciation rates and a labor surplus modification). A trans-logarithm aggregate production function model is specified and estimated. Further, it estimates TFP growth at industry level in the short-term (36 sectors during 1998-2003) with a fixed effects panel data approach.

First, it demonstrates that Chinese economy enjoys a rapid and sustainable growth with some cyclical fluctuations in the medium term during the period of 1978-2004 with on average a real GDP growth rate of 8.96% per annum. The mean of annual growth rate of Chinese real capital stock varies from 9.15% (with depreciation rate δ=5%) to 9.29% (δ=9%) while the average annual growth rate of labor working hours is 2.38%. The capital stock elasticity (elk) is increasing from 0.91 to 0.96. The labor elasticity of labor (ela) is increasing from 0.71 to 0.88. Thus, the increasing RTS varies from 1.62 (1978) to 1.83 (2004). The mean of TFP growth rate is from 6.41% (δ=5%) to 6.62% (δ=9%) during 1979-2004.

Empirically, the result above indicates that both factor inputs and TFP growth are the main determinants of Chinese economic growth post 1978. In addition to these, the main sources of TFP growth are technical efficiency change of scale economy due to the combination and gradual saving of capital and labor. It empirically reflects the industrialization process of Chinese aggregate economy. However, the negative pure technical change empirically hints at insufficient innovation in the aggregate economy during the study period. It implies that the path of economic growth is still relying on quantitative expansion with scale effect but also on quality improvement through technology innovation. It shows that Chinese industrialization and modernization is still at the primary stage. Upgrading the economic structure is a pressing issue.

Second, when the industrial sector level analysis in the short-term during 1998-2003 is concerned, it should be noted that the traditional infrastructure, heavy, chemical and textile sectors are the dominant sources of generation of value added. The 36 sectors as a whole enjoy 12.75% per year of value added increase, 26 of which experienced two figure growth rates. The main contributors of the rapid growth are the infrastructure sector (especially, ICT), medical and pharmaceutical products, ordinary machinery, etc. In the case of capital stock by industrial sector, the infrastructure sectors take the majority of the total stock. The industrial sectors as a whole enjoy 8.61% per year of capital stock increase. In the case of labor input by sectors, Textile, Basic materials, Transportation equipment, Ordinary machinery, Equipment for special purposes, and Electric supply take on more labor. However, the Chinese industrial sectors as a whole witness 0.40% per year employment reduction during the period in contrast to the growth of value added and capital stock. It reflects the reforming effect of improving efficiency with employment reduction, and the tendency of fewer job openings with capital intensive industrial development and a labor surplus.

The RTS of the industrial sectors as a whole is 0.50, which means decreasing returns to scale even though there are 8 specific sectors with increasing RTS. The industrial sectors as a whole enjoy 10.45% per year of TFP growth during 1998-2003 with obvious technology progress. This hints that both the combination of factors and technology progress are the main determinants of Chinese industrial growth during 1998-2003.

The decomposition of Chinese industrial TFP growth reveals further that the exogenous rate of technical change (TC) is 11.07% per year and the technical efficiency change (TEC) is –0.617% per year during 1998-2003. Therefore, the industrial productivity growth attributes much to the exogenous technical change. It shows that the innovation promotion efforts made by the Chinese government led to some partial returns during 1998-2003. However, the lower TEC means that there is an urgent need and great room to reallocate the resources. The short-term intensive investments bring about obvious technical change for Chinese industrial sectors. But the low institutional innovation does make a low efficiency of resources utilization.

Third, it is recommended that, in order to enhance the overall efficiency of capital by relying on market mechanisms and to improve the quality of the large labor force, especially the surplus labor force, intensive training and education could be a rational choice of public policy for the further growth of the Chinese economy. In the meantime, technology innovation should be enforced with much R&D expenditure, technology introduction and effective diffusion over the country and across the sectors, which will create much opportunity for accumulated investment as well as easing the present restrictions on employment, natural resources and the environment. It is also recommended that Chinese industrial sectors urgently need reallocation of the present resources via fair market competition, policy guided structural adjustment, the establishment of industrial linkage and further integration and regional convergence for economic scale effect in addition to enforced innovation activities.

Finally, for future research, it is important to consider the following: the national aggregate economy could be studied at the provincial level to find out the geographical differences; other sectors could be studied, such as construction, transportation, and service sectors; some specific industrial sectors also could be investigated deeply, such as high-tech manufacturing sectors.

ACKNOWLEDGEMENTS

I wish to thank the sponsors of this study: the Commission of Science and Technology and Industry for National Defense (COSTIND) of the People's Republic of China, and the Ministry of Commerce, Industry and Energy of Republic of Korea. I am very grateful to my leaders for providing the opportunity to complete this study. They are Vice Minister Zhang Huazhu, Director General Xu Yuming, Director General Wang Yiren, Director General Tu Senlin, Director General Zhou Wusheng, and Deputy Director General Zhang Fubao. I wish to thank the Techno-Economics and Policy Program (TEPP) at the College of Engineering, Seoul National University for its organization and implementation of the governmental scholarship program. I am grateful to all faculty members of the program, in particular Professors Eunnyyeong Heo, Jeongdong Lee, Almas Heshmati, Richard, Panda, Repkine and Junseok Hwang. I also would like to thank Miss Ji Eun Choi and other administrative staff for their support. I especially thank my Chinese classmates and friends for their kind help and encouragement. They are Mr. Zhu Zhenggang, Mr. Yang Wanshan, Mr. Du Zijun, Mr.Yuzheng and Mr. Wang Boyong. Thanks should be rendered to all international and Korean clasmates at TEPP for their help and encouragements. Finally I highly appreciate my mother, my wife XU Mengli and my son FENG Chi for their heartfelt support and sacrifices. I could not have completed the study without their very precious love and encouragement.

REFERENCES

Abramovitz and Moses (1993), The Search for the Sources of Growth: Areas of Ignorance, Old and New, *Journal of Economic History*, 53(2), 217-43.

Baltagi B. H. and J. M. Griffin (1988), A General Index of Technical Change, *Journal of Political Economy* 96, 20-41.

Blanchard and Olivier (2000), Macroeconomics: Chapter 13, America: *Prentice Hall International*, Inc.

Bergheim S. (2005), Global growth centers 2020 Formel-G for 34 economies, Deutsche Bank Research, March 23..

Borensztein E. and D. J. Ostry (1996), Accounting for China's growth performance, *American Economic Review* 86(2), 224– 228.

Cai F., Du Y. and Gao W. S. (2004), Employment Elasticity, Natural Unemployment and Macroeconomic Policy, Xinhua Abstract, No.23.

Caruso M. (2002), Procyclical Productivity and Output Growth in China: *An Econometric Analysis, Open economies Review* 13, 251-274.

China: National Statistics Publishing House.

Chow G. C. (1993), Capital Formation and Economic Growth in China, *Quarterly Journal of Economics* 108,809–842.

Coe D. and E. Helpman (1995), International R&D Spillovers. *European Economic Review* 39, 859-887.

Conceicao P., D. Gibson and M. Heitor (2000), Introduction: Knowledge, Technology, and Innovation for Development, Science, technology, and innovation policy: opportunities and challenges for the knowledge economy/ edited by Pedro Conceicao.

Dahlman C. (1994), Technology strategy in East Asian developing economies, *Journal of Asian Economics* 5, 541-572.

David T. and Owyong (1998), Productivity Growth: Theory and Measurement, *APO Productivity journal.*

Durlauf S., N. Johnson and J. Temple (2004), *Growth Econometrics*, Mimeo.

Felipe J. (1997), Total Factor Productivity Growth in East Asia: A Critical Survey, ADB.

Griliches Z. (1995), R&D and Productivity: Econometric Results and Measurement Issues, *Handbook of the Economics of Innovation and Technological Change.*

Harris R. G.(1999), *Determinants of Canadian Productivity Growth: Issues and Prospects.* Ottawa: Industry Canada.

Hobday M. (1995), *Innovation in East Asia,* Edward Elgar Publishing Ltd.

Hu A. G. (1998), *The Chinese Economy in Prospect.* Chapter 6, 99-146.

Huang C., Zhang M. Q. and Zhao Y. Y. (2005), Why the manufacturing sectors in developing countries can be competitive? The Evidence of China, 2005 *China's Economics Annual Conference*, December, 2005.

Hu Z. and M. S. Khan (1997), Why is China Growing So Fast? *IMF Staff Papers,* Vol. 44, No. 1 (March 1997), pp.103-131.

John and Xue (2004), *How High Is Urban Unemployment in China?*

Jorgenson D., F. Gollop and B. Fraumeni (1987), *Productivity And U.S. Economic Growth,* Elsevier Science Publishers.

Jorgenson D. W. (1963), Capital theory and investment behavior, *American Economic Review* 53, 247-59.

Kim L. (1998), *From Imitation to Innovation: Dynamics of Korea's Technological Learning,* Boston, America: Harvard Business School Press.

Krugman P. (1994), *The Myth of Asia's Miracle. Foreign Affairs* 73(6), 62-78.

Kumbhakar S. C., A. Heshmati and L. Hjalmarsson (1999), Parametric Approaches to Productivity Measurement: A comparison Among Alternative Models, *Scandinavian Journal of Economics* 101(3), 405-424.

Bottazzi L. and G. Peri (2005), The International Dynamics of R&D and Innovation in The short and In the Long Run, *NBER Working Paper*, No. 11524.

Liao H. and M. Holmes (2002), Productivity Growth of East Asia Economies' Manufacturing: *A Decomposition Analysis.*

Li K.W. (2003), China's Capital and Productivity Measurement Using Financial Resources.

Wang L. and Szirmai A. S. (2003), Technological Inputs and Productivity Growth in China's High-Tech Industries, Eindhoven Centre for Innovation Studies, The Netherlands. Working Paper.

Mankiw N. G. (1995), The Growth of Nations. Brookings Papers on Economic Activity 1. Washington, DC, America: Brookings Institution.

New Star Publisher (2004), China 2004, New Star Publishing House.

National Bureau of Statistics of China (2005), Chinese Statistics Yearbook 1996-2004, Nelson R. P. and H. Pack (1998), The Asian miracle and modern growth theory. Policy Research Working Paper, No.1881, Development Research Group, The World Bank.

OECD (2001), Manual of Measuring Productivity.

OECD (2005), Policy brief of Economic Survey of China.

Rawski (1999), *China: Prospects for full employment,* International Labor Office Geneva.

Rawski (2001), What's happening to China's GDP Statistics? *China Economic Review,* No.4.

Ruttan and Vernon W. (2001), Technology, Growth and Development—An Induced Innovation Perspective, Published by Oxford University Press, Inc.

Sharp A. (1998), Productivity: Key to Economic Success. Available: *www.csls.ca.*

Solinger (2002), Why We Cannot Count the "unemployment", The China Quarterly, Oxford.

Solow R. (1957), Technical Change and Aggregate Production Function, *Review of Economics and Statistics.*

Todaro M. P. (0000), Economic Development, Chapter 3.

Wu Y. R. (2000), Is China's economic growth sustainable? A productivity analysis. *China Economic Review* 11, 278-296.

Wang L. (2004), The Measurement of Chinese Industrial Sector Capital Stock, *World Economic Statistics Research* 1, (in Chinese).

Wang Y. and Yao Y. D. (2003), Sources of China's Economic Growth 1952-1999 incorporating human capital accumulation, *China Economic Review* 14, 32-52.

Xiong Z. Y. and Yu D. (2004), *A simple measurement of Chinese unemployment rate. Statistical Research,* No.7.

Zhang J. (2003), Investment, investment efficiency, and economic growth in China, *Journal of Asian Economics* 14, 713-734.

In: Recent Developments in the Chinese Economy
Editor: Almas Heshmati, pp. 135-172
ISBN: 1-60021-449-5
© 2007 Nova Science Publishers, Inc.

Chapter 5

A GRAVITY MODEL OF CHINA'S TRADE FLOWS

Zhengang Zhu *

Techno-Economics and Policy Program
College of Engineering
Seoul National University

ABSTRACT

Using panel data estimation technique, this study applies an augmented gravity model to analyze China's trade with 26 OECD members -- China's major trading partners, over the period 1996-2003. At the aggregate level, this study finds empirical support for the New Trade Theory and Heckscher-Ohlin Theory. Further, the gravity equation is applied to the bilateral trade of top ten sectors and also to the bilateral trade in ICT goods, following the newly developed definition by OECD. The empirical findings at sectoral level reinforce the estimation results at the aggregate level. However, failure or confirmation of the theoretical foundation of gravity equation to a specific country is not the ultimate purpose of this study. In addition, the empirical findings carry important and meaningful policy implications. This study makes significant contributions in three aspects. Firstly, to the best of my knowledge, this study is the first one to apply the gravity model to China, as a specific country, to explain its trade patterns and determinants. Secondly, a trade complementarity index is calculated and introduced in the gravity equation in an attempt to find out the peculiarity of China's trade patterns. Finally, in view of the heated debate on the theoretical foundation of the gravity equation, this study aims at finding an empirical support for an appropriate trade theory by applying the gravity model to the bilateral trade between China, the largest developing country, and selected 26 OECD members from the developed world.

Key words: gavity model, panel data, trade complementarity index, aggregate and sectoral trade flows, OECD, China

---

* Zhu Zhengang, Director, Department of Foreign Trade, Ministry of Commerce, Dong Chang An Street, Beijing, China, Post Code:100731.

I gratefully acknowledge the financial support provided by the Ministry of Industry, Commerce and Energy of Korea.

1. INTRODUCTION

The gravity model is among the most popular models used for international trade analysis. It has proved to be robust and successful in a variety of empirical applications. However, acceptance of a theoretical justification for the gravity model of trade has not been forthcoming, and debate continues over the consistency of the gravity model with standard economic trade theories.

There is a comprehensive literature on the gravity model and its applications. Deardorff (1995) argues that the neoclassical model might be better suited in the case of trade between a developed country and a developing one where factor endowments are quite different and intra-industry trade rather limited. Krugman (1979) concludes with important implications that the intra-industry trade occurs between countries with similar GDPs, and consumers will spread their expenditures over more product varieties, which will result in decreasing the consumption of each variety. Moreover, trade will lead to a reduction in the number of firms in each country.

Helpman and Krugman (1985) find that the gravity model equation is consistent with theories of trade based upon models of imperfect competition and with the Heckscher-Ohlin (hereafter referred as H-O) model. Hummels and Levinsohn (1995) prove that the gravity equation is not only suitable in explaining trade among developed countries, but also efficient in explaining the trade flows among developing countries where inter-industry trade is dominant with scarce monopolistic competition. Evenett and Keller (2002) argue that as long as production is not perfectly specialized across countries, both of the H-O model and differentiated products model are likely to account for the empirical success of the gravity equation.

Baltagi et al. (2003) apply a full interaction effects design to the gravity model when analyzing bilateral trade flows between the triad (EU15, USA and Japan) and their 57 most important trading partners (including China). Their model finds empirical support for the New Trade Theory (hereafter referred as N-T-T) and Linders' hypothesis (Linder, 1961). More recently, Debaere (2005) showed that increasing similarity in GDPs among OECD country pairs leads to higher bilateral trade to GDP ratios. His finding is partially consistent with the prediction of Helpman (1987), whose model explains intra-industry trade that is prevalent among developed countries. Besides, Debaere shows that Helpman's prediction is rejected for non-OECD countries, among which intra-industry trade is not critical.

Therefore, based on the wide range of empirical findings, the gravity equation is found to be able to characterize a large class of models, making the debate on the trade theories underlying different equations applied to different trading partners quite heated. Since most trade theories, such as the H-O theory, N-T-T and Linder's Hypothesis, can possibly generate the gravity equation, it is of great necessity to find out the proper trade model to fit China's trade flows.

The model used in this study is augmented in that the standard gravity model includes only income and distance variables. Apart from the Distance variable, this model also introduces two other explanatory variables, namely overall bilateral country size and similarity in country size, following the measurement methodologies of Egger (2000) and Baltagi et al (2003). The sum of the two countries' real GDP proxies the bilateral overall country size (LogGDPS), while a similarity index measuring the relative country size

(LogSIM) is calculated from China and the selected 26 OECD members[1]. An additional variable, Trade Complementarity Index (TCI), which is calculated to measure the degree of trade complementarities between China and each OECD member, is introduced in the augmented gravity model in an attempt to capture the relevance of the complementarities between countries in the determination of trade flows. However, it should be noted that apart from the aforementioned variables, many other factors which are not within the scope of this study affect trade.

In this study, different models including pooled OLS without Group Dummy Variables, LSDV or LS with Group Dummy Variables and Periods Effects, and Random Effect model are specified. All estimated models show a significant positive impact of the N-T-T variables (GDPS, SIM) and a negative impact of Distance variable on China's trade flows. A significantly positive impact of TCI on bilateral trade has been found in all equations at aggregate level. Thus, the gravity equation in this study finds empirical support for the N-T-T and H-O Theory, indicating that intra-industry trade and inter-industry trade are both critical in China's international trade patterns.

The empirical findings of this study, made by applying the gravity model to the bilateral trade between China as the largest developing country and OECD members as the developed world, agree with Helpman and Krugman (1985) and Evenett and Keller (2002), but contrast with Deardorff (1995) and Debaere (2005). In addition to the estimation at the aggregate level, this study also applies the gravity equation at the sectoral level, namely the top ten sectors[2] in China's trade flows. The estimation results show that all the top ten sectors are characterized with monopolistic competition and increasing returns to scale. These results also reinforce the findings from the estimations at the aggregate level.

Following the newly developed classification by OECD in 2003, this study applies the gravity equation to China's trade flows in ICT arena with respect to the growing importance and instrumental role of ICT sector. Failure or confirmation of the theoretical foundation of gravity equation to China is not the ultimate purpose of this study. The empirical findings carry important policy implications which could be quite interesting for policy-makers.

All gravity equations applied to China's trade flows, whether at the aggregate country level or at the industrial level, have found empirical support for N-T-T. It is well-known that, the N-T-T assumes marginal costs to lie below average costs for any level of output. Hence, a larger firm is always more competitive than a smaller one. This implies that competition between firms engaged in China's trade activities will become more intense. Thus, relatively large sized firms have good chances of surviving and succeeding. Besides, based on N-T-T, trade will lead to a reduction in the number of firms in each country. For the policy-makers, some effective strategies should be designed to encourage economies of scale and operation of scale at firm level.

Considering the negative coefficient of Distance variable, it is very clear that all firms have an incentive to save transport costs by production near the market. If we allow them to do so, each firm will start production in both countries – implying two-way direct foreign investment. For the policy-makers, some new rules and regulations are urgently needed to

[1] These countries and regions include Australia, Austria, Belgium, Canada, Czech, Germany, Denmark, Spain, Finland, France, Greece, Hong Kong, Hungary, Ireland, Italy, Japan, Korea, Mexico, Netherlands, Norway, New Zealand, Poland, Sweden, Switzerland, United Kingdom, and the United States of America.

[2] The top ten sectors are selected based on China's trade flows at two-digit H.S. code in 2003. They include: HS27, HS29, HS39, HS61, HS62, HS72, HS84, HS85, HS87, HS94.

encourage, support and guide the development of such investment activities, including improving the policy support system for venture capital and regulating cross-border capital transactions, etc.

Concerning China's model of international trade with monopolistic competition, the consumers prefer an increasing number of choices, and each firm must produce a variety of goods with an increasing return to scale technology. Therefore, firms should invest in product innovation in order to enhance demand for their products.

On the other hand, the empirical support for H-O theory also carries meaningful policy implications. It is well-known that, variation in factor endowments among countries has been the basis of traditional trade theories that offer the rationale for trade. Under the H-O theory, countries with abundant labor endowment, such as China, will continue to export labor-intensive products, such as textile and clothing, to capital-abundant economies, such as OECD members. Meanwhile, they will import large amount of capital-intensive and technology-intensive goods.

In general, whether China's trade flows follow the N-T-T model and/or H-O model depends greatly on the nature of economic structures and trade complementarities relationship between China and its trading partners. It goes without saying that, with China's implementation of market diversification strategy, both inter-industry trade and intra-industry trade will co-exist in the long run.

This study makes significant contributions in three aspects. Firstly, to the best of my knowledge, this study is the first one to apply the gravity model to China as a specific country, to explain its trade patterns and determinants. Secondly, in addition to the standard gravity model, a trade complementarity index is calculated and introduced in the gravity equation in an attempt to identify the peculiarity of China's trade patterns. Finally, in view of the large debate upon the theoretical foundation of the gravity equation, this study aims to find empirical support for appropriate trade theory by applying the gravity model to the bilateral trade between China, the largest developing country, and selected 26 OECD members from the developed world.

This study consists of six sections. The first section is an introduction to this study. Section 2 briefly reviews China's trade performance. Section 3 deals with the theoretical foundations of the gravity model. Section 4 introduces the methodology and the data used in the empirical analysis. Section 5 presents the empirical results and section 6 concludes the study.

2. Overview of China's Trade Performance

2.1. China's Overall Trade Flows and its Increasing Share in World Trade

Chinas' foreign trade has experienced rapid expansion together with its rapid economic growth has made the country to target the world as its market. Before economic reforms began at the end of 1978, China conducted minimal trade with the outside world, exporting just enough raw materials and simple manufactured goods to cover payments for imports of strategic minerals and other necessities not available at home. Deng's policy of opening up to the outside world induced a steady increase in China's trade with the rest of the world. During the 1980s, the value of imports exceeded that of exports as capital goods were brought in to equip the domestic manufacturing industry. During the 1989-1991 slowdown, demand for imports fell below that of exports, and China's external trade has since remained in surplus (except in 1993), resulting in the accumulation of considerable foreign exchange reserves. Joining the World Trade Organization (WTO) in 2001 contributed to the rapid growth in imports, but exports also expanded at a fast pace. Foreign exchange reserves reached a record US$769 billion at the end of September 2005.

Table 1. 1996-2005.1-9 Chinas' trade performance (Unit: billion US$)

Year	Total		Export		Import		
	Total value	Growth (%)	Value	Growth (%)	Value	Growth (%)	Balance
1996	289.88	3.2	151.05	1.5	138.83	5.1	12.22
1997	325.16	12.2	182.79	21.0	142.37	2.5	40.42
1998	323.95	-0.4	183.71	0.5	140.24	-1.5	43.48
1999	360.63	11.3	194.93	6.1	165.70	18.2	29.23
2000	474.30	31.5	249.20	27.8	225.09	35.8	24.11
2001	509.65	7.5	266.10	6.8	243.55	8.2	22.55
2002	620.77	21.8	325.60	22.4	295.17	21.2	30.43
2003	851.21	37.1	438.37	34.6	412.84	39.9	25.53
2004	1154.79	35.7	593.37	35.4	561.42	36.0	31.95
2005.1-9	1024.50	23.7	546.42	31.3	478.08	16.0	68.34

Source: General Administration of Customs of the PRC, China's Customs Statistics

With the rapid growth of China's trade volume in recent years, its share in world trade has become more significant. Over the study period, the share has increased from 2.65% in 1996 to 5.58% in 2003.

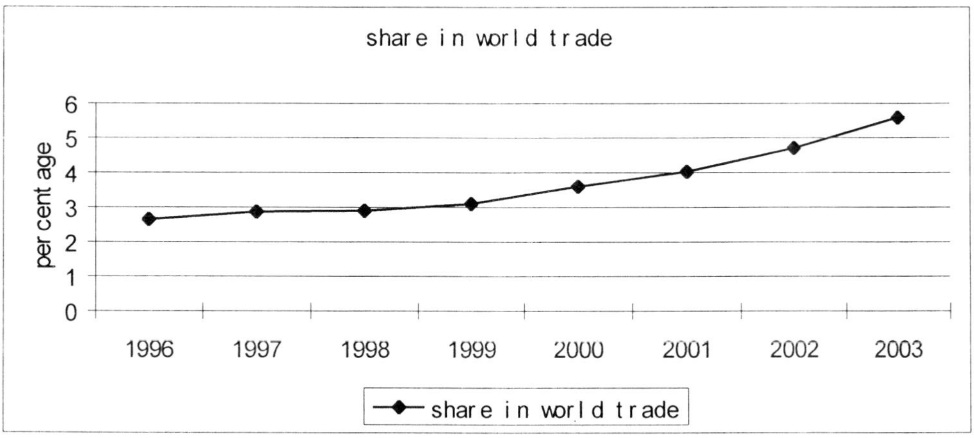

Sou

Source: OECD International Trade by Commodity Statistics – Data 2005

Figure 1. China's share in world trade.

Chinas' overall structure experienced significant changes with the rapid growth of foreign trade. Its exports were firstly dominated by basic primary products, and then by light-industrial and textile products, now changing to machinery and electronic goods and hi-tech products.

Table 2. 2001-2004 Export and Import Structural changes of Machinery and Electronic goods (MandE) and Hi-tech products (Hi-tech) (Unit: Billion US$)

Year	Export		Share in total export (%)		Import		Share in total import (%)	
	MandE	Hi-tech	MandE	Hi-tech	MandE	Hi-tech	MandE	Hi-tech
2001	118.8	46.5	44.6	17.5	120.5	64.1	49.5	26.3
2002	157.1	67.7	48.2	20.8	155.6	82.7	52.7	28
2003	227.5	110.2	51.9	25.1	225.0	119.2	54.5	28.9
2004	323.4	165.5	54.5	27.9	301.9	161.4	53.8	28.8

Source: General Administration of Customs of the PRC, China's Customs Statistics

On January 2005, China's average import tariff rate dropped to 9.4 percent, leaving only a few remaining goods to reach their final bound rate in 2006. In particular, tariffs on ICT products, such as computers, semiconductors, and telecom equipment, dropped from an average of 13.3 percent to zero, which would significantly boost China's already-large market for imported ICT products.

2.2. China's Bilateral Trade with 26 OECD Members

OECD members remained the major trading partners with China during the whole study period, although the relevant trade share demonstrated a slightly decreasing trend (changed from 75% in 1996 to 68% in 2003). Therefore, conducting a gravity analysis based on bilateral trade between China and OECD members will enable us to identify the main determinants and characteristics of China's trade flows.

2.3. The Trade Share of Top Ten Sectors

Throughout the study period, the top ten sectors occupy a significant share (above 50%) in the total bilateral trade between China and OECD members, and demonstrate a steady increasing trend, changing from 53% in 1996 to 64% in 2003.

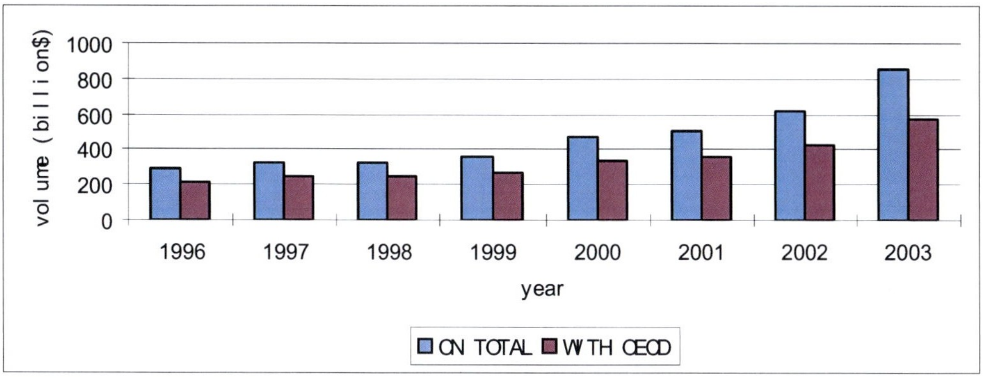

Source: OECD International Trade by Commodity Statistics – Data 2005

Figure 2. Comparison of China's bilateral trade with OECD and China's total trade volume (Unit: billion US$).

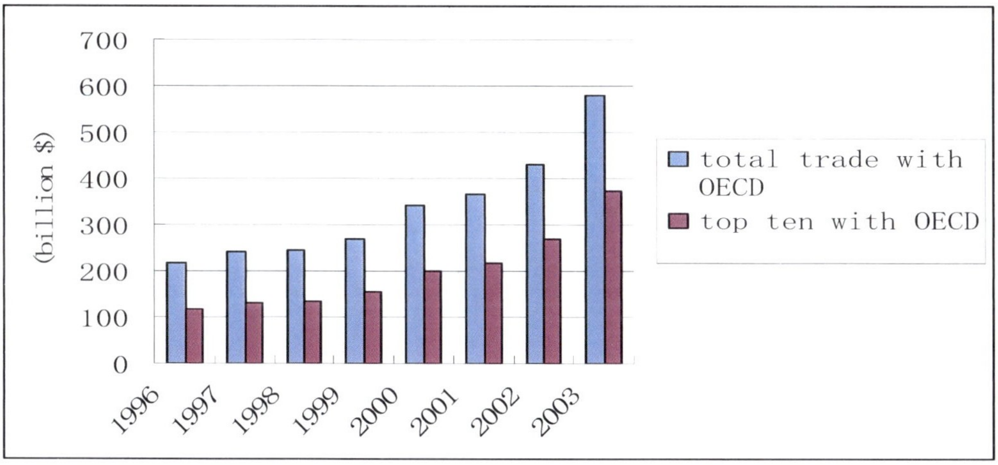

Source: OECD International Trade by Commodity Statistics – Data 2005

Figure 3. Comparison of total bilateral trade and the selected top ten sectoral trade (Unit: billion US$).

2.4. Bilateral Trade in the ICT Sector

ICT has been reshaping the global economy over the last 20 years, and it is also true for the role of ICT in China. ICT industry remains a pillar industry for China. It realized a value-added output cxcccding $76 billion in 2003. The Chinese government is very supportive of the developing ICT industry in China. It addressed this development for the first time in its Tenth Five Year Plan (2001-2005), with measures such as promotion of the development of the software and integrated circuit industries, and the improvement of China's information infrastructure. Therefore, the Chinese government has made telecom and IT development a national priority and enacted preferential policy initiatives to promote telecommunications modernization.

With the fast development of ICT industry, China's bilateral trade with OECD members in ICT sector has shown an amazingly increasing trend over the study period. The growth rate of ICT trade with OECD members was 14.6% in 1997, 19% in 1998, 30.5% in 1999, 41.5% in 2000, 13.5% in 2001, 23% in 2002, and 46% in 2003. The share of ICT trade in the total bilateral trade between China and 26 OECD members sharply increased from 12.8% in 1996 to 24.7% in 2003. This shows that the ICT trade has made a great contribution to China's trade flows.

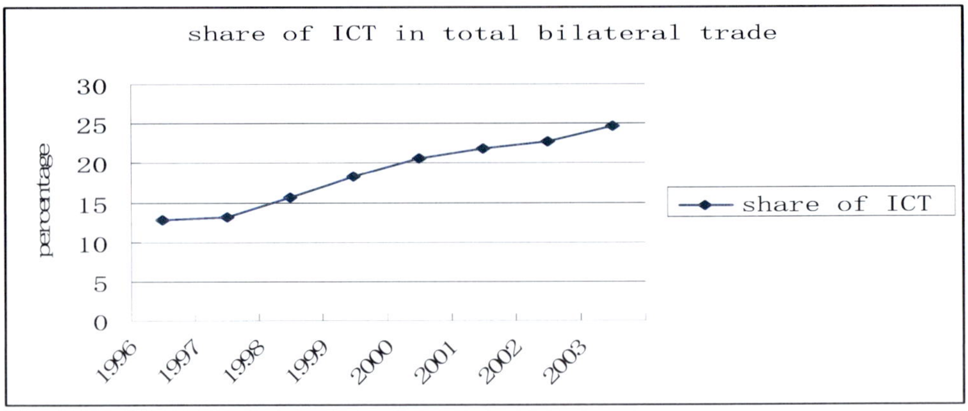

Source: OECD International Trade by Commodity Statistics – Data 2005

Figure 4. Share of ICT in total bilateral trade between China and OECD.

U.S., Japan, Hong Kong, Korea, and Germany are the main trading partners with China in ICT field, although the shares with Japan and Hong Kong indicate a sharp decreasing trend over time.

In 1996, the top five trading partners in the context of ICT products were: Japan (22.9%), Hong Kong (17.4%), USA (16.9%), Korea (5.76%) and Germany (4.05), altogether 67.01%. While in 2003, the top five changed to: USA (16%), Hong Kong (14.9%), Japan (14.5%), Korea (6.57) and Germany (4.17%), altogether 56.14%, meaning that China's ICT trade is likely to get somewhat diversified.

3. Three Theoretical Foundations of the Gravity Model

Economic and social "laws" or relations have often been borrowed from the natural sciences—physics or biology—mainly because of their hard scientific and directly intuitive characters. The gravity equation or model belongs to this category. In the 17th century, Newton defined the law of gravitation stating that two celestial bodies or planets were subjected to an attraction force that depended positively on the product of their masses and negatively on their distance. As far as the economic translation or meaning of force, mass or distance is concerned, there are some quite straightforward solutions. First of all, force is the amount of goods (and in some cases services) that is exported and moves from one country to another. Mass is usually translated into the gross domestic product of any given country.

Based upon Newton's Law of Gravitation, the gravity model predicts that the flow of people, ideas or commodities between two locations is positively correlated to their size and negatively correlated to the distance. Tinbergen (1962) and Pöyhönen (1963) were the first to apply the gravity model to international trade flows.

Table 3. Share of each OECD member in China's total ICT Trade (%)

	1996	1997	1998	1999	2000	2001	2002	2003
Australia	0.51	0.44	0.53	0.45	0.39	0.42	0.53	0.62
Austria	0.13	0.14	0.15	0.15	0.15	0.16	0.21	0.25
Belgium	0	0	0	0.37	0.36	0.49	0.34	0.37
Canada	1.09	0.96	0.96	1.10	0.76	0.81	0.63	0.63
Czech	0.02	0.02	0.05	0.04	0.03	0.14	0.26	0.30
Denmark	0.07	0.08	0.09	0.12	0.09	0.09	0.09	0.10
Finland	0.34	0.80	1.09	1.92	2.10	1.68	0.72	0.58
France	1.11	1.26	1.61	1.51	1.62	1.60	1.18	1.85
Germany	4.05	3.41	3.75	3.65	3.87	3.85	3.64	4.17
Greece	0.02	0.03	0.03	0.04	0.02	0.03	0.03	0.03
H.K.	17.4	16.6	13.3	12.4	13.9	14.3	15.5	14.9
Hungary	0.03	0.10	0.19	0.35	0.47	0.39	0.48	0.63
Ireland	0.08	0.12	0.18	0.25	0.35	0.60	0.57	0.71
Italy	0.67	0.63	0.68	0.83	0.69	0.71	0.63	0.49
Japan	22.9	20.4	17.9	17.6	16.3	15.9	150	14.5
Korea	5.76	6.05	5.05	6.16	6.43	6.30	7.13	6.57
Mexico	0.14	0.33	0.52	0.43	0.67	0.83	0.93	0.74
Netherlands	2.13	2.13	2.19	2.43	2.31	2.33	2.40	2.97
Norway	0.03	0.04	0.05	0.06	0.04	0.03	0.04	0.04
N.Z.	0.05	0.03	0.04	0.05	0.06	0.06	0.06	0.06
Poland	0.14	0.06	0.07	0.09	0.08	0.07	0.06	0.05
Spain	0.37	0.35	0.35	0.36	0.24	0.24	0.17	0.24
Sweden	2.51	2.10	2.95	2.26	1.88	1.04	0.32	0.36
Swiss	0.17	0.15	0.14	0.14	0.14	0.13	0.10	0.11
U.K.	2.08	1.97	2.34	2.64	2.49	2.21	1.50	1.46
USA	16.9	16.6	17.8	18.4	16.6	16.4	16.3	16.0

Source: OECD International Trade by Commodity Statistics – Data 2005

The standard gravity model, which is used by Deardorff (1998), is specified as follows:

$$\text{Trade}_{ij} = A\frac{(GDP_i \cdot GDP_j)^{b_1}}{(DISTANCE_{ij})^{b_2}} \qquad (1)$$

where Trade_{ij} is the value of bilateral trade (=exports + imports) between country i and j, GDP_i and GDP_j are countrys' i and j GDP respectively, $DISTANCE_{ij}$ is a measure of the bilateral distance between the two countries, and A is a constant of proportionality. Transforming equation (1) into logarithmic form hence linear expression, the estimable equation then becomes:

$$\log(trade_{ij})=A+b_1 \log(GDP_i \cdot GDP_j)+b_2 \log(distance_{ij})+\varepsilon_{ij} \qquad (2)$$

where A, b_1 and b_2 are coefficients to be estimated, the error term ε_{ij} captures any other shocks and chance events that may affect bilateral trade between the two countries. This is the core gravity model equation where bilateral trade is predicted to be a positive function of income and a negative function of distance.

Gravity models have achieved indisputable success in explaining various types of inter-regional and international flows in social sciences, including international trade. The gravity equation is quite often used in explaining the structure and pattern of international trade flows because of the rather small "costs" and great "benefits"—meaning that; necessary data are quite simple and easily available and the results are quite consistent with the facts.

While the gravity equation has been used in the empirical literature since the econometric studies done by Tinbergen (1962) and Pöyhönen (1963), the theoretical justification behind the core gravity model has been a gradual process.

The first attempt to derive the gravity equation from economic theory was made by Anderson (1979). In his article "A theoretical Foundation for the Gravity Equation" James Anderson states that: Probably the most successful empirical trade device of the last twenty-five years is the gravity equation. In his study he assumes Cobb–Douglas (and CES) homothetic preferences identical across countries, perfect product specialization under the Armington assumption (each country produces only one specialized good) and perfect competition: prices are the same in all countries. The gravity equation is derived from an expenditure system under constraints given by the importing countries' and the exporting countries' (via their balance of payments) incomes taking into account the costs related to distance.

A country imports goods because its production and demand are not equal in quantity and/or quality. Due to many different factors and causes, an economy has some advantages in producing a given commodity and this result into specialization and trade. This product specialization can occur because countries have different factor endowments as portrayed in H–O models, or because firms enjoy increasing returns to scale in production as in IRS models, or because of technology differences as in Ricardian models. Complete specialization along the Armington assumption would require quite large differences of factor proportions according to the first type of models; while in the second one there is no need for such a hypothesis in order to get the result. Nevertheless, in many instances only imperfect specialization is assumed.

The traditional thinking is that the neoclassical model might be better suited in the case of trade between a developed country and a developing one where factor endowments are quite different and intra-industry trade rather limited (Deardorff 1995). However, trade flows between similar countries might be better interpreted in a monopolistic competition approach.

Variation in factor endowments among countries has been the basis of traditional trade theories that offer the rationale for trade. As a factor-endowments model, H-O theory is used to explain the occurrence of trade in homogeneous products, in other words, depending on the factor intensity of the country, each industry sector is dominated by either import or export after opening trade. This trade pattern is sometimes called inter-industry trade. Under the H-O theory, countries with abundant labor endowment, such as China, will export labor-intensive products, such as textile and clothing, to capital-abundant economies, such as OECD members.

On the other hand, it is very common for the simultaneous export and import of any goods that belong to the same industrial sector in bilateral trade, which is named as intra-industry trade. In this regard, there are many researchers (Dixit and Stiglitz 1977; Lancaster 1980; Helpman 1987; Helpman and Krugman 1985) taking an approach which is different from traditional H-O theory, by assuming imperfect competition and increasing returns to scale. The larger the country is in terms of its GDP/GNP, for instance, the larger the varieties of goods offered. The more similar the countries are in terms of GDP/GNP, the larger is the volume of the bilateral trade (because of specialization). Thus, with economies of scale and differentiated products, the volume of trade depends in an important way on country size in terms of its GDP/GNP (Paas 2000). This is the concept of N-T-T. Dixit and Stiglitz (1977) built a Chamberlinian model that included monopolistic competition and the variety of commodity. Following Dixit and Stiglitz's treatment of monopolistic competition, Krugman (1979) used an even more succinct Chamberlinian formulation and extended the analysis to include explicit trade implication. Krugman concluded with important implications that if intra-industry trade occurs between countries with similar GDP, consumers will spread their expenditures over more product varieties, which will cause the consumption of each variety to fall. Moreover, trade will lead to a reduction in the number of firms in each country.

Several trade theorists have found that the gravity model equation is consistent with theories of trade based upon imperfect competition models and H–O model. Helpman and Krugman (1985) find that a differentiated product framework with increasing returns to scale can theoretically justify the gravity equation. The product differentiation could arise by country of origin, by economies of scale, or from technological or factor endowment differences. Two determinants characterize N-T-T models in the spirit of Krugman (1980) or Helpman and Krugman (1985), namely economies of scale combined with product differentiation and transportation costs. Helpman (1987), Bergstrand (1990) and Hummels and Levinsohn (1995) were among the first to illustrate this point empirically using the gravity model.

Feenstra et al. (1998) further derived a gravity specification from a reciprocal-dumping model of trade with homogeneous goods. Feenstra showed another kind of product differentiation model coming from factor endowment differences. Deardorff (1998) completed the theoretical foundation of the gravity model by showing that the gravity equation is consistent with H-O trade model in homogenous goods with perfect competition.

Hummels and Levinsohn (1995) conducted a model identifying empirical test with a set of non-OECD countries where monopolistic competition was not so plausible. They proved that the equation is also efficient in explaining the trade flows among developing countries where inter-industry trade is dominant with scarce monopolistic competition. Their findings questioned the uniqueness of the product differentiation model in explaining the success of the gravity equation and proved that a variety of other models, including the H-O model, can serve as alternatives.

In another study Feenstra et al. (2001) showed that while gravity equations could be derived for both differentiated and homogeneous goods, the different theories underlying the equation lead to measurably different estimation in key parameter values.

Evenett and Keller (2002) tackled the model identification problems by trying to empirically separate between H-O theory and the increasing returns trade theory as driving forces behind the success of the gravity equation. They argued that little production is perfectly specialized due to factor endowment differences and that as long as production is not perfectly specialized across countries, both of the H-O model and differentiated products model are likely to account for the empirical success of the gravity equation. As a result, estimation parameters of the gravity analysis are critically dependent upon the model identification.

Baltagi et al. (2003) suggest a gravity model with full interaction effects designed to analyze bilateral trade flows, their full interaction model finds empirical support for the N-T-T and Linder's hypothesis.

More recently, Debaere (2005) showed that the increasing similarity in GDP among OECD country-pairs leads to a higher bilateral trade to GDP ratios. His finding provides some support for the prediction of Helpman (1987), whose model explains intra-industry trade that is prevalent among developed countries. In other words, similar countries have more intense commercial relations. However, Debaere shows that Helpman's prediction is rejected for non-OECD countries, among which intra-industry trade is not critical.

Thanks to the aforementioned development of theoretical foundation, it is generally accepted that a number of trade models are responsible for the empirical success of the gravity equation. While the H-O theory would account for the success of the gravity equation in explaining bilateral trade flows among countries with large factor proportion differences and high shares of inter-industry, the differentiated product model would serve well in explaining the bilateral trade flows among countries with high shares of intra-industry trade (Frankel 1997, p53: Deardorff 1998; Evenett and Keller 2002).

In general, based on the wide range of empirical findings, the gravity equation is found to be able to characterize a large class of models, thus making the debate on the trade theories underlying different gravity equation with different trading partners even more vehement. Since most trade theories such as the H-O theory, N-T-T and Linder's Hypothesis can possibly generate the gravity equation, it is of great necessity to find out the proper trade model that fit China's trade flows.

4. Application of the Gravity Model to China's Trade Flows

Most empirical studies using gravity model verify the bilateral trade flows of country pairs in N×N countries setting. In this study, I take China as a reference country and apply the gravity equation to explain Chinas' bilateral trade flows with 26 OECD members who are its major trading partners. The application of the equation in the case of China is done simply by fixing country i = China, while leaving j = 1,2,...,N in a N×1 setting. In the gravity equation, most of the variables are in logarithmic form of real value terms with an exception of the dummy variables and those variables with relatively small numbers.

4.1. Specification and Estimation of The Model

The model I used in this study is augmented in that the standard gravity model only includes income and distance variables. Specifically, two explanatory variables, namely overall bilateral country size and similarity in country size following the measurement methodology of Egger (2000) and Baltagi et al (2003), are introduced in the augmented gravity model. The sum of the two countries' real GDP proxies overall bilateral size (LogGDPS) and a similarity index measures the relative country size (LogSIM). In this study, an additional explanatory variable, the Trade Complementarity Index (TCI) is added in order to identify whether China's trade pattern is based on the H-O model or on the differentiated products/increasing returns to scale model.

To find out the most appropriate model when applying the gravity equation to China's trade flows, all variables are first tested for multicollinerity. To check whether there is multicollinearity in the model, regression is conducted on each independent variable of the model on the remaining independent variables and R-squared computed. If any of these R-squared is greater than the original R-squared, then we can conclude that there is severe multicollinearity in the model. The results show that the model does not have any multicollinearity problem. After that, I specify several models separately. These include; a Pooled OLS model, LSDV model, Fixed Effect Model (FEM) and Random Effect Model (REM),. The Lagrange Multiplier Test is applied here to verify whether the test is in favor of FEM/REM against the classical regression model or not. Further, the Hausman test is conducted to verify whether the test is in favor of the FEM against the REM., A high value of Hausman test would be in favor of FEM against REM, while a low value of Hausman test would be in favor of REM against FEM.

In general, the REM transformation removes less of the variation due to differences in means among units than the LSDV transformation does, preserving more of the information in the data. A greater efficiency of GLS can also be seen by considering that the LSDV transformations "uses up" N-1 degrees of freedom of the data which it is equivalent to including N-1 extra dummy variables.

On the other hand, consistency of the REM depends on the assumption that the unit-specific errors are uncorrelated with other regressors in the model. If they are correlated, the estimates are inconsistent. The FEM does not require the assumption that the individual-specific effects are uncorrelated with the other regressors, as they are viewed as the coefficients of regular dummy variables which are allowed to co-vary with other regressors.

To be more specific, in the fixed-effect (within) model the assumption is that every explanatory variable is correlated with the individual-specific effect. FEM estimation is consistent whether those correlations exist or not, while REM are only consistent (and efficient) if no explanatory variable is correlated with individual-specific effect. The way the FEM avoids the problem is by not using the cross-sectional information in the data (differences between two different individuals, if the panel consists of individual information at different moments), but only the variation within individuals. To do so, the variables are transformed into deviations of individual means. Unfortunately, since the explanatory variable—"Distance", is of time invariant characteristics, when transformation is done to the variable "Distance", it would end up with rows full of 0's and the variable "Distance" has to be consequently dropped from the analysis. That is to say, "within" variation cannot be used in case of time invariant characteristics because there is no such a variation. Therefore, instead of FEM, REMs with one-way design and two-way design are applied. In the case of REM, the random error is heterogeneity specific to a cross-sectional unit—in this case, country. This random error is constant over time. In general, REM has the distinct advantage of allowing for time-invariant variables to be included among the regressors.

The general gravity equation applied in this study is specified as follows:

$$\log\left(TRADE_{ijt}\right) = \alpha + \beta_1 \log\left(GDPS_{ijt}\right) + \beta_2 \log\left(SIM_{ijt}\right) + \beta_3 \left(TCI_{ijt}\right) + \beta_4 \log\left(DIST_{ij}\right) + \varepsilon_{ijt} \tag{4}$$

The REM of one-way design includes a general intercept. Perfect collinearity is avoided by the assumption that the expectation of the unit-specific errors is zero. The model is estimated by GLS. The REM model of the two-way design includes the random unit-specific and time-specific components of the random error term.

On viewing Distance as a time-invariant variable, it is dropped from the gravity equations. In their study "On Theories Explaining the Success of the Gravity Equation" Evenett and Keller (1998) conclude that their findings are not sensitive to the omission of trade resistance (transport costs) in the gravity equation. Therefore, with the dropping of the Distance variable, there is no pre-assumption (for REM or FEM) made on the model. To find out an appropriate model, several equations are specified, including a classical regression model (pooled), fixed effect model with individual effects only, fixed effect model with time effects only, fixed effect model with individual and time effects, and random effect model, separately. The Lagrange Multiplier test will verify whether the FEM/REM is in favor of or against the classical regression model. Further, the Hausman test is conducted to determine between the REM and the FEM.

The general gravity equation without the distance variable is specified as:

$$\log\left(TRADE_{ijt}\right) = \alpha + \beta_1 \log\left(GDPS_{ijt}\right) + \beta_2 \log\left(SIM_{ijt}\right) + \beta_3 \left(TCI_{ijt}\right) + \varepsilon_{ijt} \tag{5}$$

For any unobservable variable which is constant over the period of observation, the effect of such time-invariant omitted variables by an individual-specific intercept. The individual-specific intercept controls for any combination of time-invariant variables that have been omitted either knowingly or not knowingly from the regression model. There are two approaches to estimation namely, the FEM and the REM.

In FEM, the unit-specific effects are treated as fixed constants. In this model there is no general intercept to avoid perfect collinearity with the set of N dummy variables. The implementation of the FEM is usually called the LSDV (Least Squares Dummy Variables) model. The REM includes a general intercept. Perfect collinearity is avoided by the assumption that the expectation of the unit-specific errors is zero.

4.2. Generalizations of the Model

The above-specified models can be extended by allowing for a time-specific component in addition to a unit-specific one. The FEM of such an extended model includes a general intercept. Exact collinearity is avoided by constraining both the unit-specific and the time-specific components to sum up to zero. The REM model of the two-way design includes the random unit-specific and time-specific components of the error term.

As for the aforementioned models, TRADEijt = bilateral trade volume (=exports + imports) between country i and j. i stands for China, and j =1,2,...,N stands for trade partners.

$$\log(GDPS_{ijt}) = \log(GDP_{it} + GDP_{jt}). \tag{6}$$

$$\log(SIM_{ijt}) = \log[1 \text{x} (\frac{GDP_{it}}{GDP_{it} + GDP_{jt}})^2 \text{x} (\frac{GDP_{jt}}{GDP_{it} + GDP_{jt}})^2]. \tag{7}$$

$$TCI_{ijt} = \frac{\sum[X_{kit} \times M_{kjt}]}{\sqrt{\sum[X_{kit}^2 \times M_{kjt}^2]}} \tag{8}$$

The sum of GDPs serves as a proxy for the two economies' economic size, both in terms of production capacity and size of market. Larger economies, with a great production capacity, are more likely to achieve economies of scale and increase their exports based on comparative advantage. They also possess large domestic markets being able to absorb more imports. Thus, an increase in the sum of the two economies' GDPs is expected to increase bilateral trade volumes. Therefore, it is expected that the estimated coefficient of $\beta1>0$.

SIM, Similarity variable (Egger, 2000), measures similarity level of countries in terms of their economic sizes (GDPs) and present a way to compare supply and demand relative sizes. Disaggregated indexes which are comparative index at sectoral or product level would be a more appropriate measure to explicitly compare supply efficiency with demand preferences. But due to data limitation and in view of the focus of the study, I will restrict myself to using the variable in aggregated level. The index is bounded between 0 (absolute divergences in size) and 0.5 (equal country size).

The similarity index controls for the relative size of partner countries in terms of output and hopefully it captures the bilateral intra-industry trade (Egger, 2000). Thus, the larger the SIM index, the more similar are the countries in terms of output and the higher their intra-industry trade. Therefore, it is expected the estimated coefficient of $\beta2>0$.

The distance used in this study is the great circle distance between the capital cities of China and its trading partners. In other words, in my N×1 model, all distances are measured from China and expressed in km[3]. The geographical distance variable is a trade resistance factor that represents trade barriers such as transport costs, time, cultural unfamiliarity and market access barriers, etc. Economists have offered major explanations as follows: firstly, distance is a proxy for transport costs; secondly, distance indicates the time elapsed during shipment; thirdly, distance is correlated with synchronization costs, that is to say, when factories combine multiple inputs in the production process, they need those inputs to arrive in time or else bottlenecks emerge. Therefore, sourcing inputs nearby lowers synchronization costs; fourthly, distance is correlated with communication costs; fifthly, distance may be correlated with transaction costs, meaning that distance is correlated with the costs of searching for trading opportunities and the establishment of trust between potential trading

[3] The information about geographical distance can be found from: *http://www.indo.com/distance/*

partners; and lastly, greater geographic distances are correlated with larger cultural differences. Therefore, it is expected the estimated coefficient of $\beta 4<0$.

Most of the previous literature interpreted the coefficient of distance variable as the elasticity of trade with respect to level of geographical distance. It is worth noting that the key addition to the new trade theory model is costs of trade. Krugman (1980) argued that this framework provides a clear contrast between models based on comparative advantage and those based on increasing returns. In a comparative advantage model, a country with unusually strong demand for a good leads that country to import that good. However, when there are economies of scale, there is a non-trivial location decision. Producers want to locate near unusually strong sources of demand in order to cut trade costs. It turns out that this effect is in fact a magnification of the demand deviation itself, leasing countries with unusually strong demand to become exporters of a good, all else equal.

The TCI variable is designed and served to identify the underlying trade model of my empirical estimation. The TCI measures the degree of trade complementarities between two countries.

There are several designs of the measurement of TCI, Michaely (1994), for example, introduced the Complementarity index K which is defined as:

$$K = 100 - \sum \left(\frac{\left| M_{ik} - X_{ij} \right|}{2} \right) \tag{9}$$

where Xij is the share of good i in exports by country j; and Mik, the share of good i in imports by country k. When a country's export share exactly matches another country's import share, the index is equal to 100. On the contrary, the trade complementarity index is zero in case there is no good exported by one country but imported by the other.

Another measurement of the Trade Complementarity Index (TCI) for product/good k, exported from country i to country j, is defined as:

$$TCI_{ij} = \frac{X_i^k / X_i}{M_w^k / M_w} \bullet \frac{M_j^k / M_j}{M_w^k / M_w} \tag{10}$$

where,

X_i^k = country i's exports of good k,

X_i = total exports of country i,

M_j^k = country j's imports of good k,

M_j = total imports from country j,

M_w^k = world imports of good k,

M_w = total world imports.

Following Gormely and Morrill (1998), TCI between country i and country j is calculated as:

$$TCI_{ijt} = \frac{\sum\left[X_{kit} \times M_{kjt}\right]}{\sqrt{\sum\left[X_{kit}^{2} \times M_{kjt}^{2}\right]}} \quad (11)$$ [4]

where i and j refer to a country and its trading partner: i = China, and j = 1,2,...,N k means a commodity group: k = 1,2,...,n; Xkit = share of commodity group k in the exports of country i at time t; Mkjt = share of commodity group k in the imports of country j at time t.

The TCI value ranges from 0 (perfectly competitive trade structure between country i and country j) to 1 (perfectly complementary trade structure). When two trading partners have same export shares TCI becomes 0, while a country's export shares are identical to its partner's imports shares (i.e., Xki = Mkj), the TCI is 1. Since TCI is a value measured between "0" and "1", its distribution among countries can be relatively small to take on a natural logarithm. Therefore, I include the normal value.

The TCIijt in this study is calculated based on two-digit H.S code classification It is applied to measure the degree of trade complementarities between China and the 26 OECD members. The implication of introducing the trade structure variable is to combine trade pattern with trade flows.

The TCI coefficient β3 is positive when trade volume increases with the rising trade complementarities, which can precisely represents the H-O trade model of inter-industry trade. On the other hand, β3 is negative when the trade volume increases with the falling trade complementarities. In other words, TCI refers to the case where trade volume increases with increasing competitive trade structure. Hence, it represents the differentiated product model with intra-industry trade.

Most of the evidence that gravity model works well comes from aggregated data, where total bilateral trade is regressed on GDP and distance. Only a few studies have been done on examining gravity equations at disaggregated or industrial level.

Bergstrand (1989) derived the gravity equation at the industry level by combining economic geography and factor proportions theory.

Dascal (2002) applied a gravity model approach in order to analyze the main factors affecting the trade flows of wine in the EU. It has been clearly shown in the empirical literature that gravity models can be successfully applied to a single commodity market. Dascal (2002) study utilized pooled cross-sectional and time series data in a one-way fixed effects model that accounted for country-pair heterogeneity. The results revealed that wine trade was positively influenced by an increase in GDP.

Shafer (1986) argues that sectoral analysis is offered as "a parsimonious categorization of international engagement that permits powerful assertions about states' prospects in the international division of labor".

In addition to the regression analysis, this study also investigates on how well the gravity equation fits at the disaggregated level by using aggregate trade data. In doing so, the top ten sectors from China's total bilateral trade flows are selected and the gravity equation for each of the sectors is applied on the Pooled OLS equation (1). All variables in the equation remain

[4] Note that in this formula, there exists a widely known index;-the index of trade concentration or Hirschman Index measuring a degree to which a country j exports is dispersed over various products (UNCTAD, 2004, and Ng and Yeats, 2003), that is calculated as: $H_j=\sqrt{(\sum X_{ki}^2)}$. This index is normalized so that its values range between 0 and 1. Values closer to one indicate more concentrated trade structures.

the same except the dependent variable; that is, the total trade volume TRADEijt which is replaced by a sectoral trade volume TRADEsijt where s = 1,2,...,10. The top ten sectors in China's trade flows are selected based on trade statistics of 2003. Arranged in descending order of sequence, these sectors include: electric machinery etc. (HS85); nuclear reactors, boilers, machinery etc. (HS84); plastics and articles thereof (HS39); apparel articles and accessories, not knit (HS62); iron and steel (HS72); organic chemicals (HS29); apparel articles and accessories, knit or crochet (HS61); vehicles, except railway or tramway (HS87) and furniture (HS94).

In view of the significance of ICT, a specific analysis is made for ICT trade. In 1998, OECD members agreed on a definition of the ICT sector as a combination of manufacturing and services industries that capture, transmit and display data and information electronically. As principles of this definition, the products of a candidate industry must be intended to fulfill the function of information processing and communication including transmission and display or must use electronic processing to detect, measure and/or record physical phenomena or to control a physical process. At a 2003 meeting, OECD's Working Party on Indicators for the Information Society discussed a revised list of ICT goods and finalized in December 2003. In this study, considering the growing importance of ICT sector, following OECD's definition, I apply the gravity equations to the bilateral trade in the context of ICT between China and selected OECD members in order to identify the determinants and characteristics thereof.

4.3 Data and its Sources

As for the data used in this study, the real bilateral trade flows, measured in thousands of U.S. dollar, is obtained from the 2005 OECD International Trade by Commodity Statistics, and deflated using GDP price index from IMF International Financial Statistics. The data covers the period from 1996 to 2003. The data source for GDP is IMF International Financial Statistics, with all values expressed in real terms of thousands of U.S. dollars and deflated using the GDP price index from IMF International Financial Statistics. TCI is based on two-digit H.S. code coverage (99 sectors altogether).

The reason I use OECD trade statistics is that OECD statistics provide consistent and reliable statistics by applying a general procedure and, also provide consistent data for various disaggregated sectors, which will enable me to conduct not only the gravity analysis at aggregate level but also at disaggregated level.

The trade statistics for ICT products is derived based upon the full list of six-digit HS categories (altogether there are 179 categories), which include telecommunications equipment, computer and related equipment, electronic components, audio and video equipment and other ICT goods.

5. DISCUSSION OF RESULTS

5.1. Analysis on Trade Complementarity Index (TCI)

Over the study period, the trade complementarities between China and the selected OECD members are increasing, except for Belgium, Greece, Italy and Japan. In general, the calculated TCI shows that the bilateral trade pattern between China and the 26 OECD members is complementary, rather than competitive. However, among these OECD members, there are quite some differences in terms of the degree of complementarities. For example, China's TCI with the U.S., Greece and Korea in 2003 are 0.7762, 0.5844 and 0.7504 respectively, meaning that China maintains a relatively complementary trade relationship with the U.S., a relatively competitive trade relationship with Greece, and Korea in-between.

For Australia, Austria, Czech, Denmark, Finland, Germany, Hong Kong, Hungary, Ireland, Mexico, Netherlands, Norway, Poland, Sweden, and United Kingdom, the calculated TCI maintains at relatively high level and shows a steady increasing trend over the study period, indicating that the trade relationship between China and the these members is becoming more complementary over time: For Belgium, Greece, Italy, Japan, New Zealand and Spain, calculated TCI remains at relatively low level and even shows a decreasing trend over the study period, indicating that trade relationship between China and these members is getting more competitive: Compared with the afore-mentioned OECD members, the calculated TCI between China and; Canada, France, Korea, Switzerland, and U.S.A. remains at a moderate level:

5.2. Analysis on Similarity Index (SIM)

Similarity variable (Egger, 2000) measures similarity level of countries in terms of their economic sizes (GDPs) and present a way to compare supply and demand relative sizes. Similarities or differences are very important factors in leading trade. The larger this SIM index, the more similar two countries are in terms of GDP, and the higher the share of trade. The index is bounded between 0 (absolute divergences in size) to 0.5 (equal country size).

In general, the calculated SIM shows that China enjoys quite a similar relative economic size with Canada, France, Germany, Italy, Korea, Mexico, Netherlands, Spain, and United Kingdom(almost identical with Italy and U.K.); while quite dissimilar with Czech, Finland, Greece, H.K., Hungary, Ireland, New Zealand, Norway, Poland, and USA; with Australia, Austria, Belgium, Denmark, Japan, Sweden, and Switzerland lying in-between.

Scandinavian Countries

In Denmark's case, SIM remains at moderate level and shows a decreasing trend over the study period, changing from 0.3103 in 1996 to 0.2248 in 2003, implying that both countries are getting dissimilar in their relative country size.

In Finland's case, SIM remains at low level and demonstrates a decreasing trend, changing from 0.2459 in 1996 to 0.1849 in 2003. This means that, both countries are getting dissimilar in their relative country size.

In Norway's case, SIM maintains at a relatively low level over the study period, ranging from 0.2168 to 0.2857, meaning that both countries are dissimilar in their relative country size.

In Sweden's case, SIM maintains at a moderate level and shows a decreasing trend, changing from 0.3873 in 1996 to 0.2884 in 2003, meaning that both countries are getting dissimilar in their relative country size over time.

European Countries

In Austria's case, SIM remains at moderate level and clearly shows a decreasing trend over the study period. It changes from 0.3561 in 1996 to 0.2582 in 2003 indicating that both countries are getting dissimilar in their relative country size over time.

In Belgium's case, SIM also remains at moderate level and shows a slightly decreasing trend. It changes from 0.3844 in 1996 to 0.2907 in 2003 indicating that both countries are gradually getting dissimilar in their relative country size over time.

In France's case, SIM remains at a high level over the study period and clearly shows an increasing trend, changing from 0.443 in 1996 to 0.4946 in 2003. This implies that both countries are quite similar in their country size.

In Germany's case, SIM also remains at relatively high level over the study period, changing from 0.3673 in 1996 to 0.4657 in 2003, meaning that both countries are getting more similar in their relative country size.

In Ireland's case, SIM also remains at low level during the whole study period, ranging from 0.1428 to 0.1693, meaning that both countries are dissimilar in their relative country size.

In Italy's case, SIM remains at quite a high level over the study period and shows an increasing trend, changing from 0.4752 in 1996 to 0.4999, meaning that both countries are becoming almost identical in their relative country size.

In Netherlands's case, SIM remains at a moderate level, ranging from 0.3632 to 0.4551, meaning that both countries are getting similar in their relative country size.

In Switzerland's case, SIM shows a sharply decreasing trend over the study period, changing from 0.4035 in 1996 to 0.2856 in 2003, meaning that both countries are getting dissimilar in their relative country size.

In United Kingdom's case, SIM maintains at quite high level and demonstrates an increasing trend over the study period, changing from 0.4772 in 1996 to 0.4954 in 2003, indicating that both countries are becoming almost identical in their relative country size.

In Spain's case, SIM maintains at a high level ranging from 0.4409 to 0.4924, meaning that both countries are quite similar in their relative country size.

In Greece's case, SIM remains at low level over the study period, ranging from 0.1611 to 0.23, meaning that both countries are dissimilar in their relative country size.

In Poland's case, SIM also maintains at a relatively low level, ranging from 0.2161 to 0.2484, meaning that both countries are dissimilar in their relative country size.

In Czech's case, SIM remains at a very low level during the whole study period, with its values ranging from 0.0840 to 0.1229, meaning that both countries are quite dissimilar in their relative country size.

In Hungary's case, SIM remains at quite a low level during the whole study period, ranging from 0.0727 to 0.1017, which means that both countries are quite dissimilar in their relative country size.

North and South American and Pacific Countries

In Australia's case, SIM remains at relatively high level although it shows a slightly decreasing trend, changing from 0.451 in 1996 to 0.3866 in 2003, indicating that both countries are still similar to a certain level in their country size.

In Canada's case, SIM remains at high level although it shows slightly decreasing trend, changing from 0.4939 in 1996 to 0.4699 in 2003. This means that, both countries are quite similar in their relative country size.

In USA's case, SIM remains at low level during the study period and shows a slightly increasing trend, changing from 0.1643 in 1996 to 0.2033 in 2003, meaning that two countries are still dissimilar in their relative country size.

In New Zealand's case, SIM maintains at quite low level and shows a decreasing trend, changing from 0.1461 in 1996 to 0.0981 in 2003, meaning that both countries are quite dissimilar in their relative country size.

In Mexico's case, SIM remains at a moderate level and shows an increasing trend over the study period, changing from 0.372 in 1996 to 0.4206 in 2003. This means that both countries are getting similar in their relative country size.

Asian Countries

In Hong Kong's case, SIM also remains at low level and shows a decreasing trend over the study period, changing from 0.2735 in 1996 to 0.1874 in 2003, meaning both economies are getting dissimilar in their relative country size.

In Japan's case, SIM remains at a moderate low level and shows an increasing trend over the study period, changing from 0.2385 in 1996 to 0.3692 in 2003, indicating that both countries are getting similar over time in their relative country size.

In Korea's case, SIM remains at relatively high level although it shows a decreasing trend over time, changing from 0.4851 in 1966 to 0.4165 in 2003, meaning that both countries are still similar in their relative country size.

5.3. Regression Results Analysis

5.3.1. Estimation Results at Aggregate Level

The regression results at aggregate level are summarized in Table 4.

In general, all the gravity coefficients are economically and statistically significant with sensible interpretations under different specifications. Regression results show that all of the estimated coefficients are statistically significant at 1% level, and their signs remain constant among different specifications. This means that the overall performance of the model seems quite good and the gravity model is effective in explaining China's bilateral trade flows with its 26 OECD members and that the gravity model is well applicable to a single country case.

The signs of the coefficients of the log of GDPs are positive, showing that wealthier countries trade more than their less wealthier counterparts. The log of the sum of two countries' GDPs is highly significant in determining China's trade volume. The estimated coefficient of $\beta 1$ on the GDP variable is stable and its values in different equations range from 1.9293 to 2.4679. This result is consistent with the basic hypothesis of the gravity model that the trade volumes will increase with an increase in economic size.

Table 4. Regression Results at Aggregate Level

Explanatory variables	OLS Model	REM (one-way)	REM (two-way)
LogGDPS	1.9293*** (0.0901)	2.4679*** (0.0995)	2.2180*** (0.6760)
LogSIM	0.8310*** (0.0979)	0.8351*** (0.1183)	0.7636*** (0.0775)
TCI	2.6449*** (0.6168)	2.4124*** (0.3639)	2.8775*** (0.2973)
LogDIST	-1.1975*** (0.0857)	-1.1822*** (0.2322)	-1.1880*** (0.0895)
Constant	-16.2163*** (2.1108)	-27.6009*** (2.8219)	-22.6908*** (1.5588)
F-test	237.95***		
Lagrange Multiplier Test		609.40***	610.00***
Adjusted R^2	0.8208	0.8242	0.8242

Notes: 1) The numbers in parenthesis are standard errors. 2) *** and ** and * mean significant at 1%, 5% and 10% level, respectively.

The estimated coefficient means that, holding other variables constant, a 1 percent point increase in GDP will result in more than one percent point increase in China's bilateral trade flows. Thus, the increase in China's bilateral trade volume is more proportionate to the increase in GDPs. This is characterized by a monopolistic competition and/or scale economy (Harrigan 2003). It shows that a country enjoying scale economies will trade a bigger volume, meaning a higher level of intra-industry trade.

The log of SIM, a similarity index of two trading partners' GDPs as a measure of relative country size, is also found to have a significant and positive impact on China's trade flows, its' values within different equations range from 0.7636 to 0.8351. The positive sign of the SIM coefficient means that the larger the SIM index is and the more similar two countries are in terms of GDP, the higher is the share of trade.

The distance variable is statistically significant with the expected negative sign, showing that geographical distance is an important resistance factor for China's bilateral trade flows. The greater is the distance, the smaller the trade flows. The coefficient β4 of the log of the distance turned out to be very similar to those estimated by other previous studies (Frankel 1997; Wall 1999; Buch et al. 2004). Grossman (1998) points out that most empirical gravity studies show a surprisingly large size of the estimated coefficient on the distance variable. Hence my result, which ranges from -1.1822 to -1.1975, is no exception.

The coefficient on the trade structure variable is aimed to empirically identify the underlying trade model of China's trade flows, The TCI coefficients are positive in all gravity equations and show a high statistical significance, meaning that trade volumes between China and the selected OECD members increase with the rising trade complementarities. From this point of view, it implies that China's trade pattern follows H-O trade model, which assumes that two countries in a complementary economic relationship are more likely to expand their bilateral trade volume through inter-industry trade. TCI can also be viewed as the relative factor endowment differences.

In summation, at aggregate level the gravity model finds empirical support for the N-T-T and H-O Theory.

5.3.2. Estimation Results of Equations without Distance Variable

Firstly, the results from the classical regression (CR) model (pooled) were obtained. The Lagrange Multiplier test shows a high value of LM hence, favors FEM/REM over the CR model, while the Hausman test shows a low value which in turn favors the REM against the FEM. The regression results are summarized in Table 5.

Table 5. Regression results without Distance variable

Explanatory variables	OLS Model	REM (one-way)	REM (two-way)
LogGDPS	1.9288*** (0.1259)	2.5302*** (0.1055)	2.3917*** (01609)
LogSIM	0.9851*** (0.1359)	0.8885*** (0.1261)	0.8945*** (0.1302)
TCI	3.9253*** (0.8521)	2.3099*** (0.3725)	2.1678*** (0.3973)
Constant	-27.5413*** (2.7233)	-39.2052*** (2.0375)	-36.1518*** (3.2552)
F-test	129.26***		
Lagrange Multiplier Test		669.01***	671.71***
Hausman Test		4.01 (prob=0.2607)	2.89 (prob=0.4083)
Adjusted R^2	0.6502	0.6553	0.6553

Note: 1) The numbers in parenthesis are standard errors. 2) *** and ** and * mean significant at 1%, 5% and 10% level, respectively.

All the coefficients of explanatory variables are stable and statistically highly significant at 1% level. The results for the models with distance variable and models without distance variable are similar with regard to the signs and order of magnitude of the coefficients. In other words, the signs of all coefficients are consistent with the previous findings, meaning that it has reinforced the previous regression results.

The signs of the GDPs are positive and the sum of two countries' GDPs is highly significant in determining China's trade volume. The estimated coefficient β1 on the GDP variable is stable and its values in different equations range from 1.9288 to 2.5302. The estimated coefficient means that, holding other variables constant, a 1 percent point increase in GDP will result in more than one percent point increase in China's bilateral trade flows. Thus, the increase in China's bilateral trade volume is more proportionate to the increase in GDPs.

The log of SIM, is also found to have a positive and a significant impact on China's trade flows. Its values within different equations range from 0.8885 to 0.9851.

The TCI coefficients show a high statistical significance and are positive in all the gravity equations, meaning that trade volumes between China and the selected OECD members' increases with the rising trade complementarities.

The TCI coefficients show a high statistical significance and are positive in all gravity equations. Its values range from 2.1678 to 3.9253, meaning that trade volumes between China and the selected OECD members increase with the rising trade complementarities. It implies that China's trade pattern follows H-O trade model, which assumes that two countries that are in a complementary economic relationship are more likely to expand their bilateral trade volume through inter-industry trade. TCI can also be viewed as the relative factor endowment differences.

Therefore, the gravity equation without Distance variable at aggregate level also finds empirical support for the N-T-T and H-O Theory.

5.4. Gravity Estimation at Disaggregate Level

By running OLS regression, Table 6 summarizes the regression results at the disaggregated level.

Table 6. OLS regression results for the selected top ten sectors

	LogGDPS	LogSIM	TCI	LogDIST	Constant	Adj-R2
HS85	2.1198*** (0.1107)	1.1179*** (0.1203)	6.2209*** (0.7576)	-1.3474*** (0.1053)	-23.2029*** (2.5928)	0.8086
HS84	1.6318*** (0.1059)	1.4205*** (0.1150)	6.0484*** (0.7247)	-1.0756*** (0.1007)	-14.8514*** (2.4803)	0.7812
HS27	2.3635*** (0.3614)	3.6514*** (0.3927)	0.5435 (2.4737)	-2.2103*** (0.3437)	-16.9322** (8.4656)	0.5313
HS39	1.5954*** (0.1102)	1.5144*** (0.1197)	0.8550 (0.7541)	-1.7176*** (0.1048)	-6.1547** (2.5808)	0.8036
HS62	1.7529*** (0.2913)	1.2458*** (0.3165)	4.8125** (1.9939)	-1.5841*** (0.2770)	-13.8375** (6.8237)	0.3528
HS72	2.2267*** (0.2810)	1.8192*** (0.3053)	2.0808 (1.9236)	-1.9745*** (0.2672)	-18.9448*** (6.5830)	0.4933
HS29	1.5467*** (0.2066)	1.6809*** (0.2245)	3.1994** (1.4141)	-1.1826*** (0.1965)	-11.5977** (4.8395)	0.4965
HS61	1.4267*** (0.2397)	0.6927*** (0.2605)	4.0851** (1.6412)	-1.4545*** (0.2280)	-8.3802 (5.6167)	0.3422
HS87	2.2762*** (0.2322)	1.6428*** (0.2523)	5.4059*** (1.5895)	-1.0993*** (0.2208)	-30.3802*** (5.4397)	0.5244
HS94	1.8340*** (0.2044)	1.5813*** (0.2467)	4.6247*** (1.4249)	-0.6319*** (0.1939)	-24.2463*** (4.8105)	0.4778

Notes: 1) The numbers in parenthesis are standard errors. 2) *** and ** and * mean significant at 1%, 5% and 10% level, respectively.

The overall performance of the model seems to be reasonably good with the values of adjusted R-squared ranging from 0.3422 to 0.8086, most of the explanatory variables are statistically significant at conventional levels, and their signs remain the same among different specifications, meaning that the gravity model is effective in explaining China's bilateral trade flows at sectoral level.

Among the top ten sectors, three sectors, namely HS85, HS84, and HS39, have relatively higher R-squared values than other sectors. It is worth to mention that the electric machinery (HS85) and nuclear reactors and boilers (HS84) accounted for around 40% of China's overall trade flows in 2003, thus making them the most significant sectors in recent years.

The signs of the coefficients of GDPs are positive and the log of the sum of the two countries' GDPs is highly significant in determining China's trade volume in all the top ten sectors. The estimated coefficient $\beta 1$ on the GDP variable is stable and its values in different sectors range from 1.4267 to 2.3635. This means that the trade volumes for these sectors will increase with an increase in economic size. Among the ten sectors, the mineral fuel and oil respond most sensitively to GDP variable, while knitted apparel responds relatively least sensitively to GDP variable.

The log of SIM is also found to have a significant and a positive impact on all top ten sectoral trade flows. Its values range from 0.6927 to 3.6514 within different sectors, meaning that the sectoral trade volumes between China and OECD members increase with rising similarities.

The Distance variable is statistically significant at 1% level and has a negative coefficient in all sectors and therefore behaves coherently in the way predicted by theory regardless of the sector, varying in magnitude between -0.6319 and -2.2103, meaning that the determinant of distance is very crucial for all top ten sectors. The coefficient β4 of the log of the distance turned out to be very similar to those estimated by other previous studies (Frankel 1997; Wall 1999; Buch et al. 2004). Apart from mineral fuel and oil etc., the iron and steel products and plastics are also sensitive to distance. Furniture product is least affected by Distance variable. Other products are in-between.

With the significant positive impact of variables, LogGDPs and LogSIM combined with the negative impact of Distance on bilateral trade, the gravity equation at disaggregate level finds empirical support for N-T-T.

TCI is found to have positive impact on trade flows on all sectors. However, the coefficient of TCI variable is statistically significant at 1% level only for HS85, HS84, HS87 and HS94 sectors; statistically significant at 5% level for HS62, HS29, and HS61 sectors; while not statistically significant for HS27, HS39 and HS72 sectors. It is worth noting that, at sectoral level, the coefficient of TCI is no longer a measure for model identification, but a simple measure of sectoral trade flows with respect to overall bilateral trade structure. The implication of introducing the trade structure variable here is to combine overall trade pattern with sectoral trade flows.

5.5. Gravity Estimation of ICT Sector

Following OECD's definition (2003), the gravity equation is applied to ICT trade using trade statistics of ICT products. The OLS regression results are reported in Table 7.

Table 7. Regression Result of ICT Sector

Explanatory Variables	OLS coefficient (std error)
LogGDPs	2.4519*** (0.2080)
LogSIM	0.9268*** (0.2260)
TCI	12.1960*** (1.4240)
LogDIST	-1.3300*** (0.1978)
Constant	-35.4843*** (4.8734)
Observations	208
Adjusted R2	0.6176

Notes: 1) The numbers in parenthesis are standard errors.2) *** and ** and * mean significant at 1%, 5% and 10% level, respectively.

The coefficient on GDP variable is statistically significant and has a positive sign, showing that the economies of scale is one of the most important determinants in China's trade flows in ICT field. The estimated coefficient means that, holding other variables constant, a 1 percent point increase in GDP will result in roughly a 2.4519 percent point increase in China's bilateral ICT trade flows. This is characterized by a monopolistic competition and/or scale economy (Harrigan, 2003). Thus a country like China enjoying scale economies will trade a bigger volume, meaning a higher level of intra-industry trade in ICT sector.

Another variable SIM, is also found to have a significant positive impact on ICT trade flows, meaning that the more similar in relative country size, the bigger trade share in ICT sector. As the similarity index controls for the relative size of partner countries in terms of output and hopefully capturers the bilateral intra-industry trade (Egger, 2000), the positive coefficient of SIM indicates that the larger the index, the more similar are the countries in terms of output and the higher their intra-industry trade.

TCI is found to have relatively large and positive impact on trade flows in ICT sector, and it is statistically significant at 1% level, meaning that the overall trade pattern is significantly correlated with China's ICT trade flows.

Transportation cost is found to be a significant factor in influencing China's ICT trade negatively. The estimated coefficient on log distance has the anticipated negative sign and is slightly over one, indicating that trade between China and its trading partner falls by slightly over 1 per cent for every 1 percent increase in the distance between them. This is consistent with the prevalent theoretical expectations. The closer the trading partner is, the more the trade flows could emerge.

6. Conclusions

6.1. Summary of Findings

This study is an attempt to analyze the trade performance of China with the developed world (selected 26 OECD members) through the gravity equation approach. Generally, the gravity equations work well in dealing with China's trade flows. All variables have the expected signs, which are statistically significant in most (if not all) equations.

In this study, I estimate the equation in several ways, including different estimation methods and different specifications of the gravity model. All these robustness checks confirm that the key results do not delicately depend on the exact way that the equation is specified or estimated.

With regard to the estimation at aggregate level, this study has found that two variables, GDP and SIM, are statistically highly significant in all equations and have a positive coefficient. Besides, the estimation results in this study find a significant negative effect of distance, which implies that shorter distance can induce increased trade, which is consistent with theoretical expectations. Therefore, the gravity equation at aggregate level finds empirical support for the N-T-T.

The trade structure variable TCI has a positive coefficient, and is statistically significant in most equations. At aggregate level, the positive coefficient of TCI indicates that China's trade follows H-O model with dominant inter-industry trade and some vertical intra-industry trade.

The empirical support for the N-T-T and H-O theory implies that both intra-industry trade and inter-industry trade are critical in China's international trade patterns. Therefore, by applying the gravity model to the bilateral trade between China as the largest developing country and OECD members as the developed world, it is hoped that the findings of this present study can contribute to the debate about the theoretical foundation underlying the gravity equation.

In summation, the empirical findings in this study are consistent with Helpman and Krugman (1985) and Evenett and Keller (2002), all of whom argue that both the H-O model and differentiated products model are likely to account for the empirical success of the gravity equation, and the product differentiation can arise from country of origin, economies of scale, technological or factor endowment differences. However, the empirical findings of this study are at odds with Deardorff (1995) and the recent work by Debaere (2005), whose finding provides some support for the prediction of Helpman (1987). That is, intra-industry trade is prevalent among developed countries, and thus similar countries have more intense commercial relations. However, Debaere shows that Helpman's prediction is rejected for non-OECD countries, among which intra-industry trade is not critical.

With regard to the sectoral estimation, the overall performance of the model seems to be reasonably good with most of the explanatory variables being statistically significant at conventional levels, and their signs remain constant among different specifications, meaning that the gravity model is effective in explaining China's bilateral trade flows at sectoral level. The estimation results at sectoral level reinforce those at aggregate level.

In view of the growing importance and instrumental role of ICT sector, this study has applied the gravity equation to China's trade flows in ICT goods, following the newly developed definition by OECD (2003). The estimation results show that China's bilateral trade in ICT field is positively related to the GDPs and SIM, and negatively related with Distance. And the overall trade pattern is significantly correlated with China's ICT trade flows.

6.2. Policy Implications

All the regression results show that the increase in China's trade volume is more than proportionate to the increase in GDP. China's economic growth has increased by 9.5% on average over the past two decades. According to OECD's Economic Survey of China (2005), China's rapid pace of economic change is likely to be sustained for some time. Thanks to the continued evolution of economic policies, especially in the areas of the allocation of capital, labor mobility, urbanization and the creation of an improved framework for the development of the private sector of the economy. Therefore, with the sustained economic growth, China will continue to gain higher trade growth rates and hence, become substantially integrated with the world economy.

With regard to the negative coefficient of the Distance variable, it is very clear that all firms have an incentive to start their production near the market to save transport costs. If allowed, they will commence manufacture in both countries, which implies two-way direct foreign investment. For the policy-makers, release of existing restrictions on outward investment is quite necessary. Thus, some new rules and regulations are urgently needed to encourage, support and guide the development of such investment activities, including further improving the policy support system for venture capital and regulating cross-border capital transactions, and etc.

All gravity equations applied to China's trade flows, whether at aggregate country level or at industrial level, have found empirical support for N-T-T. As we know, the N-T-T assumes that marginal costs lie below average costs for any level of output. Hence, a larger firm is always more competitive than a smaller one. This leads to the intuitive result that competition among the firms engaged in China's trade activities, including domestic firms and joint ventures, will become extremely intense. The large sized firms have better chances to survive and succeed than those small sized firms. Besides, based on N-T-T, trade will lead to a reduction in the number of firms in each country. For the policy-makers, some effective strategies should be designed to encourage scale economy and scale operation at firm level.

In view of China's model of international trade with monopolistic competition, the consumers prefer an increasing number of choices, and therefore each firm must produce a variety of goods with an increasing return to scale technology (Krugman 1980; Helpman and Krugman 1985). Thus, firms should invest in product innovation, in order to enhance demand for their products. For example, one of the most significant strategies for SK, the largest oil refining company in Korea, to enter into the Chinese market is so-called product-differentiation strategy, which focuses mainly on some environmental-friendly products. This strategy has proved quite effective and successful in recent years.

On the other hand, the empirical support for H-O theory also has meaningful policy implications. As we know, variation in factor endowments among countries has been the basis of traditional trade theories that offer the rationale for trade. Under the H-O theory, countries with abundant labor endowment, such as China, will export labor-intensive products, such as textile and clothing, to the capital-abundant economies, such as OECD members. In turn, they will import large amount of capital-intensive and technology-intensive goods.

In general, whether China's trade flows follow the N-T-T model and/or H-O model depends greatly on the nature of economic structures and trade complementarities relationship between China and its trading partners. It is quite clear that with China's implementation of market diversification strategy, both inter- and intra-industry trade will co-exist in the long run.

6.3. Limitations of this Study and Suggestions for Further Research

Due to data limitations, this study has focused only on the trade flows between China and 26 OECD members, and all non-OECD trading partners have not been included. The previous researches using gravity equation indicate that the gravity model could be very sensitive to changes in the sample, i.e. the addition or omission of countries/regions could have important impact on the overall estimation. This in turn provides a strong argument in favor of including as many countries as possible in the sample in order to avoid any bias from omitting countries which are essential to capture the characteristics and determinants of overall China's trade flows.

Theoretically and empirically, similar with most of the previous studies in this field, the study in this study has focused on the general or integrated determinants, such as GDP, size of the economy, etc. In other words, industrial characteristic is seldom addressed or taken into account. The generalization gives rise to some questions when the intra-industry trade is examined. Especially for horizontal intra-industry trade (IIT) and vertical IIT, in spite of the clear indications in the theory, the empirical studies investigating the determinants of IIT have not distinguished vertical IIT from horizontal IIT. Although this study has found empirical support for N-T-T and H-O theory, it fails to figure out whether the horizontal IIT or the vertical IIT is the dominant effect. This necessitates further study, including further investigation of horizontal and vertical IIT in China's trade flows by introducing the some newly established IIT index in my future gravity equation. Future research will depend partly on the source of data and their level of disaggregation, as well as the methodological criteria adopted.

Since the world's international economies, including China, are much more complicated than the economies created for the literal study, many experiments can provide some insights into how models are able to organize the data. Thus, despite the progresses that have been made, the determinants and empirical significance of China's trade performance are yet to be fully understood. As Harrigan (2003) put it, we are still in the very early stages of empirically understanding specialization and the volume of trade, but the work that has been done can serve as a starting point for further research.

ACKNOWLEDGEMENTS

I have been working on the present research since I came to Seoul National University two years ago. Since then many people have become involved in my research and helped me in different ways. I owe all of them a great debt of gratitude. I feel most deeply indebted to all professors in TEPP who have been a constant source of support and encouragement. Special thanks go due to Prof. Jeong-Dong Lee, Prof. Eunnyeong Hoe and Prof. Almas Heshmati, who have been patient, kind and skillful, and have always been most generous with their time and private libraries. Their invaluable comments and suggestions have led to numerous improvements in this study. Without their guidance, this study would not have come to fruition. Heartfelt thanks are also go to my wife Jia Bo and my son Zhu Ning, whose limitless love and encouragement have upheld me greatly. Any remaining shortcomings you may perceive, of course, are my own responsibility.

REFERENCES

Anderson J. E. (1979), A Theoretical Foundation for the Gravity Equation, American *Economic Review* 69(1), 106-116.

Baltagi B. H., P. Egger and M. Pfaffermayr (2003), A generalized design for bilateral trade flow models, *Economics Letters* 80(3), 391-397.

Bergstrand J. H. (1989), The Generalized Gravity Equation Monopolistic Competition, and the Factor-Proportions Theory in International Trade, *Review of Economics and Statistics* 71, 143-153.

Bergstrand J. H. (1990), The H-O-Samuelson model, the Linder hypothesis and the determinants of bilateral intra-industry trade, *Economic Journal* 100, 1216-1229.

Buch C., M. Kleinert and F. Toubal (2004), The Distance Puzzle: On the Interpretation of the Distance Coefficient in Gravity Equations. *Economics Letters* 83, 293-298.

Dascal D. (2002), An analysis of EU wine trade: a gravity model approach. *International Advances in Economic Research.*

Deardorff A. V. (1995), Determinants of Bilateral Trade: Does Gravity Work in a Neoclassical World?, NBER Working Papers 5377, *National Bureau of Economic Research*, Inc.

Deardorff A. V. (1998), Determinants of Bilateral Trade: Does Gravity Work in a Neoclassical World?, In Jeffrey A. Frankel (Ed.), *"The Regionalization of the World Economy"* Chicago; University Press.

Debaere P. (2005), Monopolistic competition and trade, revisited: testing the model without testing for gravity, *Journal of International Economics* 66, 249-266.

Dixit A. K. and J. E. Stiglitz (1977), Monopolistic Competition and Optimum Product Diversity, *American Economic Review* 67, 297-308.

Egger P. (2000), A Note on the Proper Econometric Specification of the Gravity Equation, *Economics Letters* 66, 25-31.

Evenett S. J. and W. Keller (1998), On Theories Explaining the Success of the Gravity Equation, Working Paper 6529, *National Bureau of Economic Research.*

Evenett S. J. and W. Keller (2002), On Theories Explaining the Success of the Gravity Equation, *Journal of Political Economy* 110(2), 281-316.

Feenstra R. C., J. R. Markusen and A. K. Rose (1998), Understanding the Home Market Effect and the Gravity Equation: The Role of Differentiating Goods, *NBER Working Paper* No.6804.

Feenstra R. C., J. R. Markusen and A. K. Rose (2001), Using the Gravity Equation to Differentiate Among Alternative Theories of Trade, *Canadian Journal of Economics* 34(2), 430-447.

Frankel J. A. (1997), Regional Trading Blocs in the World Economic System. Institute for International Economics, Washington, D.C.

Gormely J. P. and J. M. Morrill (1998), Korea's International Trade in Goods: The Potential for Increase Exports to and Imports from Trade Partners. Korea Institute for Industrial Economics and Trade: Seoul.

Grossman G. M. (1998), "Comment on Deardorff." In Jeffrey A. Frankel ed., The Regionalization of the World Economy. Chicago: University of Chicago Press. pp. 29-31

Harrigan J. (2003), Specialization and the Volume of Trade: Do the Data Obey the Laws? in E. Kwan Choi and James Harrigan ed., Handbook of International Trade, Blackwell Publishing, pp.165-85.

Helpman E. and P. Krugman (1985), Market structure and foreign trade: Increasing returns, imperfect competition and the international economy. Cambridge, MA, MIT Press.

Helpman E. (1987), Imperfect Competition and International Trade: Evidence from Fourteen Industrial Countries. *Journal of the Japanese and International Economy.* Cambridge, MA, MIT Press.

Hummels D. and J. Levinsohn (1995), Monopolistic competition and international trade: Reconsidering the evidence, *Quarterly Journal of Economics* 110 (3), 799-836.

Krugman P. (1979), Increasing returns to scale, monopolistic competition and international trade, *Journal of International Economics* 110, 799-836.

Krugman P. (1980), Scale economies, product differentiation, and the pattern of trade, *American Economic Review* 70, 950-959.

Lancaster K. (1980), Intra-industry trade under perfect monopolistic competition, *Journal of International Economics* 10, 151-175.

Linder S. B. (1961), An Essay On Trade and Transformation. John Wiley, New York.

Michaely M. (1994), Trade Preferential Agreements in Latin America: Ex-ante Assessment. The World Bank Latin American and Caribbean Region, Washington, D.C.

Paas T. (2000), Gravity Approach for Modeling Trade Flows between Estonia and the Main Trading Partners, Working Paper, No. 721, Tartu University Press, Tartu.

Pöyhönen P. (1963), A Tentative Model for the Volume of Trade between Countries, Weltwertschaftliches Archiv 90(1), 93-99.

Shafer D. M. (1986), Undermined: the implications of mineral export dependence for state formation in Africa, Third World Quarterly 83, 916-952.

Tinbergen J. (1962), Shaping the World Economy: Suggestions for an International Economic Policy, New York: 20th Century Fund.

UNCTAD, Handbook on Statistics 2004, Geneva: New York and Geneva: United Nations.

Ng F. and A. Yeates (2003), Major Trade Trends in East Asia: What Are Their Implications for Regional Cooperation and Growth?, World Bank Policy Research Working Paper No 3084, Washington, D.C. The World Bank

Wall J. H. (1999), Using the Gravity Model to Estimate the Costs of Protection, January/February Review of Federal Bank of Saint Louis.

APPENDICES

Appendix 1. The Calculated Trade Complementarity Index (TCI) and Similarity Index (SIM)

Year	Partner	TCI	SIM
1996	Australia	0.6780	0.4510
1997	Australia	0.6719	0.4327
1998	Australia	0.6974	0.3980
1999	Australia	0.7376	0.4005
2000	Australia	0.7781	0.3769
2001	Australia	0.7854	0.3512
2002	Australia	0.7745	0.3574
2003	Australia	0.7914	0.3866
1996	Austria	0.7007	0.3561
1997	Austria	0.7244	0.3065
1998	Austria	0.7564	0.2962
1999	Austria	0.7763	0.2851
2000	Austria	0.8051	0.2524
2001	Austria	0.8167	0.2371
2002	Austria	0.8248	0.2365
2003	Austria	0.8226	0.2582
1996	Belgium	0.6071	0.3844
1997	Belgium	0.6170	0.3393
1998	Belgium	0.6351	0.3280
1999	Belgium	0.6417	0.3181
2000	Belgium	0.6513	0.2842
2001	Belgium	0.6598	0.2685
2002	Belgium	0.5766	0.2676
2003	Belgium	0.5719	0.2907
1996	Canada	0.6121	0.4939
1997	Canada	0.6056	0.4865
1998	Canada	0.6520	0.4759
1999	Canada	0.6720	0.4770
2000	Canada	0.7298	0.4783
2001	Canada	0.7250	0.4682
2002	Canada	0.6955	0.4611
2003	Canada	0.7137	0.4699
1996	Czech	0.7287	0.1229
1997	Czech	0.7341	0.1002
1998	Czech	0.7884	0.0972
1999	Czech	0.7927	0.0966
2000	Czech	0.8280	0.0840
2001	Czech	0.8479	0.0853
2002	Czech	0.8620	0.0964
2003	Czech	0.8830	0.1088
1996	Denmark	0.7402	0.3103
1997	Denmark	0.7600	0.2676
1998	Denmark	0.7929	0.2561
1999	Denmark	0.8259	0.2463

2000	Denmark	0.8672	0.2187
2001	Denmark	0.8812	0.2074
2002	Denmark	0.8888	0.2060
2003	Denmark	0.8904	0.2248
1996	Finland	0.7456	0.2459
1997	Finland	0.7563	0.2140
1998	Finland	0.7916	0.2084
1999	Finland	0.8154	0.1984
2000	Finland	0.8532	0.1765
2001	Finland	0.8630	0.1669
2002	Finland	0.8559	0.1672
2003	Finland	0.8267	0.1849
1996	France	0.7025	0.4430
1997	France	0.7320	0.4741
1998	France	0.7523	0.4791
1999	France	0.7537	0.4844
2000	France	0.7850	0.4959
2001	France	0.7833	0.4986
2002	France	0.7745	0.4987
2003	France	0.7745	0.4946
1996	Germany	0.7629	0.3673
1997	Germany	0.7628	0.4165
1998	Germany	0.7845	0.4269
1999	Germany	0.7891	0.4380
2000	Germany	0.8239	0.4651
2001	Germany	0.8369	0.4760
2002	Germany	0.8335	0.4773
2003	Germany	0.8369	0.4657
1996	Greece	0.6364	0.2301
1997	Greece	0.6765	0.2181
1998	Greece	0.7092	0.1945
1999	Greece	0.7004	0.1945
2000	Greece	0.6584	0.1691
2001	Greece	0.6482	0.1611
2002	Greece	0.5929	0.1661
2003	Greece	0.5844	0.1921
1996	Hong Kong	0.8766	0.2735
1997	Hong Kong	0.8732	0.2662
1998	Hong Kong	0.9458	0.2466
1999	Hong Kong	0.9394	0.2446
2000	Hong Kong	0.9429	0.2373
2001	Hong Kong	0.9524	0.2174
2002	Hong Kong	0.9492	0.2042
2003	Hong Kong	0.9311	0.1874
1996	Hungary	0.7174	0.0896
1997	Hungary	0.7485	0.0820
1998	Hungary	0.7897	0.0799
1999	Hungary	0.8173	0.0796
2000	Hungary	0.8708	0.0727
2001	Hungary	0.8994	0.0751
2002	Hungary	0.9155	0.0879

2003	Hungary	0.9255	0.1017
1996	Ireland	0.7057	0.1585
1997	Ireland	0.6926	0.1525
1998	Ireland	0.7288	0.1505
1999	Ireland	0.7805	0.1554
2000	Ireland	0.8163	0.1428
2001	Ireland	0.8814	0.1439
2002	Ireland	0.9220	0.1534
2003	Ireland	0.8921	0.1693
1996	Italy	0.6778	0.4752
1997	Italy	0.6745	0.4909
1998	Italy	0.6905	0.4946
1999	Italy	0.6776	0.4974
2000	Italy	0.6838	0.4999
2001	Italy	0.6884	0.4990
2002	Italy	0.6730	0.4990
2003	Italy	0.6668	0.5000
1996	Japan	0.7007	0.2385
1997	Japan	0.6802	0.2836
1998	Japan	0.7297	0.3155
1999	Japan	0.7292	0.2998
2000	Japan	0.7160	0.2996
2001	Japan	0.7229	0.3406
2002	Japan	0.7180	0.3663
2003	Japan	0.6877	0.3692
1996	Korea	0.6932	0.4851
1997	Korea	0.6953	0.4616
1998	Korea	0.7022	0.3770
1999	Korea	0.7462	0.4242
2000	Korea	0.7401	0.4332
2001	Korea	0.7272	0.4066
2002	Korea	0.7616	0.4153
2003	Korea	0.7504	0.4165
1996	Netherlands	0.7068	0.4551
1997	Netherlands	0.7080	0.4181
1998	Netherlands	0.7278	0.4106
1999	Netherlands	0.7516	0.4033
2000	Netherlands	0.8017	0.3773
2001	Netherlands	0.8031	0.3632
2002	Netherlands	0.7657	0.3653
2003	Netherlands	0.8411	0.3893
1996	New Zealand	0.6510	0.1461
1997	New Zealand	0.6968	0.1292
1998	New Zealand	0.7149	0.1004
1999	New Zealand	0.7057	0.0989
2000	New Zealand	0.7418	0.0849
2001	New Zealand	0.7203	0.0777
2002	New Zealand	0.6909	0.0820
2003	New Zealand	0.6971	0.0981
1996	Norway	0.6830	0.2857
1997	Norway	0.6838	0.2537

1998	Norway	0.7160	0.2310
1999	Norway	0.7532	0.2310
2000	Norway	0.7482	0.2273
2001	Norway	0.7991	0.2168
2002	Norway	0.8109	0.2238
2003	Norway	0.8323	0.2322
1996	Poland	0.6644	0.2484
1997	Poland	0.6672	0.2302
1998	Poland	0.7041	0.2358
1999	Poland	0.7288	0.2296
2000	Poland	0.7491	0.2161
2001	Poland	0.7780	0.2278
2002	Poland	0.7827	0.2236
2003	Poland	0.7868	0.2259
1996	Spain	0.6392	0.4924
1997	Spain	0.6336	0.4745
1998	Spain	0.6391	0.4695
1999	Spain	0.7715	0.4659
2000	Spain	0.6455	0.4475
2001	Spain	0.6639	0.4409
2002	Spain	0.6563	0.4431
2003	Spain	0.6655	0.4658
1996	Sweden	0.7182	0.3873
1997	Sweden	0.7247	0.3402
1998	Sweden	0.7646	0.3256
1999	Sweden	0.7795	0.3188
2000	Sweden	0.8087	0.2954
2001	Sweden	0.8190	0.2615
2002	Sweden	0.8120	0.2637
2003	Sweden	0.8097	0.2884
1996	Switzerland	0.7114	0.4035
1997	Switzerland	0.7096	0.3494
1998	Switzerland	0.7201	0.3382
1999	Switzerland	0.7398	0.3240
2000	Switzerland	0.7501	0.2953
2001	Switzerland	0.7220	0.2850
2002	Switzerland	0.7215	0.2856
2003	Switzerland	0.7394	0.2963
1996	U.K.	0.7148	0.4772
1997	U.K	0.7083	0.4805
1998	U.K	0.7338	0.4820
1999	U.K	0.7595	0.4841
2000	U.K	0.8323	0.4900
2001	U.K	0.8155	0.4954
2002	U.K	0.7957	0.4954
2003	U.K	0.8102	0.4928
1996	USA	0.7428	0.1643
1997	USA	0.7464	0.1755
1998	USA	0.7759	0.1795
1999	USA	0.7772	0.1797
2000	USA	0.8056	0.1829

2001	USA	0.7955	0.1899
2002	USA	0.7907	0.1960
2003	USA	0.7762	0.2033
1996	Mexico	0.7754	0.3720
1997	Mexico	0.7815	0.3992
1998	Mexico	0.8250	0.3994
1999	Mexico	0.8544	0.4124
2000	Mexico	0.8740	0.4422
2001	Mexico	0.8902	0.4451
2002	Mexico	0.8979	0.4368
2003	Mexico	0.9120	0.4206

Appendix 2. List of Industrial Sectors, 2-Digit H.S. Code

1. Chapter 01: Live Animals
2. Chapter 02: Meat And Edible Meat Offal
3. Chapter 03: Fish, Crustaceans And Aquatic Invertebrates
4. Chapter 04: Dairy Prods; Birds Eggs; Honey; Ed Animal Pr Nesoi
5. Chapter 05: Products Of Animal Origin, Nesoi
6. Chapter 06: Live Trees, Plants, Bulbs Etc.; Cut Flowers Etc.
7. Chapter 07: Edible Vegetables And Certain Roots And Tubers
8. Chapter 08: Edible Fruit And Nuts; Citrus Fruit Or Melon Peel
9. Chapter 09: Coffee, Tea, Mate And Spices
10. Chapter 10: Cereals
11. Chapter 11: Milling Products; Malt; Starch; Inulin; Wht Gluten
12. Chapter 12: Oil Seeds Etc.; Misc Grain, Seed, Fruit, Plant Etc
13. Chapter 13: Lac; Gums, Resins And Other Vegetable Sap And Extract
14. Chapter 14: Vegetable Plaiting Materials And Products Nesoi
15. Chapter 15: Animal Or Vegetable Fats, Oils Etc. And Waxes
16. Chapter 16: Edible Preparations Of Meat, Fish, Crustaceans Etc
17. Chapter 17: Sugars And Sugar Confectionary
18. Chapter 18: Cocoa And Cocoa Preparations
19. Chapter 19: Prep Cereal, Flour, Starch Or Milk; Bakers Wares
20. Chapter 20: Prep Vegetables, Fruit, Nuts Or Other Plant Parts
21. Chapter 21: Miscellaneous Edible Preparations
22. Chapter 22: Beverages, Spirits And Vinegar
23. Chapter 23: Food Industry Residues And Waste; Prep Animal Feed
24. Chapter 24: Tobacco And Manufactured Tobacco Substitutes
25. Chapter 25: Salt; Sulfur; Earth And Stone; Lime And Cement Plaster
26. Chapter 26: Ores, Slag And Ash
27. Chapter 27: Mineral Fuel, Oil Etc.; Bitumin Subst; Mineral Wax
28. Chapter 28: Inorg Chem; Precandrare-Earth Metandradioact Compd
29. Chapter 29: Organic Chemicals
30. Chapter 30: Pharmaceutical Products
31. Chapter 31: Fertilizers
32. Chapter 32: Tanning And Dye Ext Etc; Dye, Paint, Putty Etc; Inks

33. Chapter 33: Essential Oils Etc; Perfumery, Cosmetic Etc Preps
34. Chapter 34: Soap Etc; Waxes, Polish Etc; Candles; Dental Preps
35. Chapter 35: Albuminoidal Subst; Modified Starch; Glue; Enzymes
36. Chapter 36: Explosives; Pyrotechnics; Matches; Pyro Alloys Etc
37. Chapter 37: Photographic Or Cinematographic Goods
38. Chapter 38: Miscellaneous Chemical Products
39. Chapter 39: Plastics And Articles Thereof
40. Chapter 40: Rubber And Articles Thereof
41. Chapter 41: Raw Hides And Skins (No Furskins) And Leather
42. Chapter 42: Leather Art; Saddlery Etc; Handbags Etc; Gut Art
43. Chapter 43: Furskins And Artificial Fur; Manufactures Thereof
44. Chapter 44: Wood And Articles Of Wood; Wood Charcoal
45. Chapter 45: Cork And Articles Of Cork
46. Chapter 46: Mfr Of Straw, Esparto Etc.; Basketware And Wickerwrk
47. Chapter 47: Pulp Of Wood Etc; Waste Etc Of Paper And Paperboard
48. Chapter 48: Paper And Paperboard And Articles (Inc Papr Pulp Artl)
49. Chapter 49: Printed Books, Newspapers Etc; Manuscripts Etc
50. Chapter 50: Silk, Including Yarns And Woven Fabric Thereof
51. Chapter 51: Wool And Animal Hair, Including Yarn And Woven Fabric
52. Chapter 52: Cotton, Including Yarn And Woven Fabric Thereof
53. Chapter 53: Veg Text Fib Nesoi; Veg Fib And Paper Yns And Wov Fab
54. Chapter 54: Manmade Filaments, Including Yarns And Woven Fabrics
55. Chapter 55: Manmade Staple Fibers, Incl Yarns And Woven Fabrics
56. Chapter 56: Wadding, Felt Etc; Sp Yarn; Twine, Ropes Etc.
57. Chapter 57: Carpets And Other Textile Floor Coverings
58. Chapter 58: Spec Wov Fabrics; Tufted Fab; Lace; Tapestries Etc
59. Chapter 59: Impregnated Etc Text Fabrics; Tex Art For Industry
60. Chapter 60: Knitted Or Crocheted Fabrics
61. Chapter 61: Apparel Articles And Accessories, Knit Or Crochet
62. Chapter 62: Apparel Articles And Accessories, Not Knit Etc
63. Chapter 63: Textile Art Nesoi; Needlecraft Sets; Worn Text Art
64. Chapter 64: Footwear, Gaiters Etc. And Parts Thereof
65. Chapter 65: Headgear And Parts Thereof
66. Chapter 66: Umbrellas, Walking-Sticks, Riding-Crops Etc, Parts
67. Chapter 67: Prep Feathers, Down Etc; Artif Flowers; H Hair Art
68. Chapter 68: Art Of Stone, Plaster, Cement, Asbestos, Mica Etc.
69. Chapter 69: Ceramic Products
70. Chapter 70: Glass And Glassware
71. Chapter 71: Nat Etc Pearls, Prec Etc Stones, Pr Met Etc; Coin
72. Chapter 72: Iron And Steel
73. Chapter 73: Articles Of Iron Or Steel
74. Chapter 74: Copper And Articles Thereof
75. Chapter 75: Nickel And Articles Thereof
76. Chapter 76: Aluminum And Articles Thereof
77. Chapter 77: Lead And Articles Thereof
78. Chapter 78: Zinc And Articles Thereof

79. Chapter 79: Tin And Articles Thereof
80. Chapter 80: Base Metals Nesoi; Cermets; Articles Thereof
81. Chapter 81: Tools, Cutlery Etc. Of Base Metal And Parts Thereof
82. Chapter 82: Miscellaneous Articles Of Base Metal
83. Chapter 83: Nuclear Reactors, Boilers, Machinery Etc.; Parts
84. Chapter 84: Electric Machinery Etc; Sound Equip; Tv Equip; Pts
85. Chapter 85: Railway Or Tramway Stock Etc; Traffic Signal Equip
86. Chapter 86: Vehicles, Except Railway Or Tramway, And Parts Etc
87. Chapter 87: Aircraft, Spacecraft, And Parts Thereof
88. Chapter 88: Ships, Boats And Floating Structures
89. Chapter 89: Optic, Photo Etc, Medic Or Surgical Instrments Etc
90. Chapter 90: Clocks And Watches And Parts Thereof
91. Chapter 91: Musical Instruments; Parts And Accessories Thereof
92. Chapter 92: Arms And Ammunition; Parts And Accessories Thereof
93. Chapter 93: Furniture; Bedding Etc; Lamps Nesoi Etc; Prefab Bd
94. Chapter 94: Toys, Games And Sport Equipment; Parts And Accessories
95. Chapter 95: Miscellaneous Manufactured Articles
96. Chapter 96: Works Of Art, Collectors' Pieces And Antiques
97. Chapter 97: Special Classification Provisions, Nesoi

In: Recent Developments in the Chinese Economy
Editor: Almas Heshmati, pp. 173-220
ISBN: 1-60021-449-5
© 2007 Nova Science Publishers, Inc.

Chapter 6

INCOME INEQUALITY IN CHINA[1]

Almas Heshmati [2]
University of Kurdistan Hawler and Techno-Economics and Policy Program
College of Engineering, Seoul National University
San 56-1, Shinlim-dong, Kwanak-gu
Seoul 151-742, South Korea

1. INTRODUCTION

There is an ongoing and increasing interest in measuring and understanding the level, causes and development of global income inequality. The increasing interest has been considerable particularly during the 1990s. This period was signified by a shift in research which previously focused on economic growth, the identification of the determinants of economic growth and convergence in GDP per capita across countries to analyse the distribution of income, its development over time and identification of factors determining the world-wide distribution of income. This shift in focus is specifically from the issues of convergence or divergence of per capita income to the long-term equalisation or polarisation of income across regions and countries of the world.

This shift in research orientation is not only a reflection of technological change and raised human capacity to create growth, wealth and in the effective use of resources, but also as a result of awareness of the importance of redistribution and poverty reduction. Rapid technological changes, heterogeneous economic growth and differences in countries potential to take advantage of those opportunities together with their poor redistributive policies and institutions have however resulted in large and growing disparities in the living standards within and foremost between countries of the world. The growing disparity is the key background that calls for the analysis of possible trends in global income inequality.

---

[1] This chapter is to a large extent extractions from Heshmati (2006), "Global Trends in Income Inequality", Nova Science Publishers Inc. that ere found relevant to income inequality in China.

[2] E-mail: *heshmati@snu.ac.kr*

There are a number of comprehensive surveys of income inequality and poverty. Subramanian (1997a) presents a number of essays on the measurement of inequality and poverty, with an approach that has introduced readers to the theory and applications in the measurement of inequality and poverty. Both conceptual and technical issues of measurement are addressed and the relevance of these concerns in the context of developing country's experience explored. The chapter by Anand (1997) presents a review of the measurement of income inequality including indices (among others) based directly on the Lorenz diagram, the effect on inequality of changes in income, the ranking of income distribution and the comparison of inequality. Another edited comprehensive and related volume on different aspects of inequality measurement is by Silber (1999). This volume begins with a foreword by Amartya Sen, discussing some conceptual issues in particular the relationship between economic inequality and non-income influences whose consequences are difficult to transform into practical implications.

The rest of the chapter is organized as follows. Section 2 is a review of several inequality indices used in the analysis of income inequality. Section 3 looks at the measurement and decomposition of income inequality by sub-groups and income sources. Alternative ways of measuring inequality among individuals and inter- and intra-country inequality and the distribution of income is addressed in Section 4. A similar decomposition but based on continents and sub-continents around the world are reviewed in Section 5. Empirical results found in the literature on inequality at the regional level in China and summary in a selection of other large countries and those based on the WIID material is found in Section 6. The data issues, data quality and consistency, variable definitions and measurements, various adjustment procedures are discussed in Section 7. Section 8 contains summary and conclusions.

1.1. The Objectives and Scopes of this Study

This chapter attempts to fill the gap in existing literature by focusing on the empirical analysis of income inequality in China. In particular it addresses a number of issues crucial to the studies of income inequality. These are the concepts, measurements and decomposition of inequality, the world distribution of income and inequality measured at different levels such as at the global, continental/sub-continental, international, intra-national and regional levels. Experiences gained from the analysis of these issues are then reflected in the discussion of income inequality in China.

Inequality has several dimensions. We economists are mostly concerned with the income and consumption dimensions of inequality. Several inequality indices can be derived from the Lorenz diagram which is shown and discussed in Section 2. The most widely used index of inequality is the Gini coefficient. Subramanian (1997b) and Cowell (2000) provide comprehensive reviews the notion and the measurement of inequality. Non-income inequality, although often income related, includes items like skill, education, opportunity, happiness, health and wealth. The effects of inequality on non-income factors of earnings and health are equally important but these are not directly in the scope of this study.

Different methods have been developed to decompose inequality (Pyatt 1976; Shorrocks 1980, 1982 and 1984; Fields 2000; Morduch and Sicular 2002), and changes in poverty (Kakwani and Subbaro 1990; Jian and Tandulkar 1990; Datt and Ravallion 1992; Shorrocks and Kolenikov 2001). A decomposition of changes in poverty into growth and redistribution is important in the evaluation of inequality and its impact on growth and on poverty among regions, sub-groups and sectors. In the above studies inequality is decomposed by sub-groups, income sources, causal factors and by other characteristics of the observation units. Inequality can also be decomposed at different levels of aggregation. At the national level it can be decomposed into within-subgroup and between-subgroup components while at the international level it can be decomposed into within-country and between-country components.

In recent years availability of household surveys has been improved and several standardized databases have been created. These allow for the analysis of income distribution at disaggregate per capita household levels. Income distribution is otherwise often analyzed at three levels of aggregation, namely global, international and intra-national. Global or world income inequality refers to inequality differences between all individuals in the world (Milanovic 2002; Schultz 1998; Quah 1999; Bourguignon and Morrisson 2002; Sala-i-Martin 2002b, Heshmati 2006a), while international income inequality refers to the economic disparity between countries (Acemoglu 2002; Cornia and Kiiski 2001; Gottschalk and Smeeding 1997; Milanovic 2001). At the intra-national level inequality refers to the distribution of income among people within individual countries (Cameron 2000; Gustafsson and Shi 2002; Liebbrandt, Woolard and Woolard 2000; and others).

In addition to the extreme level of global and international, income inequality can be measured at an intermediate level, equivalent to continental and sub-continental areas (Heshmati, 2005). This investigation examines both between and within regions consisting of continents or sub-continents. There is evidence that poverty and inequality has developed differently among transition economies (Milanovic and Ytzhaki 2001; Ivaschenko 2002; Wan 2002), East Asian countries (Kakwani and Krogkaew 2000; and You 1998); the European Union (Gottschalk and Smeeding 2000; Lindert and Williamson 2001; Mahler 2001), Latin American (LondoNo and Szekely 2000; Wood 1997) and sub-Saharan African (Milanovic and Yitzhaki 2001; Svedborg 2002) countries. In several of these studies, inequality and poverty are related to a number of determining factors. These results are further contrasted to those obtained based on the World Income Inequality Database (WIID).

Income inequality can also be measured at a within-country regional level. Due to the limited space, here the focus is on inequality in income distribution in China. In such studies, focus is on large countries like China (Tsui 1993; Xu and Zou 2000; Lee 2000; Gustafsson and Shi 2002), Russia (Commander, Tolstopiatenko and Yemtsov 1999; Yemtsov 2002; Luttmer 2001; Fedorov 2002), India (Mishra and Parikh 1997; Jha 2000; Datt and Ravallion 1992) and the USA (Patridge, Rickman and Levernier 1996; Moffitt and Gottschalk 2002). China and India experienced rapid economic growth after economic reform, accompanied by increased inequality and a reduction in poverty. This inequality can further be decomposed into components associated with inter- and intra-sector and provincial components and their determinants in turn identified.

A number of databases are frequently used in applied growth and income inequality research. Descriptions of such databases are found in Summers and Heston (1991), Barro and Lee (1996), Deininger and Squire (1996) and Atkinson and Brandolini (2001). Despite the differences in objectives, country coverage, sources, units of measurement and income definitions, each database plays an important and complementary role in growth and inequality studies. Each set of data of course has benefits and limitations. Different data properties are discussed in Section 7.

1.2. The Limitations of this Study

Due to space limitation, this chapter despite its broad coverage excludes reviews of two important areas including the relationship between inequality, poverty and growth and the link between inequality, poverty and globalization. There is an investigation of the relationship between different combinations of openness, growth, inequality and poverty (Sachs and Werner 1995; Dollar and Kraay 2001; Person and Tabellini 1994; Deininger and Squire 1998; Goudie and Ladd 1999; van der Hoeven and Shorrocks 2003; and others), that in general find a positive relationship between openness and growth but differences between and within countries in the impact of growth on the poor. In recent years the research and debate has focused on the extent the poor benefits from this economic growth (Ravallion 1998, 2001; Ravallion and Chen 2003; Ravallion and Datt 2000; Quah 2001), where one opinion argues that the benefits of economic growth to the poor are undermined or offset by inadequate redistributive policies and the increase in inequality. Another opinion is that despite increased inequality liberal economic policies and open markets raise the income of everyone in a society, reducing the incidence of poverty.

Empirical results on the relationship between growth, inequality and poverty show that outcomes of policy measures are heterogeneous in their impacts. In general, it is rather difficult to measure the effects of inequality and growth on the developing countries' efforts to reduce poverty in the course of economic development. Economic growth benefits the poor but at the absence of effective redistribution policies, it might deteriorate the income distribution. Initial conditions, institutions, specific country structures, and time horizons each play a significant role in targeting policies to make economic growth pro-poor. Regression results based on the WIID database in Heshmati (2004a) suggest that income inequality is declining over time. Inequality is also declining with the growth of income. There is a significant regional heterogeneity in the levels of inequality and its development over time.

Globalization describes changes in international economy and world politics. The process has made the developed economies more and strongly interrelated. Evidence suggests that there is a large heterogeneity in the degree of globalization over time and across countries and regions. This heterogeneity causes disparity in development, especially when linked with negative effects like rising inequality within and between countries. Research on the link between globalization and world inequality and poverty is plentiful (Lindert and Williamson 2001; O'Rourke 2001; O'Rourke and Williamson 2000; Maddison 2001; Williamson 2002; and Solimano 2001), however an analysis of the link at the empirical level, with a few exceptions (Heshmati 2006b; Mahler 2001; Agenor 2003; and Andersen and Herbertsson 2003) is more scarce. Globalization is generally expected to reduce poverty through faster growth in more integrated economies. Heshmati (2004b) investigates the usefulness of new indices of globalization to compare countries by their integration in the world economy, and also for between and within region comparisons. They are used in regression analysis to study the causal relationship between income inequality, poverty and globalization. A negative relationship is found between income inequality and the aggregate globalization indices.

Globalization reduces poverty and increases the poorest share of income and thereby reducing inequality.

Conditional results from a regression analysis of the relationship between inequality, poverty and globalization in Heshmati (2004b) show that the globalization index explains only 7-11 per cent of the variations in income inequality, and 9 per cent of variations in poverty among the countries. When controlling for regional heterogeneity, it is found that the regional variable plays an important role in the explanation of variations in inequality and poverty.

2. MEASUREMENT OF INCOME INEQUALITY

This section is a review of the recent advances in the measurement of inequality. Inequality has several dimensions. Economists are mostly concerned with the income and consumption dimensions. Several inequality indices including the most widely used index of inequality namely the Gini coefficient are discussed. Non-income inequality includes inequality in skills, education, opportunities, happiness, health, wealth, and others. Results from review of the literature suggest a relationship between inequality in income and non-income dimensions. This indicates that one should account for the interrelationship between the different dimensions in the measurement and analyses of inequalities.

Income inequality refers to the inequality of the distribution of individuals, household or some per capita measure of income among the population of a country. In illustrations we follow the notation found in Anand (1997). An income distribution is a vector of incomes, $x = (x_1, x_2, \ldots.., x_n)$, where x_i indicate the income of the ith individual in a society consisting of n individuals. The mean of the distribution of x and its dimensionality are written as $\mu(x)$ and $n(x)$. Here income is a continuous random variable bounded within the interval $x_0 (\geq 0)$ and $\bar{x}$. The density, distribution and the first moment functions for a continuous random variable are $f(x)$, $F(x)$, and $\Phi(x)$. Where $f(x)$, $F(x) = \int_{x_0}^{\bar{x}} f(y)dy$, and $\Phi(x) = 1/\mu \int_{x_0}^{\bar{x}} yf(y)dy$ are the proportion of the population with income not exceeding x, cumulative proportion of the population with income not exceeding x, and cumulative share in total income respectively. The mean distribution is $\mu = \int_{x_0}^{\bar{x}} yf(y)dy$.

The graph of $\Phi(x)$ against $F(x)$ is the Lorenz (1905) curve representing the inequality of income distribution. The divergence of a Lorenz curve for perfect equality and the Lorenz curve for a given income distribution is measured by some index of inequality. The most widely used index of inequality is the Gini coefficient. The distribution and inequality of income is illustrated in the Lorenz diagram, Figure 1.

The Lorenz curve plots the cumulative share of total income against the cumulative proportion of income receiving units. It is used to analyze the size distribution of income and wealth, to estimate the Gini index and other measures of inequality and poverty. However, an important drawback of the traditional models of the Lorenz curve is the lack of satisfactory fit over the entire range of a given income distribution. There are two parametric approaches to estimate the Lorenz curve (Ryu and Slottje, 1999). The estimated Lorenz curve is sensitive to the errors in survey data. Hasegawa and Kozumi (2003) propose an alternative approach of estimating the Lorenz curve with contaminated data using Bayesian non-parametric analysis and present a method for removing the contaminated observations. Results obtained using both simulated and real data suggests that this approach estimates the Lorenz curve and Gini indices adequately. Ogwang and Rao (2000) propose two hybrid Lorenz curve, namely the additive models and the multiplicative models by the combination of traditional models of a Lorenz curve.

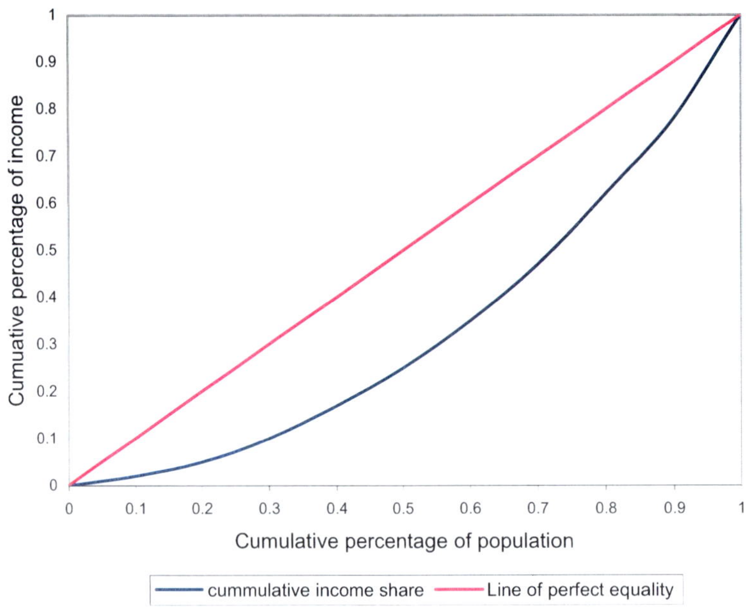

Figure 1. The Lorenz diagram.

2.1. Inequality Indices

Several inequality indices can be derived from the Lorenz diagram. The Lorenz Curve construction also gives us a rough measure of the amount of inequality in income distribution. The measure is called the Gini Coefficient (Figure 1). The Gini coefficient is a standard measure of inequality defined as the area between the Lorenz curve and the line of perfect equality divided by the area below the perfect equality line as expressed in the following formula:

$$Gini = 1 - \sum_{i=0}^{n-1} (F_{i+1} - F_i)(\Phi_{i+1} + \Phi_i) \tag{1}$$

where F and Φ are as previously defined. The index lies within the interval 0 (perfect equality) and 1 (perfect inequality). Among other notable measures of inequality are: the range, the variance, the squared coefficient of variation, the variance of log incomes, the absolute and relative mean deviations, and Theil's two inequality indices (see Anand 1997).

The range and the variance are the two common statistical measures of dispersion for a distribution in general. These are useful measures in the context of income. The range is defined as the absolute difference between the highest and the lowest income levels. The measure is normalized by dividing the range by the mean income:

$$RGE = (x_{\max} - x_{\min}) / \mu \tag{2}$$

where the arithmetic mean income is $\mu = 1/n\sum_{i=1}^{n} y_i$. The method is very sensitive to extreme observations. The variance of income is written as:

$$VAR = \mathrm{var}(y) = \frac{1}{n}\sum_{i=1}^{n}(y_i - \mu)^2 \tag{3}$$

The squared coefficient of variation is obtained by dividing the variance with squared mean:

$$SCV = VAR / \mu^2 \tag{4}$$

In similarity with the range, the variance and squared coefficient of variation are also sensitive to extreme observations. The variance of logarithm of income can be written as:

$$VLI = \mathrm{var}(\log y) = \frac{1}{n}\sum_{i=1}^{n}(\log y_i - \log \tilde{\mu})^2 \tag{5}$$

where

$$\tilde{\mu} = \frac{1}{n}\sum_{i-1}^{n} \log y_i \tag{6}$$

is the geometric mean income of the distribution. Finally, the first Theil's entropy index of inequality is defined as:

$$T1 = \frac{1}{n}\sum_{i=1}^{n}\frac{y_i}{\mu}\log\frac{y_i}{\mu} \tag{7}$$

The second measure can be written as:

$$T2 = \sum_{i=1}^{n}(1/n)\log\frac{(1/n)}{(y_i / Y)} = \frac{1}{n}\sum_{i=1}^{n}\log\frac{\mu}{y_i} \tag{8}$$

where $Y = n\mu$ is the total income. The $T2$ is analogous to $T1$ except that it reverses the role of income shares (y_i / Y) and population shares $(1/n)$. Both Theil's indices measure the divergence between income shares and population shares, but using different distance functions.

Anand (1997) discuss indices based on the Lorenz diagram and also several other indices. The Absolute Mean Difference index is among the indices based on the Lorenz diagram as an alternative definition to the Gini coefficient (AGC) and is specified as:

$$AGC = 1/2(AMDiff / \mu) \tag{9}$$

where $AMDiff = \int_0^\infty \int_0^\infty |x - y| f(x) f(y) dx dy$ is the absolute mean difference of two income distributions of x and y. The AMD is more widely known as Gini's mean difference. AGC can also be defined as one-half of the relative mean difference:

$$AGC = 1/2(AMDev / \mu) \tag{10}$$

where $AMDev = \int_0^\infty |y - \mu| f(y) dy$ is the absolute mean deviation. These absolute and relative definitions are equivalent. Another measure of inequality based on the Lorenz diagram is the value of the maximum discrepancy (p^*) between the line of perfect equality and the Lorenz curve and is written as:

$$MD = \left[p^* - L(p^*)\right] = 1/2(AMDev / \mu) = RMDev / 2 \tag{11}$$

where $RMDev$ is the relative mean deviation. Another divergence measure proposed is based on the area of the largest triangle between the Lorenz curve and the line of equality and the area below the line of perfect equality. This measure reduces to the value of MD.

The indices above have different properties that can be used in their ranking, relevance and performance evaluation. There are three basic properties that one would expect the above indices of inequality to satisfy: mean or scale independence, population size independence and the Pigou-Dalton condition. According to the first two properties the index remains invariant if everyone's income or if the number of people at each income level is changed by the same proportion, respectively. The third condition states that the value of an index is reduced if there is a rank preserving transfer of income from a richer to a poorer person.

The Gini coefficient and the squared coefficient of variation satisfy all three conditions, while the relative and absolute mean difference and the range measures satisfy only the first two conditions but violate the Pigou-Dalton condition, if formulated in a strict sense, by ignoring the distribution inside the range. The variance measure violates the mean independence property. Unlike the variance of income, the variance of log income is a mean independent measure. The two Theil's inequality measures also satisfy each of the three desirable properties.

Generalization of the Gini coefficient in the sense of transfer sensitivity is important. A generalization of the Gini coefficient, called the extended Gini coefficient, was proposed by Kakwani (1980), Donaldson and Weymark (1980) and Yitzhaki (1983). The generalized Gini is further discussed by Xu (2000) and Zitikis and Gastwirth (2002). The new index accommodates differing aversions of inequality. Empirical estimation of the extended index has been limited to the covariance formula suggested by Lerman and Yitzhaki (1989). The extended Gini is equal to the original Gini coefficient when the aversion factor is 2.

3. Decomposition of Income Inequality

This Section is a review of recent developments of different approaches to decompose inequality by subgroups, income sources, causal factors and other unit characteristics. Different methods of decomposing changes in poverty into growth, redistribution, poverty standard and residual components are described. In parametric approaches the dynamics of income accounting for transitory and permanent changes in individual and household earnings conditional of various covariates are also reviewed. Statistical inferences for inequality measurement including delta and bootstrapping and other methods to provide estimates of the sampling distribution are presented.

The origin of the modern inequality decomposition literature is to be found in Shorrocks (1980, 1982 and 1984),[3] where he examined decomposition of inequality by income sources such as earnings, investment income and transfer payments; by population subgroups like single persons, married couples, and families with children; or by subaggregates of observations which share common characteristics like age, household size, region, occupation, or some other attributes. He shows that a broad class of inequality measures can be decomposed into components reflecting only size, mean and inequality value of each population subgroup or income source.

In decomposing income inequality, Shorrocks (1983) examines the relative influence of income components and evaluates the performance of different decomposition rules using US data. The method based on the Gini coefficient can be written as:

$$I(Y) = \frac{2}{n^2 \mu} \sum_{i=1}^{n} \left(i - \frac{n+1}{2} \right) Y_i \tag{12}$$

where $Y_i = \sum_{k=1}^{K} Y_i^k$ is the sum of these income components k for individual i. The inequality decomposition rules for factor components can be generated for inequality measures of the form:

$$I(Y) = \sum_{k=1}^{K} \sum_{i=1}^{N} a_i(Y) Y_i^k = \sum_{k=1}^{K} S_k \tag{13}$$

[3] The current state of knowledge regarding the theory and the application of inequality decomposition techniques in a spatial and regional context is reviewed by Shorrocks and Wan (2004).

where S_k is a contribution of factor k to the overall income inequality, a_i is the weight attached to individual i income component k, Y_i^k. The proportional factor contribution on aggregate income is expressed as:

$$s_k = S_k / I(Y) = \text{cov}(Y_k, Y) / \sigma^2(Y) \tag{14}$$

with $\sum_k s_k = 1$. Empirical results are based on panel data obtained from the PSID consisting of 2,755 households observed in the period 1967-76. Analysis of the distribution of net family incomes results in the identification of ten factor components.

The effects of growth on income poverty have been studied by accounting for the changes in the distribution of income. Income poverty $P(z, \mu, L)$ is expressed in terms of poverty line (z), mean income level (μ) and the relative distribution of income (L). The Lorenz curve represents the structure of relative income inequalities. Assuming the poverty line is fixed at a given level, income poverty is given by $P(\mu, L)$. The total change in poverty (Δp) is then decomposed into two components. The first component is the growth component due to changes in the mean income while holding the Lorenz curve constant at some reference level, and the second is a redistribution component due to changes in the Lorenz curve while keeping the mean income constant at some reference level.

There are a number of ways of decomposing the total change in poverty. Kakwani and Subbaro's (1990) decomposition approach for given poverty line is:

$$\begin{aligned} \Delta p = p_1 - p_0 &= P(\mu_1, L_1) - (\mu_0, L_0) \\ &= \{P(\mu_1, L_0) - P(\mu_0, L_0)\} + \{P(\mu_1, L_1) - P(\mu_1, L_0)\} = G + R \end{aligned} \tag{15}$$

where μ and L are mean income and the Lorenz curve characterizing the distribution of income respectively. The subscripts 0 and 1 denote the two (consecutive or non-consecutive) initial and final periods of observation, and G and R are contributions from the growth and redistributive components respectively. In analyzing the impact of economic growth on poverty in India, Kakwani and Subbaro measures separately the impacts of the changes in average income and income inequality on poverty. They examine trends in the distribution and the growth of consumption and assess their relative impacts on the poor and ultra poor, over the period 1972-83 and across the 15 major states of India. Results suggest that the beneficial effect of growth on the incidence of poverty during 1973-77 was outweighed by adverse movements in the inequality of consumption. States differ in needs, capacities, social policy, intervention programmes and performance.

For the same decomposition purpose Jian and Tendulkar (1990) proposed:

$$\begin{aligned} \Delta p = p_1 - p_0 &= P(\mu_1, L_1) - (\mu_0, L_0) \\ &= \{P(\mu_1, L_1) - P(\mu_0, L_1)\} + \{P(\mu_0, L_1) - P(\mu_0, L_0)\} \end{aligned} \tag{16}$$

The two decompositions differ by the differences in the reference point: base year versus final year, of the growth and redistribution components. In the choice of the base year in multiple time period comparisons, one might take the quality of the data point and its relevance into consideration. Datt and Ravallion (1992) found the above decompositions of poverty changes as being time path dependent, arising through and dependent on the choice of reference levels. To make the changes path independent they proposed:

$$\begin{aligned}\Delta p = p_1 - p_0 &= P(\mu_1, L_1) - (\mu_0, L_0) \\ &= \{P(\mu_1, L_0) - P(\mu_0, L_0)\} + \{P(\mu_0, L_1) - P(\mu_0, L_0)\} + E\end{aligned} \tag{17}$$

where E is an extra residual component appended to (8). The residual exists whenever the poverty measure is not additively separable between μ and L. It is the difference between the growth (redistribution) components evaluated at the terminal and initial Lorenz curves (mean incomes) respectively. The residual does not vanish unless μ and L remain unchanged over the decomposition period, or apportioned between the two components. The two growth and redistribution components differ by the base year or reference level chosen as a benchmark. In their application of the decomposition method, Datt and Ravallion used three measures of poverty (headcount, poverty gap and Foster-Greer-Thorbecke – FTG) where the Lorenz curve is parametrized as beta and general quadratic functional form. The poverty measure and their decompositions are estimated for rural and urban India during 1977-78, 1983, 1986-87, and 1988 and for Brazil in 1981-88.

In a similar decomposition approach, but relaxing the assumption of fixed poverty line, Shorrocks and Kolenikov (2001) investigate how changes in mean income, inequality and the poverty standard have affected the level of poverty in Russia. The total change in poverty is defined as:

$$\begin{aligned}\Delta p = p_1 - p_0 &= P(\mu_1, L_1, z_1) - (\mu_0, L_0, z_0) = G + R + S + E \\ &= \{P(\mu_1, L_0, z_0) - P(\mu_0, L_0, z_0)\} + \{P(\mu_0, L_1, z_0) - P(\mu_0, L_0, z_0)\} \\ &+ \{P(\mu_0, L_0, z_1) - P(\mu_0, L_0, z_0)\} + E\end{aligned} \tag{18}$$

where μ, L and z are respectively the mean income, the Lorenz curve and the poverty rate characterizing the distribution of income. The G, R, S and E are respectively contributions from the growth, redistribution, poverty standard effects and the extra residual or overlapping components. Shorrocks and Kolenikov quantify the contributions of these factors to year-by-year changes in the poverty rate and its development in Russia since 1985. Based on household data for the period 1985-99, rising inequality is identified as the principal cause of the high poverty rate in Russia.

It is possible to decompose inequality by income sources and population subgroups. The results are however sensitive to the choice of different inequality indices resulting in the development of alternative decomposition approaches. It is important to distinguish between the transitory and permanent components of earnings. In the long-term some effects of transitory shocks average out, while others persist. Economic policy aiming to change earnings inequality should distinguish shocks that households are able to smooth out and target those that they can not smooth out by accounting for subgroup heterogeneity and earnings instability. These parametric approaches are conditional of various covariates. The main benefits of parametric approaches are that the changes are conditional on various attributes not captured by the growth and the redistribution of components. Furthermore, confidence intervals for the effects are estimated. The main disadvantage is the assumption of functional forms of the relationship and its specification.

4. The World Income Inequality

This Section covers a range of measures and methods frequently employed in empirical analysis of global income inequality and global income distribution. Different determining factors of inequality along with quantification of their impacts and empirical results from different case studies are presented. These results are further contrasted to those obtained based on the WIID. A number of issues crucial to the studies of global income inequality are also addressed. Inequality can be measured at different levels of aggregation: global, international and intra-national. We analyse income at each of the three levels, discuss the benefit and limitations of each approach, present empirical results found in the literature and, compare the results with those based on the WIID.

4.1. Distribution of Income Among the World's Individuals

An analysis of the dynamics of distribution of income across people worldwide would ideally be based on data on individual incomes accruing over time. One could then estimate the entire income distribution across individuals and characterize its dynamics through time. Such data representative of populations, consistent over time and across countries is not available. A similar data (the LIS and the HEIDE), but at smaller scale for the OECD and transition countries is available. There are, however, major differences in defining various pre- and post-taxes income components and transfers by countries and over time. In the absence of appropriate databases, several researchers have attempted to develop alternative empirical frameworks based on aggregative statistics of the underlying data to serve in different ways as a substitute in the analysis of global income distribution and income inequality.

There are number of ways of estimating income distribution and global income inequality and of constructing world indices of income distribution. One procedure is to use national household income (or expenditure) survey collected mainly since the mid 1980s providing direct income information by quintiles and deciles for individual countries to construct world income distribution over time (Milanovic 2002). A short, unequal and unbalanced time periods is among the limitations of this approach.

A second approach is to use the mean income or GDP per capita for individual countries complemented by Gini coefficient or standard deviation as the measurement of income dispersion within the country and make an assumption of log-normality to construct income distribution for individual countries (Schultz 1998 and Quah 1999).

A third approximation is to use a known actual income distribution of representative countries and apply it to other countries with geographical and economic similarities but with missing data (Bourguignon and Morrisson 2002). Among the limitations of this approach are variations in intertemporal patterns of income distribution and changing counterfactual countries over time.

The fourth way is to use aggregate GDP data and within-country income share to assign a level of income to each person in the world in order to estimate income distribution and global income inequality using different indices (Berry, Bourguignon and Morrrisson 1983 and Sala-i-Martin 2002b). The second and fourth alternatives are similar in the use of per capita GDP but they differ by additional information on within-country income shares used.

The fifth approach is to divide the global population into percentiles in terms of per capita income (Park (2001). In this approach, global income inequality refers to inequality among the global population. This method is similar to the second approach. Recently Dikhanov and Ward (2002) combined micro and macro approaches to reconstruct the world's income distribution.

The above approaches are criticised for several reasons. Results based on a few yearly observations are likely to be sensitive to the changing economic situation of countries, and various data and estimation methods. The uneven survey quality, the differences in the survey's definitions of income and expenditure, the assumption of equality of individuals within each decile, the problem of mixing of income and expenditure, and the use of a single PPP exchange rate affect the quality of analysis. However, these studies might serve to establish the benchmark for analysis of world inequality. The limitations of these studies are the short time period and the lack of income surveys with a satisfactory country population and a continuous time period coverage. Despite their limitations, these studies can serve to establish a benchmark for world income inequality and poverty.

4.2. Inter-National Distribution of Income

The inter-national inequality refers to the distribution of income between countries. The common approach is to use the mean income or GDP per capita for individual countries complemented by the Gini coefficient or the standard deviation as measure of income dispersion within the country and within-country income shares to construct income distribution for individual countries. Sala-i-Martin (2002a) uses aggregate GDP data and within-country income shares to estimate the worldwide distribution of income, computes poverty rates and estimates the global income inequality for the period 1970-1998. Inequality is decomposed into within and between-country inequality components. The results also show the reduction in global inequality between 1980 and 1998. Most global disparities are due to cross-country rather than within country characteristics. The main source of between-country reductions is the growth in the Chinese economy. The within-country inequality has slightly increased. The lack of growth in the African economies might cause further divergence and an increase in global inequality.

Unlike in Sala-i-Martin, the results by Maddison (2001) showed evidence of rising disparities in the world economy due to the divergence in economic performance across regions and countries over time. Bourguignon and Morrisson (1999) study showed that the increase in total inequality during the entire period of 1820-1990 is driven by a rise in inequality between countries. The inequality between countries is the dominating factor in the evolution of the world income inequality. Milanovic (2002) in a comparison of income in 1988 and 1993 shows that between 75-88 per cent of inequality is attributed to the differences in mean income between countries and only 12-25 per cent is explained by the inequality within countries. Capeau and Decoster (2003) relate the diverging tendencies to income measures, the use of weights and the assumption of inequality among citizens irrespective of the location.

Several factors have been identified and attempts have been made to quantify their impacts on the inter-national income inequality. In a number of recent studies, the inequality effects of population weights on the Gini coefficient, the regional cost of living, openness, technology spillovers, specialization in production, economic growth, initial condition, skill-biased technology and wages, supply and demand of human capital and redistributive policies are investigated. Inter-national distribution of income based on the Gini coefficients of national per capita GDP for the period 1950 to 1998 and 120 countries has been computed by Milanovic (2001). The temporal patterns of inequality differ by whether the Gini coefficient is weighted by population or not. The unweighted Gini coefficient shows a declining inequality between 1965 and 1978 and an increasing trend in inter-national inequality after 1978. The picture differs if the Gini coefficients are computed by weighting the GDP per capita by regional population shares. The weighted results show a declining world inequality due to the faster growth in the Indian and Chinese economies than the world economy. The increases in inequality are also found to be sensitive to the differences in regional cost-of-living (Ravallion and Datt, 2000).

4.3. The WIID Data

The data used here are obtained from the UNU-WIDER World Income Inequality Database (WIID) which is an expanded version of the Deininger and Squire (1996) database. The WIID contains information on income inequality, income shares, and a number of variables indicating the source and the quality of data for 146 countries. The countries are observed on an irregular basis mainly during the period 1950 to 1998. To avoid distortions for graphing the trend in global income inequality over time, the lower part of the data in 1950 is truncated. The number of excluded observations covering 1867-1949 is only 25 or 1.5 per cent of the sample. A statistical summary of the WIID data is presented in Table 1.

The Gini coefficient is measured in percentage points. It is the mean of multiple observations for a country in a given year. The multiplicity of observations is due to the differences in income definitions, data sources, reference units, and the population coverage. In constructing global inequality, we have adjusted the Gini coefficient for the population as:

$$Gini_t = \sum_{i=1}^{N} (pop_{it} / pop_t)\, Gini_{it} = \sum_{i=1}^{N} ps_{it} Gini_{it} \tag{19}$$

where pop_{it} is the population of country i in period t and ps_{it} is the corresponding population share. Aggregate population in a given year (pop_t) is the reference population for the global population. However, since our sample does not cover all countries in the world in every year, the population adjusted Gini measure is very sensitive to the exit and entry of countries with a large population like China and India.

To provide a better picture of the distribution of world inequality and its development over time we report the unweighted mean, median, standard deviation and populations weighted mean Gini coefficient in Figure 2. The deciles observations are transformed to quintile income shares to make the income distribution comparable across countries and over time. This procedure results in maximum number of comparable observations that can be obtained from the data but at the cost of losing information. In Figure 3 the mean quintile income shares over time are presented. As an alternative measure of inequality the ratio of the highest to the lowest quintiles is computed (see Table2).

4.4. Global Trend in Inequality

Simple descriptive statistics based on the WIID database are presented in Table 1. The summary statistics of the Gini coefficient for observations with and without income share distributions are given separately and jointly as well. The mean Gini coefficient for observations with income shares (36.43) is lower than for those without income shares (38.11). There is a large variation in the distribution of income among the countries and over time. The income share of the poorest 20 percent varies in the interval 0.016 and 0.157, with a mean and a standard deviation of 0.069 and 0.036 respectively. The income share of the richest 20 per cent is 0.441 with relatively small standard deviation of 0.082. The disparity in income shares results in a Q5/Q1 ratio with a mean of 8.175 and a standard deviation of 5.758. The range varies within the interval 2.035 and 40.812.

Table 1. Statistical summary of the World Income Inequality Database (WIID)

Variable	obs	mean	std dev	minimum	maximum
Gini without income shares	1376	38.110	10.910	15.900	79.500
Gini with income shares	1358	36.433	9.273	17.830	66.000
Gini with/out income shares	1631	38.065	10.517	15.900	79.500
Income share Q1	844	0.069	0.036	0.016	0.157
Income share Q2	844	0.112	0.026	0.020	0.204
Income share Q3	844	0.157	0.025	0.070	0.255
Income share Q4	844	0.220	0.022	0.124	0.313
Income share Q5	844	0.441	0.082	0.249	0.710
Q5/Q1 ratio	844	8.175	5.758	2.035	40.812

Note: Gini coefficient with/without income shares refer to a combination of two observations for a country in a given year where one is with and the other without information on distribution of income.

Table 2. Development of global Gini coefficient and distribution of income shares over time

Year	obs	unweighted	weighted	Q1	Q2	Q3	Q4	Q5	Q5/Q1
1950	7	43.63	40.90	0.06	0.11	0.15	0.21	0.46	7.12
1951	6	40.33	36.41	0.06	0.11	0.16	0.23	0.44	7.65
1952	8	41.47	36.93	0.05	0.11	0.16	0.22	0.45	8.72
1953	11	43.32	35.70	0.06	0.11	0.15	0.21	0.47	7.62
1954	8	40.10	37.39	0.07	0.12	0.17	0.23	0.42	6.33
1955	11	45.30	36.99	0.06	0.12	0.17	0.23	0.42	6.89
1956	10	43.80	36.50	0.05	0.10	0.14	0.21	0.49	10.20
1957	15	39.36	37.26	0.06	0.11	0.15	0.21	0.47	7.61
1958	18	39.50	37.97	0.06	0.11	0.15	0.22	0.45	7.39
1959	17	44.24	37.72	0.07	0.10	0.13	0.18	0.52	7.43
1960	25	47.41	39.98	0.05	0.09	0.13	0.19	0.55	12.15
1961	21	43.45	38.01	0.06	0.10	0.14	0.21	0.48	7.79
1962	25	38.64	39.84	0.06	0.11	0.16	0.22	0.44	7.24
1963	25	39.69	35.69	0.06	0.11	0.16	0.22	0.44	7.03
1964	21	40.70	34.40	0.06	0.10	0.14	0.20	0.49	8.26
1965	25	42.71	37.84	0.07	0.11	0.15	0.22	0.46	7.03
1966	17	38.38	33.94	0.07	0.12	0.16	0.22	0.42	5.82
1967	28	40.61	36.35	0.07	0.13	0.17	0.23	0.39	5.26
1968	34	43.33	38.67	0.06	0.10	0.15	0.21	0.49	8.62
1969	36	41.95	35.85	0.07	0.11	0.16	0.21	0.45	6.86
1970	42	42.16	34.38	0.06	0.11	0.15	0.21	0.47	7.72
1971	34	42.62	40.67	0.06	0.10	0.15	0.21	0.48	8.22
1972	28	39.00	36.91	0.07	0.12	0.16	0.22	0.43	5.91
1973	31	37.34	33.64	0.06	0.12	0.16	0.23	0.42	6.68
1974	24	39.16	34.54	0.07	0.12	0.16	0.23	0.42	6.35
1975	37	39.57	34.67	0.06	0.11	0.16	0.22	0.45	7.23
1976	38	38.04	39.94	0.06	0.11	0.16	0.22	0.44	6.97
1977	33	39.40	30.51	0.07	0.11	0.16	0.22	0.44	6.63
1978	31	34.67	31.65	0.07	0.11	0.17	0.23	0.42	6.09
1979	35	37.95	31.21	0.06	0.11	0.16	0.23	0.43	7.02
1980	41	38.05	33.83	0.07	0.12	0.16	0.22	0.43	6.39
1981	56	33.33	33.60	0.07	0.12	0.16	0.23	0.43	6.57
1982	31	34.34	31.49	0.08	0.13	0.17	0.23	0.39	5.11
1983	30	36.84	31.39	0.07	0.13	0.17	0.23	0.40	5.51
1984	34	35.77	31.47	0.08	0.12	0.17	0.23	0.41	5.40
1985	35	35.09	34.44	0.07	0.13	0.17	0.22	0.41	5.56
1986	56	34.04	33.07	0.06	0.11	0.16	0.22	0.44	6.91
1987	40	34.13	32.99	0.07	0.12	0.16	0.23	0.43	6.45
1988	53	31.93	34.52	0.07	0.12	0.16	0.23	0.42	6.19
1989	66	34.76	33.98	0.06	0.11	0.15	0.22	0.45	7.14
1990	63	34.94	34.90	0.07	0.12	0.16	0.22	0.43	5.95
1991	58	36.04	34.61	0.07	0.11	0.16	0.22	0.44	6.52
1992	60	36.21	36.22	0.08	0.11	0.16	0.22	0.43	5.36
1993	59	37.75	35.31	0.09	0.11	0.16	0.22	0.43	5.06
1994	56	37.95	35.15	0.08	0.10	0.15	0.21	0.47	6.08
1995	60	38.82	37.37	0.08	0.10	0.15	0.21	0.45	5.74
1996	53	39.32	35.36	0.08	0.10	0.14	0.21	0.47	6.20
1997	38	36.46	34.67	0.08	0.11	0.15	0.21	0.46	5.93
1998	15	37.72	40.12	0.09	0.12	0.16	0.22	0.42	4.86
Mean	49	39.02	35.65	0.07	0.11	0.16	0.22	0.45	6.80

Notes: The weighted Gini coefficient refers to the population weighted mean value calculated based on the country observations in a given year. The Q1- Q5 are quintile income shares. The ration Q5/Q1 is a measure of the extent of income share inequalities in the world.

There is a large disparity in inequality over time (see Table 2). It should be noted that the numbers here reflect average multiple observations for countries in a given year. The choice of measurement and the units of observations are not accounted for here. Therefore, the data lack uniform quality criteria and contains inconsistencies in distributions, definitions, sources, levels and coverage across countries and over time. If one chooses to use a consistent segment of the data, the resulted sample will be very small and hardly sufficient to serve as a base for a discussion of global trends in income inequality.

The median value of Gini coefficient (37.74 per cent) is on average 1.5 per cent lower than the mean value (39.02 per cent). The mean, median, standard deviation, minimum, maximum and range of unweighted and mean weighted Gini coefficient for the period 1950 to 1998 are presented Figure 2. It shows that the mean and the median inequality follow the same pattern and are declining over time. The dispersion in inequality also declines after 1958.

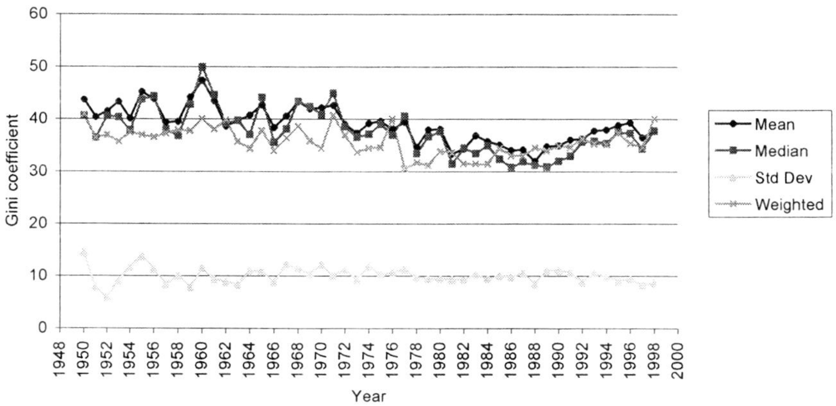

Figure 2. Global trends in income inequality.

In the measurement of global or regional inequality, it is common to weight inequality by population. The population-weighted mean Gini coefficient is much lower (35.65 per cent) than the non-weighted (39.02 per cent). The drop is caused by the inclusion of countries with large populations and relatively low inequalities. Though India and China are frequently observed, the weighing procedure is not reliable as the flow of population is very irregular over time. The average change in the Gini coefficient is 0.50 per cent indicating a small positive trend in non-weighted inequality over time. The change in Gini coefficient varies in the interval –7.76 (1952/1953) to +6.62 (1963/1964).

The distribution of income measured by quintile shares shows a large variation across countries and over time. The mean income quintile shares are 0.069, 0.112, 0.157, 0.220 and 0.441 (see Table 2). The lowest quintile share shows constant pattern prior to 1990 but increasing patterns post the 1990 period. On the other hand, the highest 3 quintiles show variations before 1970 but a decreasing pattern in the post 1970s (see Figure 3). This resulted into a continuously increasing inequality change over time combined with a declining Q5/Q1 ratio. The highest ratios are associated with countries involved in (domestic) conflicts like Iraq, Lebanon, Paraguay, Central African Republic, Guinea, Sierra Leone, South Africa and Georgia, while the lowest are associated with Egypt, Lao, Belarus and Luxembourg.

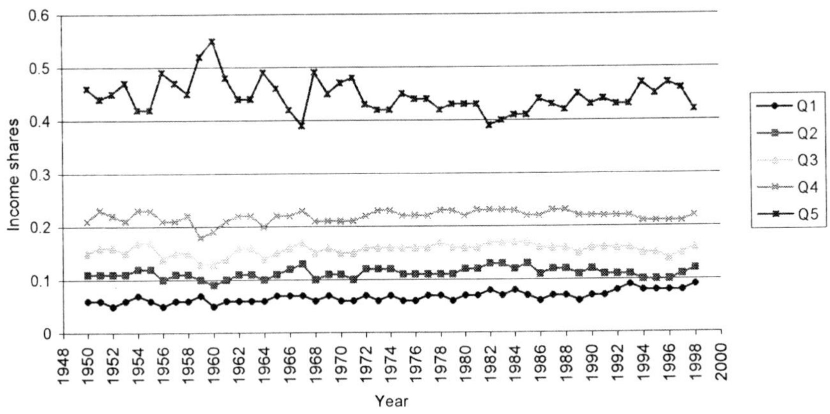

Figure 3. Development of global income shares.

Considering the global trends, due to the strong influence of the highest quintile income share, the inequality is volatile prior to 1970 and more stable and increasing during the period post 1986. There is evidence of the convergence in the mean, median and population weighted means over time (see Figure 2). In sum based on the WIID data and given applied measurement methods and data irregularities, there is no convincing sign of a significant increasing or decreasing global trend in income inequality over the last 50 years.

4.5. Factors Affecting World Distribution of Income

The literature on the distribution of income and income inequality identifies a number of factors important for the evolution of world income distribution. The factors affecting the shape of world distribution of income include inheritance, wage inequality, supply of skills, labour market institutions, mobility, redistributive policies, growth, globalization, democracy, geography and institutions. The non-uniform increase in wage inequality, the technical change biased against unskilled workers and the government's redistributive policies have resulted in the heterogeneous development of inequality among the industrialized countries. In addition to the geographical factors, the institutional structure and democracy play a role in economic development and inequality of countries.

The between-country inequality dominates the within-country component. The latter can easily be affected through policy interventions. Growth is found to increase income inequality. However, several studies conclude that the benefit of growth exceeds the disadvantages to the poor. More evidence based on better data is needed to make inferences on growth and the within-country distributional changes. Further studies are also needed to investigate the channels through which globalization affect the world income inequality. Finally, the multidimensional links and direction of the causal relationships between the determinants of income inequality other than inequality growth and openness has been neglected in the previous research.

4.6. Redistribution of World Income

Economic growth, population growth, life expectancy, and the changes in the structure of income inequality are the important factors determining the evolution of world income distribution. Empirical results show that world inequality measured as the Gini coefficient increased somewhat and poverty measured as headcount decreased. In summation, the inequality within individual countries is not increasing but the inequality between countries and regions as well as poverty concentration in some regions is increasing. Given the skewed distribution of world income and its development, this section discuss engaging and creative studies such as Kaplow (2002), Kopczuk, Slemrod and Yitzhaki (2002), Li, Squire and Zou (1998) Cornia and Court (2001), Birdsall (1998), Stiglitz (1998), Caminda and Goutswaard (2001), and Park, Wang and Wu (2002) on how to bring about necessary changes to world income distribution in a desirable way.

In view of the above and from a public finance perspective, global redistribution has the same structure as that of an individual country. World redistribution is very small and not optimal relative to world inequality. The within country redistribution has little impact on global inequality. Political and capital market factors determine the stability, changes and levels of inequality across countries. Land reform, expanding education and active regional policy are found to be effective economic reform policy measures. At a smaller regional scale such as the EU, the social security reforms show evidence of the positive impact of taxes and targeting transfers on the distribution of income and inequality within and between the member countries. The political constraint and the level of targeting are important to the success of the regional targeting programmes to reduce poverty.

In the analysis of factors causing inequality, it would be useful to broadly differentiate between factors affecting each of the within-and between-country components of inequality. In the case developing countries, the emphasis should be given to a systematic discussion of important factors such as colonialism, institutions and governance, international trade, international debt, defence spending, infrastructure for economic development, structural adjustment programs and international aid. This will allow for heterogeneous perspectives on the inequality problem, available resources and measures to reduce inequality

5. Regional Income Inequality

Income inequality can be measured at different levels of aggregation such as global, continental, international and national levels. Here we consider income inequality at the continental and the sub-continental levels. We investigate the economic disparity between regions of the world and among countries within each continent or sub-continent. The empirical results for data availability reasons are mainly based on the second half of the 20th century. The review covers a whole range of measures and methods frequently employed in empirical analysis of the global and regional income inequality and income distribution. Empirical results from different case studies are discussed and the results are contrasted to those obtained based on the WIID described previously. The distribution of Gini coefficient, quintile shares for different regions is presented in Table 3.

Table 3. Summary of Gini coefficient and quintile shares by country group, based on WIID

Region	Min	Max	Nyear	Range	Gini	WGini	Q1	Q2	Q3	Q4	Q5	Q5/Q1
MENA	1944	1997	57	53	39.01	41.31	0.07	0.10	0.15	0.21	0.47	7.09
East Asia	1953	1998	93	45	33.67	28.81	0.07	0.12	0.16	0.23	0.41	5.55
SEAsia&Pacif.	1956	1998	87	42	43.17	39.80	0.07	0.10	0.14	0.21	0.49	7.39
South Asia	1950	1997	106	47	36.94	34.49	0.08	0.12	0.16	0.21	0.42	5.13
Latin America	1948	1998	320	50	47.39	51.79	0.04	0.08	0.13	0.21	0.54	12.50
sub-Sah. Afr.	1914	1999	157	85	49.26	46.53	0.06	0.09	0.13	0.20	0.52	8.21
East Europe	1955	1998	191	43	26.14	31.57	0.10	0.14	0.18	0.22	0.35	3.54
Former Soviet	1972	1998	125	26	31.56	33.99	0.09	0.12	0.16	0.22	0.42	4.78
Industrialized	1867	1998	495	131	34.79	36.08	0.07	0.12	0.17	0.24	0.40	5.72
All regions	1867	1999	1392	132	38.06	38.26	0.07	0.11	0.16	0.22	0.44	6.88

Min First year of observation
Max Last year of observation
Nyear Number of years observed
Range The difference between the last and first years of observation
Gini Mean Gini value
WGini Population weighted mean Gini value
Q1-Q5 Income shares of the first-fifth quintiles of population
Q5/Q1 the ration of the fifth quintile share to the first quintile income share

Table 4. Distribution of Gini coefficient and quintile shares by individual country, based on WIID

Country	Idnr	Region	Min	Max	Nyear	Range	Gini	WGini	Q1	Q2	Q3	Q4	Q5	Q5/Q1
East Asia:														
China	25	2	1953	1998	26	45	29.35	28.59	0.08	0.12	0.16	0.25	0.39	5.21
HongKong	60	2	1957	1996	12	39	44.65	44.50	0.05	0.10	0.14	0.20	0.51	9.99
KoreaRep	74	2	1953	1993	17	40	34.18	34.28	0.07	0.12	0.16	0.22	0.42	5.73
Mongolia	92	2	1995	1997	2	2	30.88	.	0.10	0.12	0.16	0.22	0.40	4.02
Taiwan	129	2	1953	1996	36	43	33.04	31.92	0.08	0.13	0.17	0.23	0.38	4.59
Mean region	2	2	1953	1998	93	45	33.67	28.81	0.07	0.12	0.16	0.23	0.41	5.55
South East Asia and Pacific:														
Cambodia	19	3	1997	1997	1	0	40.40	.	0.10	0.10	0.14	0.20	0.46	4.87
Fiji	44	3	1968	1977	3	9	43.05	43.00	0.04	0.08	0.13	0.22	0.52	13.08
Indonesi	63	3	1964	1996	17	32	36.36	36.09	0.09	0.12	0.16	0.21	0.42	4.79
Lao	76	3	1992	1992	1	0	30.40	.	0.13	0.12	0.16	0.20	0.39	2.93
Malaysia	86	3	1957	1995	18	38	47.71	47.83	0.05	0.09	0.13	0.21	0.53	11.16
Myanmar	94	3	1958	1958	1	0	34.97	.	0.10	0.13	0.13	0.15	0.49	4.85
Philippi	106	3	1956	1997	12	41	46.94	46.43	0.05	0.09	0.13	0.20	0.53	10.14
PopuaNG	108	3	1996	1996	1	0	50.90	50.90	0.06	0.08	0.12	0.19	0.56	9.12
Singapor	118	3	1966	1993	15	27	42.49	42.27	0.06	0.11	0.14	0.23	0.46	7.27
Thailand	132	3	1962	1998	16	36	45.03	45.33	0.05	0.09	0.13	0.21	0.52	9.72
Vietnam	146	3	1992	1998	2	6	35.90	35.70	0.11	0.11	0.15	0.20	0.43	3.88
Mean region	3	3	1956	1998	87	42	43.17	39.80	0.07	0.10	0.14	0.21	0.49	7.39
Mean all regions			1867	1999	1392	132	38.06	38.26	0.07	0.11	0.16	0.22	0.44	6.88

Note: USSR, Yugoslavia and Czechoslovakia are excluded and East and West Germany are averaged.
Country Country
Idnr Country ID number
Region Regional location
Min First year of observation
Max Last year of observation
Nyear Number of years observed
Range The difference between the last and first years of observation
Gini Mean Gini value
WGini Population weighted mean Gini value
Q1-Q5 Income share of the first-fifth quintiles of population
Q5/Q1 the ration of the fifth quintile share to the first quintile income share

To provide a better picture of the distribution of inequality we report the first, the last, the period range and the number of years a country is observed. In Table 4 we report the Gini coefficient and the population weighted Gini coefficient together with the distribution of income. The decile observations are transformed into quintile income shares to make the income distribution comparable across countries and over time. As a second measure of inequality, the ratio of the highest to the lowest quintiles are calculated and reported.

5.1. Inter-Regional Income Inequality

The relative high degree of homogeneity in the economic development within regions combined with a high degree of heterogeneity between regions makes analysis of the inter-regional inequality an interesting dimension to be explored. Maddison (2001), using data on GDP across countries and over time reports a steady increase in the inter-regional inequalities since 1870. As a measure of the regional dispersion, the ratio of income per head of the richest to the poorest region of the world is used. The ratio has increased from 5:1 in 1870 to 19:1 in 1998. In addition to income ratios, Maddison uses income share as a second measure to compare regions of the world. The global GDP share of the Western off-shoots (US, Canada, Australia and New Zealand) increased from 10.2 per cent in 1870 to 30.6 per cent in 1950. It declined to 25.1 per cent in 1998. The Western Europe share of the global GDP decreased from 33.6 per cent to 20 per cent during the same period. Similar decrease was observed in the case of Latin America from 8.7 per cent to 2.5 per cent, while Africa's share remained constant at around 3.0-3.5 per cent. Asia's share declined prior to 1952 but it increased from 18.5 per cent in 1973 to 37.2 per cent in 1998. Eastern Europe and the former USSR enjoyed a constant share of world GDP in the range of 11-13 per cent until 1973. Thereafter, this region experienced a decline from 12.9 per cent in 1973 to 5.3 per cent in 1998. In the case of GDP shares, no correction for changes in the population size or the purchasing power parity is made.

The income inequality derived from the WIID where the sample countries are divided into 9 regions and the distribution of income by quintiles is reported in Table 3. The results show a significant interregional heterogeneity. Here we define heterogeneity as the standard deviation of the Gini coefficient. The highest rate is found to be associated with the sub-Saharan Africa (10.05 per cent) and Middle East and North Africa (8.23 per cent), while a low dispersion is observed in South East Asia (5.87 per cent), South Asia (5.375), and Eastern Europe (5.06 per cent). The variation, despite the comprehensive redistribution systems is unexpectedly high in the industrialised countries (7.90 per cent). Sub-Saharan Africa and Latin America again display the lowest levels of income (0.06 and 0.04) allocated to the first quintile of the population and the highest share to the highest quintile (0.52 and 0.54), respectively. With an exception of Eastern Europe and the former Soviet Republics, the variation in inequality within regions is stable or declining over time. South East Asia and South Asia show the least dispersion within region (see Figure 4). However, the development of inequality in Latin America, Eastern Europe and the former Soviet Republics show increasing trends in the post 1970s.

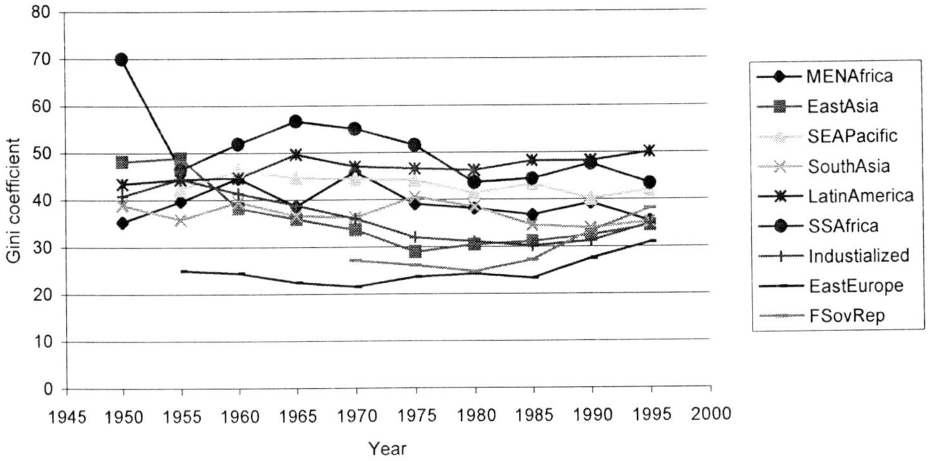

Figure 4. Trend in mean unweighted gini coeficient by region.

There are a number of other measures (other than the ratio of income per head of the richest to the poorest region and the regions' GDP share of global income) used in the studies of inter-regional income inequality. A third measure is based on the Gini coefficient of income inequality. The focus is on its variations across regions and its regional development over time. Several studies indicate that the Gini coefficient has increased. A fourth measure is based on the development of the absolute number of the poor. The number of the poor has declined but its regional concentration has increased. Land distribution and redistribution of assets are a fifth measure of inequality. A sixth measure is based on income mobility that counteracts increasing income inequality. A seventh measure can be computed based on the ratio of the regions highest to lowest quintile share of income.

Regardless of the chosen measure, the transformation of income to PPP and its adjustment for the population size, the coverage in terms of the number of countries and their populations share are important factors affecting the development of the inter-regional inequality in the world. Results based on WIID database show a large interregional heterogeneity in both the level and the development of income distribution and income inequality over time (Table 5). The inequality in Latin America, Eastern Europe and the former Soviet Republics show increasing trends in post 1970s.

5.2. Income Inequality in East Asia, South-East Asia and Pacific

Here we review a few recent studies on each geographical region. The regional classification differs from that used to group countries based on the WIID database or the classifications found in international data sources. Thus, the review here is based on a less standardized classification employed by individual researchers in the inequality literature. It has not been possible to trace studies based on household data comparing income inequality among multiple of the East and the South-East Asian countries. In the following discussion, we mainly review briefly the available single country studies.

Table 5. Distribution of Gini coefficient by individual country, based on WIID

Country	Idnr	Region	Min	Max	Nyear	Range	Min	Mean	Median	Max	StdDev	Range	Wgini	Dgini
East Asia:														
China	25	2	1953	1998	26	45	18.60	29.35	29.34	55.80	7.18	37.20	28.59	3.37
HongKong	60	2	1957	1996	12	39	37.65	44.65	45.09	52.00	4.11	14.35	44.50	1.70
KoreaRep	74	2	1953	1993	17	40	29.82	34.18	34.00	40.22	2.95	10.40	34.28	0.80
Mongolia	92	2	1995	1997	2	2	28.57	30.88	30.88	33.20	3.28	4.63	.	-6.98
Taiwan	129	2	1953	1996	36	43	28.14	33.04	30.33	55.80	7.16	27.66	31.92	-0.41
Mean region	2	2	1953	1998	93	45	18.60	33.67	31.20	55.80	7.65	37.20	28.81	.
South East Asia and Pacific:														
Cambodia	19	3	1997	1997	1	0	40.40	40.40	40.40	40.40	.	0.00	.	.
Fiji	44	3	1968	1977	3	9	42.25	43.05	42.50	44.41	1.18	2.16	43.00	-0.55
Indonesi	63	3	1964	1996	17	32	31.38	36.36	34.20	51.00	5.74	19.62	36.09	5.06
Lao	76	3	1992	1992	1	0	30.40	30.40	30.40	30.40	.	0.00	.	.
Malaysia	86	3	1957	1995	18	38	37.26	47.71	48.16	57.16	4.03	19.90	47.83	0.97
Myanmar	94	3	1958	1958	1	0	34.97	34.97	34.97	34.97	.	0.00	.	.
Philippi	106	3	1956	1997	12	41	43.06	46.94	47.35	50.26	2.42	7.21	46.43	-0.06
PopuaNG	108	3	1996	1996	1	0	50.90	50.90	50.90	50.90	.	0.00	50.90	.
Singapor	118	3	1966	1993	15	27	37.00	42.49	42.83	48.83	3.20	11.83	42.27	1.05
Thailand	132	3	1962	1998	16	36	41.08	45.03	43.91	51.43	3.16	10.34	45.33	0.64
Vietnam	146	3	1992	1998	2	6	35.70	35.90	35.90	36.10	0.28	0.40	35.70	0.19
Mean region	3	3	1956	1998	87	42	30.40	43.17	43.90	57.16	5.87	26.76	39.80	.
Mean all regions			1867	1999	1631	132	15.90	41.12	40.24	79.50	9.61	27.91	35.65	0.34

Note: USSR, Yugoslavia and Czechoslovakia are excluded and East and West Germany are averaged.

Country	Country
Idnr	Country ID number
Region	Regional location
Min	First year of observation
Max	Last year of observation
Nyear	Number of years observed
Range	The difference between the last and first years of observation
Minimum	Minimum Gini value
Mean	Mean Gini value
Median	Median Gini value
Maximum	Maximum Gini value
StdDev	Standard deviation of the Gini
Range	The difference between maximum and minimum Gini values
Wgini	Population weighted mean Gini
Dgini	Average percentage change in Gini

Warr (2001) has studied the incidence of poverty and inequality in Thailand using household and population data for the period of 1988-1999. The poverty and inequality results in a regional perspective indicate that inequality increased in post 1997. Prior to the economic crisis of 1997, there was a 21.4 per cent decline in the percentage of the poor from 32.6 per cent to 11.2 per cent. However, the poverty rate again increased during the post crisis period to 15.9 per cent in 1999. Inequality is measured by the Gini coefficient and the ratio of the highest to the lowest quintile income shares using both household and individual as the unit of observation. In the latter case, Warr accounts for the gender and ages of household members to reflect their needs. In comparison with the need-based measure, the unweighted household measure underestimates the inequality.

Despite the major reduction in poverty rate, Thailand has failed to reduce the widening gaps between individuals, areas and regions predominately the Northern region. Droughts in the dry season, the floods in the wet season, lack of support from central government, large sized household, employment patterns, low educational attainment, limited access to credit, and inadequate rural-urban linkage are among the underlying causes of poverty (Hossain 2001). Hossain focuses on the income poverty and inequality in the Northern region and suggests some employment, income and equality policy measures to mitigate regional as well as rural-urban disparities in Thailand. Cameron (2000) also finds changes in the income distribution in Java being related to the ageing of population, educational attainment and agricultural/industrial structure.

Several East Asian economies tried to couple economic growth with reductions in poverty and income disparity. The economic crisis of 1997 has deteriorated these prospects. Analysis of the relationship between growth, inequality and poverty in nine countries in the East Asia and the Pacific region is summarised by Kakwani and Krongkaew (2000). In the Australian case, the focus is on the taxes and transfers and on the growth rates of the various income components rather than on the growth rate of the total income as in the other countries. The distribution of income has remained relatively equal in Japan despite the changes in the welfare post the World War II. The regional income distribution in Korea has been very egalitarian and affected by the domination of the political and the military leaders. The increasing development of the income disparity in Taiwan is related to the industrial transformation and changes in the factor intensity of production.

It is widely believed that the East Asian economies performed exceptionally well both in generating growth and in keeping income inequality low. You (1998) investigated the income distribution in East Asia and found that only Japan, Korea and Taiwan enjoy low inequality. However, in general the East Asian countries have been successful in translating high profit shares into high savings and investment rates. The high profits and the low inequality have resulted in an even distribution of wealth. Bourguignon, Fournier and Gurgand (2001) applied a decomposition method to isolate the impact of the changes in earnings structure, labour-force participation behaviour, and the socio-demographic structure of the population on stability of the income distribution in Taiwan during 1979-1994. Wage structure, changes in female labour force participation, educational structure and changes in composition of household have in different ways served both as deriving and off-setting forces to the inequality changes.

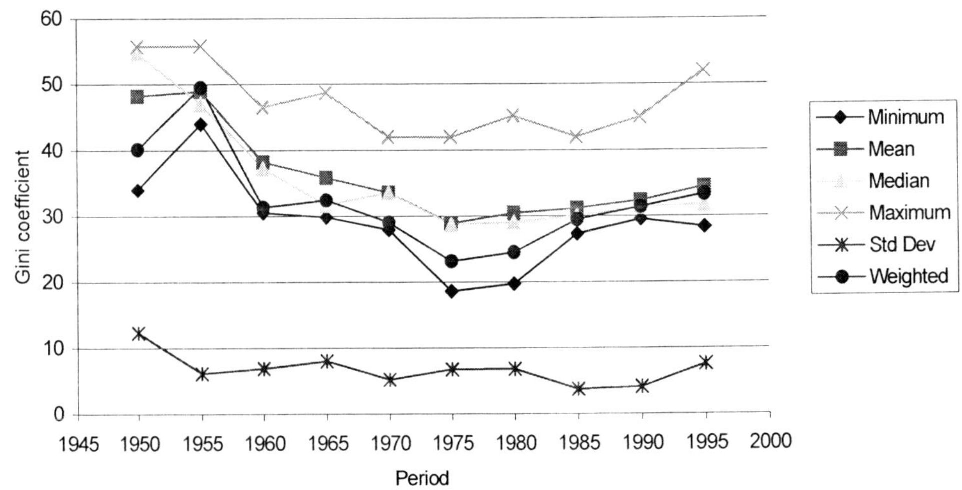

Figure 5. Development of Gini coefficient, East Asia.

Based on the WIID database, the mean income inequality in the East Asian region is quite low, 33.67 (see Figure 5). It is the highest in Hongkong (44.65) but the lowest in China (29.35). Inequality has declined in Mongolia, but it increased in China over time. The mean income inequality in the South Asian region is higher than East Asia, 36.94. Inequality is the highest in Iran (45.59) but the lowest in Pakistan (34.26). Changes in the inequality over time have been the highest in Nepal.

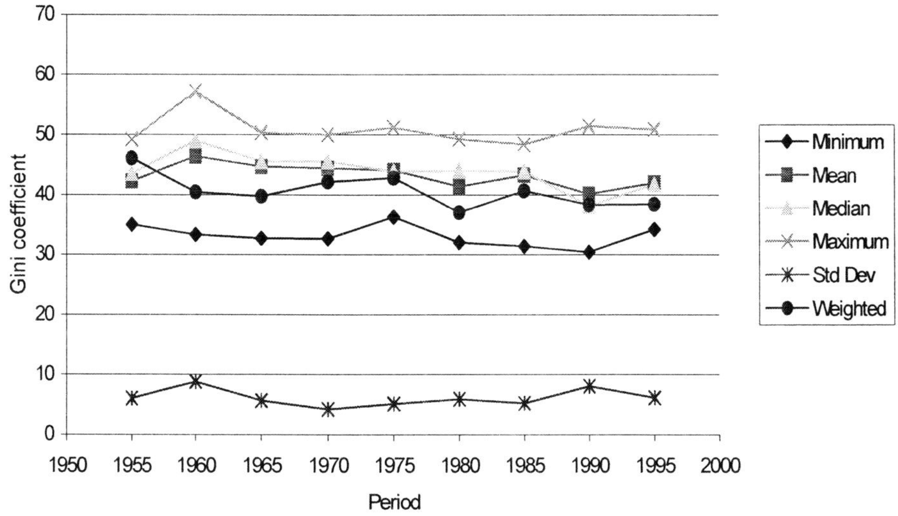

Figure 6. Development of Gini coefficient, South Asia and pasific.

The mean income inequality in South East Asia and Pacific (Figure 6) is much higher that the South Asian regions, 43.17, but not when the dispersion in inequality is concerned. Inequality is the highest in Malaysia (47.71) and Philippines (46.94). The ranking here is based on more than one survey observation and less influenced by outliers or measurement errors. The increase in inequality has been the highest in Indonesia. The ratio of the highest to the lowest quintiles with the exception of Hongkong (9.99) is below 7 in the South Asian countries. However, it exceeds 10 in several of the South East Asian and the Pacific countries including Fiji, Malaysia and Philippines. For more details on the level and variations in inequality across the three regions, see Table 4 and 5. Inequality in East Asia declined prior to 1975 but it increased in post 1980, while it declined over time in South East Asia and Pacific. There is a positive association between the level and the variation in inequality. In general, dispersion in inequality is declining over time indicating a convergence in inequality but to a higher level.

The East Asian countries have been successful in coupling growth and equality. However, the 1997 economic crisis deteriorated these prospects. The conflicting results compared to other regions development are explained by the entry of China into the world market and the advent of new technology biased against unskilled workers.

6. PROVINCIAL AND REGIONAL INEQUALITY IN CHINA

6.1. Introduction

In addition to the aggregate levels of global, continental and international listed above, income inequality can also be measured at a within-country regional level. Here the focus is on inequality in income distribution in a selection of large countries measured in terms of the population size and land area, where regions include states, provinces, federations or distinct geographical locations within a country. In certain cases, it can also be defined as more aggregated geographical coastal, central and western regions in China or geographical regions in Russia. Such studies focus on large countries like China (Tsui 1993; Xu and Zou 2000; Lee 2000; Gustafsson and Shi 2002), Russia (Commander, Tolstopiatenko and Yemtsov 1999; Yemtsov 2002; Luttmer 2001; Shorrocks and Kolenikov 2001; Fedorov 2002), India (Mishra and Parikh 1997; Jha 2000; Datt and Ravallion 1992) and the USA (Patridge, Rickman and Levernier 1996; Black and Dowd 1997; Zandvakili 1999; Moffitt and Gottschalk 2002).

China and India experienced rapid economic growth after economic reform, accompanied by increased inequality and reduction in poverty. The level and development of inequality has varied by location and sector. This inequality can further be decomposed into various components associated with inter- and intra-sector and provincial components and their determinants in turn identified. Analysis of within-country regional inequality can reveal the effects of openness, marketisation, convergence due to factor mobility, and may also indicate regional polarisation, or disintegration and widening inequality driven by structural differences between regions. Furthermore, it is important to consider heterogeneity in income inequality in both level and development over time, as well as different characteristics of sub-group dimensions. Empirical evidence suggests that inequality and poverty alter following structural adjustment programmes affecting the welfare of sub-groups of a population differently.

The empirical results reported here are based on the second half of the 20th century. The countries considered here covers transition (China and Russia), developing (India) and industrialised (USA) countries. Empirical results from the literature is further complemented and compared with those obtained from the WIID data covering post 1950s. The next sub-section presents inequality in China and a brief review of inequality in Russia, India and USA.

6.2. Households Surveys in China

Empirical studies on inequality and poverty in China is often based on two household surveys conducted by the Institute of Economics, Chinese Academy of Social Sciences, with the assistance of the State Statistical Bureau (SSB) in Beijing. The first survey of household income for 1988 was implemented in 1989 and the second for 1995 in 1996. Sample households are visited every month by an enumerator for 5 years. The sample size in the first survey was about 20,000 households and about 15,000 in the second. The rural sample covers 109 counties located in 19 provinces and the urban sample covers cities located in 11 provinces. The provinces are chosen such as to reflect the geographical differences in China.

The data allow studies of inequality and poverty by sub-groups, income sources, various household characteristics, sectors and locations. For a short description of the data, see Gustafsson and Zhong (2000) and Gustafsson and Shi (2001a).

6.3. Provincial Inequality and Growth

China has experienced rapid economic growth with major impact on inequality during the recent decade. Xu and Zou (2000) using a new panel data set about Chinese provincial urban level income inequality show that the Gini coefficient increased from 0.17 in 1985 to 0.23 in 1995. The periods' average varies in the interval 0.17 and 0.25 by provinces and 0.13 and 0.34 by years of observation. The data is obtained from urban household surveys in each of the 29 provinces and from various provincial statistical yearbooks covering the period of 1985-1995 (except 1987 and 1988). Based on average incomes for each 5 percentiles, Xu and Zou compute the Gini coefficients, percentage of income of bottom, top and the third and fourth quintiles and the ratio of top to bottom quintiles for each province.

Xu and Zou find that since the beginning of economic reforms initiated in 1978, aggregate output growth has been on the average 9.9 per cent per year while the average growth in GDP per capita was 8.8 per cent during the period of 1978-1994. The difference can be explained by changes in the population. The growth rates differ by the location between 4.8 per cent for inland and 14.2 per cent for coastal provinces. The correlation between the growth rate and Gini coefficient is 0.27 and seem to support the Kuznet's (1955) inverted U-curve. This contradicts the Alesina and Rodrik (1994) and Person and Tabellini (1994) findings based on cross-section of international data who observed a negative association between income growth and inequality. In analysing the causal mechanism relating to inequality and growth in India and China, Quah (2002) pointed out that there is no single evidence about such relation. Many other factors like macroeconomic, technological, political or institutional beyond inequality influence economic growth. Ravallion (1998) suggests that the aggregation can bias tests of whether inequality impedes growth. Ravallion empirically evaluated the effects of asset inequality on consumption growth for rural household in China. The effect is lost in regional growth models.

6.3.1. Determinants of Provincial Inequality

In the above discussion, we have reviewed researches identifying factors other than inequality that influence economic growth. Xu and Zou (2000) looks at the reverse link, i.e. the role played by output growth, increasing exposure to international trade, urbanisation, taxation, government spending, inflation, human capital formation, geography, and the sectoral structure of the economy in determining the changes in income inequality. The relation is specified as:

$$INEQ_{it} = \beta_0 + \beta_{SOE}SOE_{it} + \beta_{INF}INF_{it} + \beta_{DIS}DIS_{it} + \beta_{SCH}SCH_{it} + \beta_{GDP}GDP_{it} + \beta_{TRA}TRA_{it} + \beta_{EXP}EXP_{it} + \beta_{URB}URB_{it} + \phi_i + \varepsilon_{it} \quad (20)$$

where $INEQ_{it}$ is Gini coefficient or it can alternatively be measured as the (ratio of) quintile income shares Q5/Q1, Q5, Q1, or Q34. The ϕ_i captures unobserved province-specific effects. The explanatory variables are: the share of state-owned enterprises (*SOE*), the inflation rate (*INF*), distance of a province's capital to the nearest port by railroad (*DIS*), the share of residents with more than secondary schooling (*SCH*), GDP growth rate (*GDP*), trade measured as the ratio of value of import and export to GDP (*TRA*), the share of government expenditure as a share of GDP (*EXP*), and the change of urbanisation level of a province measured as the growth rate of the share of non-agricultural population in the province (*URB*). The results show that income distribution has been affected by the changing structure of the economy, the role of the state, and increasing urbanisation. Inequality and Q5 increased (and Q1 decreased) with reduction of SOE share of output, higher inflation, higher growth rate, and foreign trade. Government spending tends to shift resources from the rich and the poor to the middle class. Provinces furthest from the coast had larger inequality probably reflecting greater imperfection of capital market. Schooling and increasing urbanisation did not affect income inequality. It has not been possible to identify determinants of (unobserved) level differences in inequality across different provinces.

6.4. Regional and Sectoral Inequality Decomposition

Since the impacts of economic reform are regionally dissimilar in China, not only inter-provincial but also intra-provincial, intra-rural, intra-urban, and rural-urban inequality are crucial in analysing China's regional inequality. Tsui (1993) decomposes China's regional inequality into the five components mentioned above using per capita gross value of industrial and agricultural outputs for 1982. The decomposition is based on a simple principle where the overall inequality (*I*) of each attribute is the sum of within-group (*WG*) and between-group (*BG*) inequalities expressed as:

$$I(X_i) = WG_i + BG_i \tag{21}$$

where the terms within-group and between-groups are equivalent to intra-provincial and inter-provincial inequalities. The results show that both intra-provincial and inter-provincial inequalities are the important sources of China's regional inequality. Disparity among the coastal, central and western regions is insignificant but the variance within the coast is substantial. Inter-rural and inter-urban inequality accounts for a large share of intra-provincial and overall inequality but neither of intra-rural and intra-urban are crucial factors to the development of inequality. Eastwood and Lipton (2000) discuss the changes in the focus of reforms in China in post 1983. The focus shifted from rural agricultural liberalisation to the urban sector industrial liberalisation with wages more tied to labour productivity. During the period 1983-1995, substantial rises in total, intra- and inter-sectoral inequalities were observed. However, inequality was rising faster in the urban sector. Against expectations, adjustments and liberalisations have not resulted in narrowing the urban-rural gap. Gustafsson et al. (2001) find a strong relationship between age and wage indicating that seniority plays a strong role in determining earnings in urban China.

Lee (2000) re-investigates Tsui's (1993) findings using recent and more disaggregate data from China's 2165 cities and counties in 1994 but applying the same decomposition method. Per capita consumption[4] and gross value of industrial and agricultural outputs are used as a measure of income. For the decomposition of inequality index, the Theil's entropy measure is defined. The results in Lee show that: rural-urban disparity has been reduced in turn reducing the intra-provincial inequality. The dominant sources of overall inequality in output have shifted from the intra-provincial to inter-provincial inequality, from rural-urban to intra-rural inequality, from disparity within the coastal region to the gap between coastal and interior regions. Disparity among coastal, central and western regions has increased while the gap between rural and urban within each region has narrowed. Disparity among the three regions is a dominant source of regional inequality. Output and consumption measures produce different inequality levels and rankings, 0.39 and 0.33. The share of intra (inter)provincial inequality of the overall inequality is 48.5 (51.5 per cent) for output and 63.2 (36.8 per cent) for consumption measures. In the case of consumption, the intra-provincial inequality, rural-urban inequality, and disparity within the coastal region are crucial factors of the overall regional inequality. The role of intra-urban income inequality is currently significant. The coastal and rural-industry-led growth aggravates the intra-rural output inequality. Kanbur and Zhang (1999) also conclude that the contribution of rural-urban disparities to regional inequality far exceeds the contribution of increasing inland-coastal disparities. Difference in the ease of migration provides a partial explanation for the phenomenon.

Gustafsson and Shi (2002) investigate how income inequality varies within and across counties in rural China. Household data covering 18 provinces in 1988 and 1995 is used. Results show that income inequality in rural China has increased rapidly. Differences in mean income between counties within provinces, between provinces as well as diverging means by regions are major contributors to rural inequality. Part of the income inequality within China's provinces is spatial. However, Ravallion and Chen (1999) argued that the structural changes in the rural economy are not reflected in the methods used for processing the raw data. Two thirds of the increase in inequality vanishes when market-based valuation methods are used and allowances are made for regional cost-of-living differences. Using the same data as in Gustafsson and Shi (2002), Gustafsson and Zhong (2000) found that despite impressive economic growth poverty has decreased only slightly due to the changed demographic composition of the population. Basing on a common poverty line, poverty is characterised to be a rural and also a geographical problem. The effectiveness of regional targeting in China's poverty alleviation programme for the period 1981-1995 is evaluated by Park, Wang and Wu (2002). They find modest positive effects on rural income growth. Perfect targeting may not be optimal due to tradeoffs between targeting and other social objectives.

Income source is the important component in inequality. In a regression-based approach, Morduch and Sicular (2002) examined inequality decomposition by income sources. The method is illustrated based on a small farm level data from rural China and compared to Theil-T, CV and Gini decomposition methods. The role of regional segmentation, education, age and political variables is emphasised. The results are found to be sensitive to the choice of decomposition method. Wan (2001) also decomposed changes in regional income inequality in rural China into structural, real inequality and interactive effects by decomposing Gini

[4] Tsui (1993) used per capita gross value of industrial and agricultural outputs as measures of income.

index by income (wage, farming and residual) sources. Structural effects found to be the driving force underlying increased regional inequality in rural China. The pitfalls in regression-based inequality decomposition are discussed by Wan (2002). A simple procedure is suggested to rectify these pitfalls. Based on results from data on 30 Chinese regions during the period 1992-1995, Wan argues that the root of problems relating to constant and residuals are not caused by inequality, rather they lie in the construction of proposed decomposition methodologies.

6.4.1. Income Factor Decomposition of Inequality

Previous studies have suggested that non-agricultural activities have been the major cause of rural income inequality. Increase in agricultural income was considered as a policy measure to reduce rural inequality in China. Cheng (1996) used household data from 5 grain producing Chinese regions in 1994 and Lerman and Yitzhaki (1985) decomposition. The result shows that inequality within the grain producing areas was also very high, with differences in crop income as the major source of inequality. The decomposition of inequality indicates that 61 per cent of the income inequality of peasant households is due to intra-provincial while the remaining 39 per cent is from the inter-provincial inequality components.

We have already described an example of a decomposition of Gini by income source. In a second study which is based on a different approach, the Gini coefficient of household income is decomposed according to type of income. This method has been used by Gustafsson and Shi (2001b) to analyse the reasons for the rapid increase of income inequality. They investigated the effect of the processes of economic and social transition on the distribution of income in China. The Gini coefficient and the differences of the Gini coefficient between two years is computed. Results based on samples of 1988 and 1995 household surveys shows that the changes in relative size of money income due to the distribution of land by household size and its changed profile are found to be the major processes behind the rapid increase of income inequality in rural China. Changes in the urban housing allocation and an increased number of retirees in combination with higher benefits have increased inequality. Using the same data, Gustafsson and Shi (2001a) analyses the Chinese labour market to investigate how earnings[5] inequality and relative earnings have changed between 1988 and 1995. The mean logarithmic deviation (*MLD*) index and the changes in the *MLD* between the two periods are computed. The total change is decomposed into 4 components. These are interpreted as: the effect of intertemporal changes in inequality within groups (A), the effect of changes in population shares on the within-group inequality (B), the effect of changes in population shares on the relative mean earnings of the population group (C), and the relative mean earnings of the population groups (D). The overall effects of demographic changes is equal to the sum of B and C. Results show that earnings inequality has increased rapidly affecting all categories of labour as defined by ownership sector, region and education. The contribution of basic wages and subsidies to inequality increase is positive, while those of bonus and other earnings are negative.

[5] Total earning is decomposed into basic wages, bonus, subsidies and other earnings.

6.5. Convergence in Per Capita Income

China's experience with trade liberalisation after 1978 and with rapid growth in the coastal provinces, gives an indication of widening inequality among China's diverse regions. Jian, Sachs and Warner (1996) examine the tendency towards convergence in real per-capita income among the provinces of China during the period 1952-1993. No strong convergence or divergence during the initial phase of central planning (1952-1965) was observed. There is strong evidence of divergence during the 'cultural revolution' (1965-1978) with social planning in favour of richer industrial regions widening the inter-regional inequality. Regional inequality is equalised with the extent of marketization and openness that begun in 1978. Convergence due to factor mobility, flow of labour, capital and technology, increased productivity among the rural regions and convergence within the coastal provinces. A policy to further liberalisation of interior will also promote convergence. Variance decomposition of the log of real GDP in each province is obtained. Zhang, Liu and Yao (2001) investigate the time-series properties of per capita income in China's regions during the period 1952 to 1997 and compare the consistency of results with cross-sectional methods. The results based on Gini coefficient, the ratio of per capita income between regions and the coefficient of variation suggests that eastern and western regions have converged to their own specific steady states over the past 40 years. The regional gap between the east and other regions widened before the reforms but economic reforms has worsened the gap further.

6.6. Polarization Vs. Inequality Indices

To overcome the limitation of the two inequality (Gini and Generalized Entropy) indices and the three polarisation (Wolfson 1994; and Tsui and Wang 1998) indices in establishing along which dimension polarisation occurs, Kanbur and Zhang (1999) developed a polarisation index (*KZ*) by specifying clusters and measuring the extent of inequality decomposed into within-group and between-group inequality components (see also Zhang and Kanbur, 2001). Polarisation refers to clustering of the income distribution along with some key dimensions. The *KZ* index is expressed as the ratio between inequality and within inequality. The index is then calculated for each of the four dimensions: West-East, National status, Capital city size and Export share by using income and expenditure definitions. In testing the behaviour of the four indices, it is found that the polarisation indices do not produce different results from the inequality indices. The *KZ* index seems to offer more insights into changes in China's income distribution. The results show that while polarisation along West-East and national status dimensions remained constant, polarisation along capital city size and export share dimensions increased during 1983-1995. The conclusion is that regional polarisation is driven by structural differences between regions rather than geographic or political. In terms of levels, rural-urban polarisation is more serious than inland-cost, while in terms of trend, the inland-coast polarisation has increased much more than rural-urban. Birchenall (2001) applied a measure of polarisation to Colombian income distribution. Human capital accumulation reduced the dispersion of income distribution leading to a period of stagnation when mobility declined. The structural reforms made the economy less equal with increased mobility.

6.7. Policy Measures to Reduce Inequality

Khan and Riskin (2001) provide a comprehensive analysis of inequality and poverty in China in the age of globalisation. Based on the 1988 and 1995 survey data they observe major changes in the composition of income between the two survey dates. Rural household income mainly from farming has declined from 74 per cent to 56 per cent, while non-farming wages increased from 9 per cent to 22 per cent resulting in increasing income inequality. The Gini ratio for rural income grew by 23 per cent from 0.34 to 0.42 due to unequal distribution of faster-growing wage components of rural income. The corresponding increases in inequality in the urban areas were 43 per cent in seven years from 0.23 to 0.33. The increasing inequality of distribution of income caused rise in urban income inequality. The wage share of income grew from 44 per cent to 61 per cent. Other components of income like income of retirees and housing rental were subject to fast growth as well. Subsidies declined from 20 per cent of urban income to 1 per cent.

Demurger et al. (2002) examined the growth in GDP per capita for the period 1952-1998 and decomposed the location and policy growth rates in the provincial growth regressions to quantify the contribution of each factor in the period 1996-1999. Their respective contribution varies with the interval of 0-2.8 and 1.6-3.5 per cent. The highest and lowest rates are associated with the coastal and north-western provinces respectively. The authors list a number of policy measures to solve the unbalanced growth and to reduce the regional disparity. The policy measures include: extension of the deregulation from coastal to include other provinces, introduction of a registration system to prevent movements from the rural poor to prosperous areas, changes in the policy of the monopoly state bank system to allocate more resources to the western provinces, improvement in the infrastructure to overcome geographical barriers, and to increase the human capital formation. Shi (2001) estimated that the growing inequality of income distribution in both rural and urban areas has created more difficulties in reducing poverty since the mid-1980s.

6.8. Summary of Inequality in China

China has experienced rapid economic growth in the post economic reform initiated in 1978 with the implications for inequality. Research analysing income inequality in China is often based on household surveys collected in the late 80s and 90s or published statistics at regional level. The surveys are of good coverage when regional, provincial and sectoral dimensions are considered. There is a general agreement among the researches presented above that Gini coefficient increased over time and heterogeneously across provinces. The dissimilar impact of growth on inequality is not limited to inter-provincial, but also intra-provincial, intra-urban, intra-rural and rural-urban inequality. Intra-provincial, intra-rural and intra-urban inequality components contribute significantly to the overall inequality. The growing inequality has created more difficulties in reducing poverty. Income sources are differently important to the sectoral inequality. The correlation between the growth and inequality support the Kuznet's inverted U-curve relationship. In analyzing the causal mechanism relating inequality and growth, many other factors like macroeconomic, technological, political and institutional factors other than inequality might influence economic growth. Output growth, increasing exposure to international trade, urbanisation, taxation, government spending, inflation, human capital, geography and the sectoral structure of the economy determine the extent and direction of changes in inequality. The regional polarisation is driven by the structural differences between regions.

6.8.1. Regional Inequality in Russia

The Russian Household Budget Survey (HBS) conducted since 1952 by Goskomstat and the Russian Longitudinal Monitoring Survey are the main data sources used in the analysis of income inequality, income distribution and poverty in Russia. The Soviet style family budget nature of the survey was revamped in 1997. The new sample covers around 49,000 families observed in a quarterly basis. It is representative of each region (89 territorial units or Federations) of Russia for urban/rural subgroups. For a brief description of the HBS data, see Yemtsov (2002).

The level of inequality in the Russian Federation has been higher than in other transition economies since Russia entered its process of transition. The factors causing the increase in inequality are wealth transfer, changes in government expenditure, growth in earnings dispersion, shifts in the structure of income and also disruption in production. Several studies point to significant between and within regional inequality and with an increasing trend in the inequality levels. The regional inequality differences were found to be related to endowments and initial conditions, transfers, restructuring policies and economic shocks. Measurement errors due to unregistered income, growth of the informal economic activities and home production do not allow estimation of the negative growth rate and increasing incidence of poverty with accuracy. A restructuring of the education system is suggested as an important step to avoid continuous production of wrong skills and to reduce inequality. However, increasing regional inequality, regional polarisation and heterogeneous economic development together with size, ethnic and natural diversity of regions may cause further disintegration and widening regional differences in living standards in Russia. Regional polarisation is driven by structural differences between regions rather than geographical or political. Rising income dispersion is a major factor behind rising inequality in personal income. It should be noted that measures of inequality and poverty might be biased. The bias is a result of the fact that the effects of housing privatisation, relative price effects of liberalisation and wage arrears on income distribution are not accounted for.

6.8.2. Regional Inequality in India

Nearly all of the empirical studies of poverty, inequality, human development and labour studies in India are based on the National Sample Survey (NSS) data covering the India's 24 states in the post 1944. The NSS database includes details on consumer expenditure, demographic characteristics, and labour market statistics. The data consists of annual stratified sample household surveys collected and processed by the Indian bureau of statistics. The household sample size varies greatly between the surveys. For a short description and examples of the use of the data, see Jha (2000) and Datt and Ravallion (1992).

The data quality underlying inequality and poverty analysis in India qualitatively seem to be much better than those of the Russian Federation. Many Indian studies discuss both inter-regional and intra-regional inequality. The latter is further decomposed into urban and rural components. Results suggests that policies to reduce inequality should be concentrated on reducing the within state urban and rural inequalities simultaneously. A decomposition of changes in poverty shows that growth and redistribution effects on poverty were different and uneven across sectors and over time. The urban sector contributed to the raising share of aggregate poverty. The distributional shifts and economic growth have aided poverty alleviation. Changes in capital intensity have resulted in a shift in distribution of income and a rise in inequality following macroeconomic stabilisation and structural adjustment reforms. This in turn has reduced the poverty hence, reducing the effects of economic growth. To make growth more pro-poor, the rapid economic growth must be combined with better redistributive policies. Polarisation differs by states, sectors and it has developed differently over time.

6.8.3. Regional Inequality in USA

The Panel Study of Income Dynamics (PSID) has intensively been used for the analysis of income inequality and income distribution in the US. PSID is a nationally representative longitudinal study of about 8,000 families in the US. The same families and individuals are followed over time since its introduction in 1968. On an annual basis information is collected on economic, health and social behaviour. More information about the data is found at http://psidonline.isr.umich.edu/.

Access to high quality household data covering long periods of the US allows analysis of dynamics of income inequality and income distribution. Analysis of income is performed at different levels of aggregation. Historically; US South had both lower incomes and greater inequality than the Non-South. The income per capita is however converging over time. At the regional level, incomes are stochastically converging to the level of the nation. There is a significant interstate income inequality. Greater international migration, increased metropolitan share of population, changes in family structure, increased share of female headed households, increased female labour participation and institutional and cultural differences increased income inequality, while greater labour force participation reduced inequality. Race, education, age and marital status are key factors affecting inequality in the US. In addition to the sources of inequality it is important to distinguish between transitory and permanent components of inequality. Short-run inequality is influenced by the transitory shocks, while long-run inequality is declining due to the smoothing of transitory component.

6.9. Results Based on the WIID

The data underlying analysis are obtained from the WIID. Here, we focus on the inequality among selected large countries. Due to the absence of data at the within country regional level, we use time series data, although countries are not observed consecutively over time. The Gini coefficient is measured in percentage points. It is mean of multiple observations for a country in a given year. Gini coefficient was also calculated and adjusted for the share of population.

In order to provide a picture of the distribution of income and inequality, we report the first, the last, the period range and the number of years a country is observed. In addition to the mean Gini coefficient, median, minimum, maximum, standard deviation, range and annual changes in Gini are provided in Table 6 for large countries together with mean values for the region where they are located. In Table 7 we report Gini coefficient and population weighted Gini together with distribution of income. The deciles observations are transformed to quintile income shares with the objective to make the income distribution comparable across countries and over time. As a second measure of inequality the ratio of the highest to the lowest quintiles are calculated and reported in Table 7.

Table 6. Mean Gini coefficient by country and region, based on WIID

Country/Region	Min	Max	N	Range	Min	Mean	Median	Max	StdDev	Range	Wgini
China	1953	1998	26	45	18.60	29.35	29.34	55.80	7.18	37.20	28.59
East Asia	1953	1998	93	45	18.60	33.67	31.20	55.80	7.65	37.20	28.81
India	1950	1997	41	47	28.86	34.55	34.94	46.25	3.63	17.39	34.12
South Asia	1950	1997	106	47	28.86	36.94	35.75	53.00	5.37	24.14	34.49
Russian Fed.	1981	1998	13	17	25.10	34.14	36.55	44.81	7.64	19.71	39.35
East Europe	1955	1998	191	43	15.90	25.14	25.04	44.81	5.06	28.91	31.57
US	1944	1997	53	53	35.18	38.65	37.93	44.78	2.35	9.60	38.85
Industrialized	1867	1998	495	131	19.87	34.79	33.83	67.20	7.90	47.33	36.08
All regions	1867	1999	1631	132	15.90	41.12	40.24	79.50	9.61	27.91	35.65

Min First year of observation
Max Last year of observation
N Number of years observed
Range The difference between the last and first years of observation
Min Minimum Gini value
Mean Mean Gini value
Median Median Gini value
Max Maximum Gini value
StdDev Standard deviation of the Gini
Range The difference between maximum and minimum Gini values
Wgini Population weighted mean Gini

Table 7. Mean Gini coefficient and quintile shares by country and region, based on WIID

Country/Region	Min	Max	N	Range	Gini	WGini	Q1	Q2	Q3	Q4	Q5	Q5/Q1
China	1953	1998	26	45	29.35	28.59	0.08	0.12	0.16	0.25	0.39	5.21
East Asia	1953	1998	93	45	33.67	28.81	0.07	0.12	0.16	0.23	0.41	5.55
India	1950	1997	41	47	34.55	34.12	0.09	0.12	0.16	0.21	0.41	4.83
South Asia	1950	1997	106	47	36.94	34.49	0.08	0.12	0.16	0.21	0.42	5.13
Russian Fed.	1981	1998	13	17	34.14	39.35	0.09	0.12	0.16	0.22	0.41	4.56
East Europe	1955	1998	191	43	26.14	31.57	0.10	0.14	0.18	0.22	0.35	3.54
US	1944	1997	53	53	38.65	38.85	0.05	0.11	0.17	0.24	0.43	9.17
Industrialized	1867	1998	495	131	34.79	36.08	0.07	0.12	0.17	0.24	0.40	5.72
All regions	1867	1999	1392	132	38.06	38.26	0.07	0.11	0.16	0.22	0.44	6.88

Min First year of observation
Max Last year of observation
N Number of years observed
Range The difference between the last and first years of observation
Gini Mean Gini value
WGini Population weighted mean Gini value
Q1-Q5 Income shares of the first-fifth quintiles of population
Q5/Q1 the ration of the fifth quintile share to the first quintile income share

It should be noted that the point observations are not comparable across countries or for the same country over the entire time period. The data incomparability is due to differences in units of measurement, area and population coverage, and income definitions. There is a trade off between the number of observations and the consistency of the data. This is the motivation for our preferences for a maximisation of the number of observations rather than a search for maintaining data consistency.

The comparison of income inequality among the four large countries reported in Table 6 show that the mean Gini coefficient in China (29.35) and India (34.55) is lower than the regional mean values where the countries are located, while those of Russia (34.14) and US (39.65) are higher than their respective regional means. It should be noted that the country mean values are based on observations covering different sub-periods.

With the exception of Russia the mean and median values are quite close. However, the standard deviation and range between minimum and maximum Gini values differ greatly among the countries. India (3.63) and the US (2.35) shows less dispersion in Gini coefficient over time. The lowest quintile income share in the US (0.05) shown in Table 7 is lowest compared to the 0.08-0.09 among the other countries. The low Q1 combined with the high Q5 share (0.43) compared with those of the results of the other countries (0.39-0.43) result in a high Q5/Q1 ratio for the US (9.17). The corresponding for other countries is 4.56 (Russia), 4.83 (India) and 5.21 (China).

Table 8. Development of Gini coefficient and quintile income shares in China

Year	Gini	DGini	Q1	Q2	Q3	Q4	Q5	Q5/Q1	Popul	GDP
1953	55.8	.	.	.	.	.	.	.	.	.
1964	30.5	-4.1	.	.	.	.	.	.	698355	960
1970	27.9	-1.4	.	.	.	.	.	.	818315	1008
1975	26.6	-0.9	.	.	.	.	.	.	916395	1041
1977	18.6	-15.0	.	.	.	.	.	.	943455	1050
1978	22.5	21.2	.	.	.	.	.	.	956165	1111
1979	23.7	5.0	.	.	.	.	.	.	969005	1165
1980	29.4	24.3	0.08	0.12	0.18	0.25	0.37	4.6	981235	1204
1981	19.7	-32.9	.	.	.	.	.	.	993861	1231
1982	23.6	19.6	0.08	0.14	0.18	0.22	0.38	4.4	1008599	1285
1983	24.4	3.6	0.09	0.15	0.17	0.24	0.36	4.1	1023288	1348
1984	23.4	-4.3	0.10	0.14	0.19	0.23	0.34	3.4	1036803	1479
1985	29.8	27.5	0.08	0.12	0.16	0.23	0.40	4.8	1051013	1622
1986	27.3	-8.7	0.08	0.12	0.16	0.26	0.39	5.1	1066758	1706
1987	28.0	2.6	0.07	0.11	0.16	0.28	0.38	5.4	1083998	1776
1988	31.9	14.1	0.07	0.11	0.16	0.29	0.38	5.7	1101596	1864
1989	29.8	-6.6	0.06	0.12	0.16	0.24	0.42	6.5	1118623	1860
1990	32.0	7.3	0.07	0.11	0.16	0.24	0.41	6.2	1135160	1912
1991	31.0	-3.2	0.06	0.11	0.15	0.31	0.36	5.6	1150756	2064
1992	33.0	6.5	0.06	0.11	0.16	0.26	0.42	6.9	1164951	2264
1993	29.5	-10.6	.	.	.	.	.	.	1178402	2470
1994	31.5	6.8	.	.	.	.	.	.	1190918	2672
1995	35.4	12.3	0.08	0.10	0.15	0.22	0.47	6.2	1203324	2894
1996	28.3	-19.9	.	.	.	.	.	.	1215414	3062
1997	29.3	3.3	.	.	.	.	.	.	1227177	3192
1998	40.3	37.7	0.08	0.10	0.15	0.22	0.46	5.6	1238599	3282

Year Year of observation
Gini Mean Gini coefficient
DGini Change in Gini coefficient
Q1-Q5 First to Fifth quintile income shares
Q5/Q1 Ratio of the fifth to the first quintile income shares
Popul Population in 1000
GDP Read GDP per capita

In Table 8, in addition to Gini coefficient and quintile income shares, we report the percentage changes in Gini coefficient as well as the population and per capita incomes over time for the sample of four large countries. The quintile income shares are not reported in some years due to missing observations. The annual changes with the exception of US vary greatly for China, India and Russia reflecting effects of economic crises or shocks to the economy. In the case of Russia, the large changes are always leading to increasing inequality, while in the cases of China and India, large reductions in inequality can be observed in certain periods. In the US, with an exception of 1991/92 and 1996/97, annual income inequality changes is small and not exceeding 10 per cent. The growth in population is highest in India, while the growth in GDP per capita is highest in China followed by US. Worth to mention is that the 1997 level of per capita income in US (30,573) unadjusted for PPP is more than 9.5 times that of China (3,192) in 1997. Distinction should be made between relative and absolute values in comparing the four countries with respect to per capita GDP and populations.

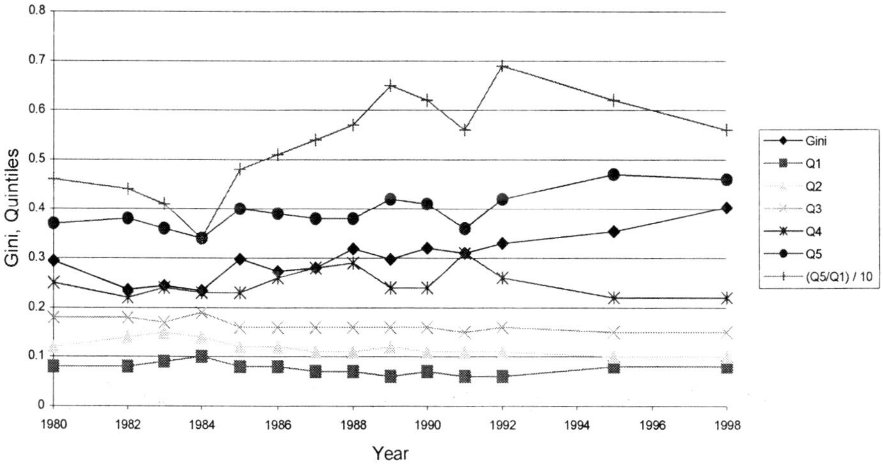

Figure 7. Development of Gini coefficient and income shares in China.

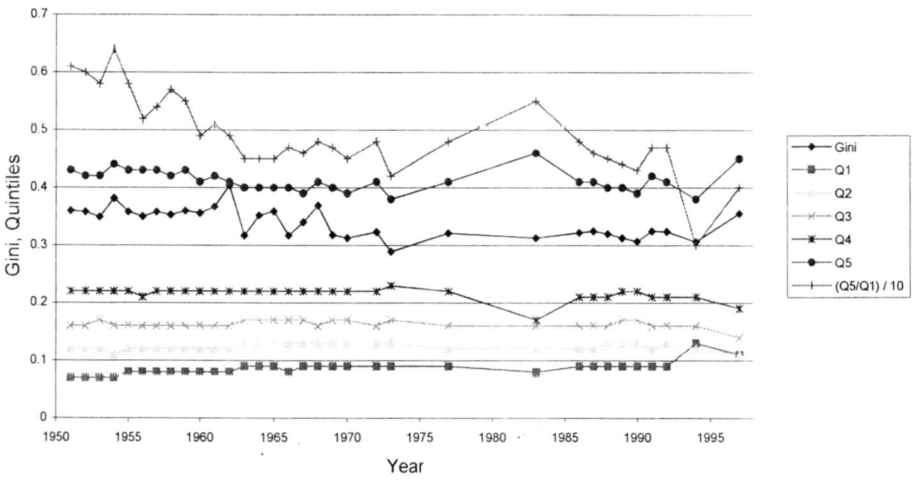

Figure 8. Development of Gini coefficient and income shares in India.

The development of Gini coefficient together with quintile income shares and the Q5/Q1 ratio for individual countries are presented in Figures 7-9. In order to make the data levels comparable, the Q5/Q1 ratio is divided by 10 and Gini coefficients are reported in decimal form in the 0-1 interval. Furthermore, the years where quintile income shares are missing are excluded from the graphs. Only years where all information is available are used in drawing the graphs. However, complete set of data including excluded observations can be viewed in Table 8.

Figure 7 shows that income share of the second and third quintiles in China are declining over time. Shifts in income have taken place mainly among the fourth and fifth quintiles. Inequality shows increasing trend in post 1985. The Q5/Q1 ratio is increasing sharply between 1984 and 1989 but it declines from 1992. Inequality in India has declined before 1972 and remained constant until 1994 then increased (see Figure 8). The income share of the first quintile in India has increased during the period 1950-1967 and 1992 onward. The Gini coefficient follows same temporal patterns as that of the fifth quintile. The Q5/Q1 ratio is declining over time before 1993. The corresponding numbers for Russia during the period 1993-98 are quite stable with an exception of 1995 when a major shift in the quintile income shares is observed. In similarity with India, the US Gini coefficient develops in the same way as income share of the fourth quintile (see Figure 10). Shifts in the income shares are from the second and the third quintiles to the fifth quintile. The Q5/Q1 ratio fluctuates greatly in post 1980. Finally, development of Gini coefficient for all four countries is shown in Figure 10. The trend in inequality in the US, China and Russia is positive, while that of India is negative but variable.

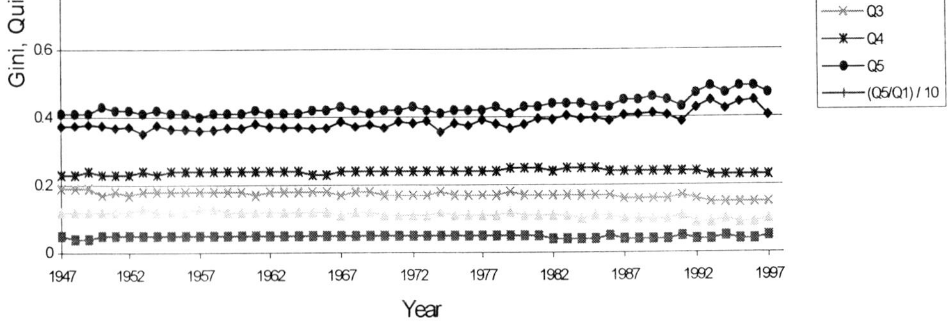

Figure 9. Development of Gini coefficient and income shares in USA.

7. DATA ISSUES

This Section focuses on the important data issues to the analysis of growth, poverty and economic inequality (Heshmati 2004c). We briefly introduce a number of major databases frequently used in applied research on growth, poverty and income inequality. A discussion of data quality, data consistency, variable definitions and measurement, changing population and household size leading to various necessary scale and price adjustment procedures will follow. The sampling design and various dimensions of sample dependency are also discussed. Based on the existing experience we identify a number of factors that are important in applied research. The focus is on those factors which impacts on reliability, precision, sensitivity and consistency of the results and conclusions drawn.

The extensive literature emerging in recent years are focused on the study of how the distribution of incomes across countries and globally has developed over time. The increased interest in income inequality may be both the cause and the effect of the availability of data. Availability of household surveys have been improved and several standardized databases created. These allow for analysis of income distribution at the most disaggregate individual or per capita household levels. Income distribution is otherwise often analyzed at an aggregate level of global, regional and international. Income inequality can also be measured at a within-country regional level. Empirical studies at each level are extremely data intensive and are based on the second half of the twentieth century.

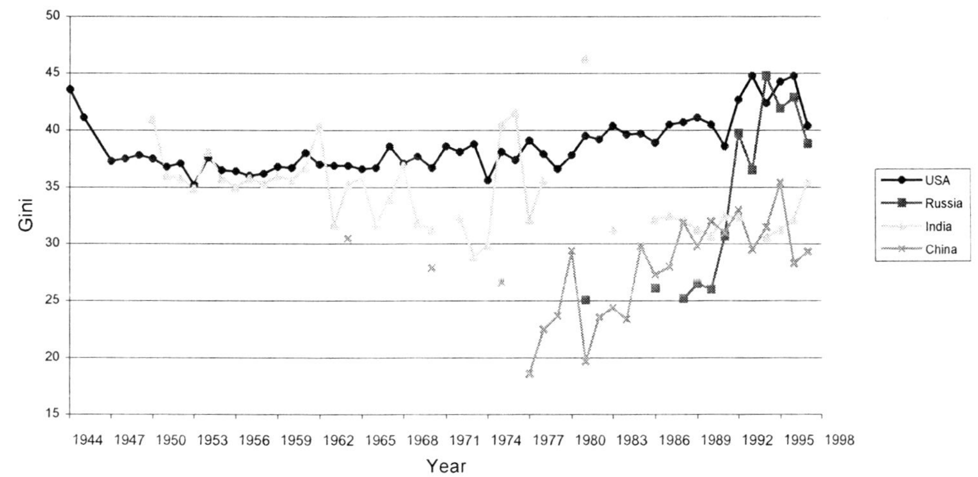

Figure 10. Development of Gini coefficient by country.

A number of databases are frequently used in applied global, international, regional, intra-national growth, poverty and income inequality research. The descriptions of such databases are found in Summers and Heston (1991), Barro and Lee (1996), Deininger and Squire (1996) and Atkinson and Brandolini (2001). Despite the differences in objectives, country coverage, sources, units of measurement and income definitions, each database plays an important and complementary role in growth and inequality studies. Each set of data has both benefits and limitations. The choice of data seems to affect the conclusions drawn about trends in inequality. Quality, consistency, income definition and measurement, changing population, household size and various variable adjustment procedures are among important issues that are discussed. Consistency across countries and over time is a key issue to the reliability of results. The measurement of income, its decomposition by source and sub-groups with satisfactory coverage, sampling and representation of population are important in the generation of consistent information about the state of income inequality. An absence of such properties might result in misleading or spurious results.

Secondary cross-national data sets play an important role in empirical economic research offering cross-country panel data analysis. The Summers and Heston (1991), Baro and Lee (1996), Deininger and Squire (1996), World Income Inequality Database, and other by World Bank, United Nations and Luxembourg Income Study (LIS) are among the widely used secondary data sets containing information on education, population, trade, finance, health, politics and income distribution. The premise and pitfalls in the use of such data-sets and how they can be best assembled and used in income inequality (in OECD countries as a case study) is discussed by Atkinson and Brandolini (2001). The primary concern of Atkinson and Brandolini is with data quality and data consistency. These are the two important but in their view neglected issues in most applied research. In the following we provide a brief description of each of the important data sets listed above. It extends the Atkinson and Brandolini (2001) study by using up-to-date relevant references and available data sources.

The databases that are frequently being used in applied income inequality and poverty research differ by objectives, country coverage, sources, units of measurement and income definitions, yet each one play an important role in inequality studies and by serving as complement to each other. Each data have of course their benefits and limitations and the choice of data affects the conclusions drawn about trends in inequality for a single or groups of countries and over time. Quality, consistency, income definition and measurement, changing population and household size and various variable adjustment procedures are among important data issues discussed here. Consistency across countries and over time is a key issue to the reliability of results in panel data studies.

Measurement of income, its decomposition by source and sub-group with satisfactory coverage, sampling and enumeration units and representative of population is important in generation of consistent information about the state of income inequality. Heterogeneity in ability, in actual consumption and consumption needs by age, gender and size of households and presence of economies of scale requires calculation of representative consumption amounts by using some measures of equivalence methods of scales. The cost of living varies by location primarily divided into urban, rural or regions. Empirical results show that estimates of income and consumption inequalities are sensitive to the cost of living index_as the price deflator.

Higher gender earnings disparity, growing positive correlation of income within families, and growing proportion of families with single adults explains large parts of the increase in overall inequality. An incorrect assumption about independent and identically distributed income over time and contemporaneous dependent across members of household produces biased results. Few existing studies show that there is a large gain in precision if one takes dependencies into account.

8. SUMMARY AND CONCLUSIONS

This chapter addressed a number of issues crucial to the measurement and analysis of global income inequality. The issues include the concepts, measurement and decomposition of inequality, and the analysis of the world distribution of income and inequality measured at different ranges of aggregation. Other areas of interest are the relationships between macroeconomic variables, inequality and poverty. The gained experiences are then reflected in the discussion of the data differences and conclusions drawn. This section summarises the results from the review of literature and our findings based on the WIID database.

Inequality has different dimensions;- both income and non-income. Here the focus is centred on income dimensions. Several inequality indices can be derived from the Lorenz diagram. The most widely used index of inequality is the Gini coefficient. Income inequality can be decomposed at different levels of aggregation. At the national and international levels, it can be decomposed into within-subgroup and between-subgroup and within-country and between-country components respectively.

Literature on inequality decomposition is developed to measure variations in inequality associating it with the underlying causal factors. Methods have been developed to decompose inequality by sub-groups, income sources, causal factors and by other unit of observational characteristics. At the national level, it is decomposed into within-subgroup and between-subgroups components, while at the international it is decomposed into within-country and between-country components. Different methods of decomposing the changes in poverty into growth, redistribution and poverty standard components are also suggested. Regression-based methods of decomposition of inequality by income sources have been proposed. Compared with unconditional approach, the latter provides possibilities to quantify the conditional roles of various characteristics in a multivariate context and to construct confidence intervals for contributions to the inequality index.

A number of ways to construct world indices of income distribution and to measure global income inequality are reviewed. Few of them compare the world's distribution of income at the individual level. A combined micro and macro approach where the mean income per capita complemented with some measures of income dispersion or income share from household surveys is often used. Economic growth, population growth, life expectancy, and the changes in the structure of income inequality are important factors determining the evolution of world income distribution. Empirical results show that the world inequality measured as Gini coefficient increased and poverty measured as headcount decreased. Inequality within individual countries is not increasing but inequality between countries and regions is increasing affecting the evolution of world income inequality. Results based on the WIID database shows no convincing sign of a significant global trend in income inequality over the last 50 years. Inequality was volatile prior to 1970 but more stable and slowly increasing in the post 1986.

In addition to global, international and national levels, we considered income inequality at regional level defined as continents or sub-continents. The same decomposition of inequality within and between regions applies. Intra-regional inequality refers to the disparity in income distribution within a region consisting of a number of countries. The East Asian countries have been successful in coupling growth and equality prior to the 1997 economic crisis. The entry of China into the world market and the advent of new technology biased against unskilled workers did have major impacts on the inter-regional development of inequality. Results based on WIID database show a large inter-regional heterogeneity in both the level and the development of income distribution and income inequality over time. Inequality in Latin America, East Europe and Former Soviet Republics showed increasing trends in the post 1970s.

The within-country income inequality at the regional level in a selection of large countries with regional division was examined. The results are mainly based on the second half of the 20th century and four large countries including China, Russia, India and USA. China has experienced a rapid economic growth post the economic reform accompanied by an increased inequality. Empirical results suggest that the level and development of inequality has been greatly different by geographical locations and economic sectors. In a number of studies, attempts have been made to identify the determinants of inequality across different provinces. There is an indication that regional polarization been driven by structural differences between regions. Regional inequality and polarization is of a more serious policy concern in Russia. Heterogeneous economic development, size, ethnic and natural diversity of regions together with restructuring policies and economic shocks caused widening regional inequality and poverty in Russia. The results might however be biased due to data quality and measurement error. Results based on the WIID database show that inequality in US has increased slightly over time. The trend in inequality in India is negative but variable. There is a positive trend in inequality in China and Russia during their post economic reform periods.

There are a number of databases that are frequently used in applied global, international, regional and also in national growth and inequality research. Despite their benefits, limitations and differences by objectives, composition of countries, country coverage, sources, unit of measurement and income definitions, each play an important and complementary role in inequality studies. The choice of data affects the conclusion drawn about the trends in inequality for a single or groups of countries and over time. Quality, consistency, income definition and measurement, changing population and household size and various adjustment procedures are among important data issues discussed here. The existing empirical results are found to be quite sensitive to these factors.

The rising global or national inequality, although undesirable, is not inevitable, as individuals, regions and countries are different by initial conditions, goals and in productivity. It is evident that the wealthy and advanced nations in the capacity of technology leaders and deriving force of development are the main beneficiaries of economic development. Despite such persisting difference, the current world's social situation argues that although living standards have improved in many places the poverty remains entrenched. This and as a result of existing technology gap will widen further the gap between the rich and the poor hence, calling for immediate action. Growth is considered as an effective means of reducing poverty. However, focusing only on economic growth is an ineffective way of achieving development and equality. Redistribution is often a neglected measure in the debate. The multidimensionality of inequality and its overall impacts on the poor in form of inequality in income, wealth, opportunity, health and education should not be neglected.

REFERENCES

Acemoglu D. (2002), Cross-country inequality trends, NBER Working Paper No. 8832.

Agénor P.R. (2003), Does globalization hurt the poor?, World Bank, *Unpublished manuscript.*

Alesina A., R. DiTella and R. MacCulloch (2001), Inequality and happiness: are Europeans and Americans different?, *NBER Working Paper* 8189.

Alesina A. and D. Rodrik (1994), Distributive politics and economic growth, Quarterly *Journal of Economics* 109, 465-490.

Anand S. (1997), The measurement of income inequality, in: S. Subramanian (ed) *Measurement of inequality and poverty,* Oxford University Press, pp. 81-105.

Andersen T.M. and T.T. Herbertsson (2003), Measuring globalization, *IZA Discussion Paper* 2003:817.

Atkinson A.B. and A. Brandolini (2001), Promise and pitfalls in the use of "secondary" data-sets: income inequality in OECD countries as a case study, *Journal Economic Literature* 39, 771-799.

Barro R.J. and J-W Lee (1996), International measures of schooling years and schooling quality, *American Economic Review* 86(2), 218-223.

Berry A., F. Bourguignon and C. Morrisson (1983), Changes in the world distribution of income between 1950 and 1977, *Economic Journal* 93(370), 331-350.

Birdsall N. (1998), Inequality and global coordination, Why inequality matters: the developing and transition economies, mimeo, *Carnegie Endowment for International Peace*, Washington D.C.

Birchenall J.A. (2001), Income distribution, human capital and economic growth in Colombia, *Journal of Development Economics* 66, 271-287.

Bourguignon F. and M. Fournier and M. Gurgand (2001), Fast development with a stable income distribution in Taiwan, 1979-94, *Review of Income and Wealth* 47(2), 139-163.

Bourguignon F. and C. Morrisson (1999*), The size distribution of income among the world citizens, mimeo, DELTA*, Paris.

Bourguignon F. and C. Morrisson (2002), Inequality among world citizens: 1820-1992, *American Economic Reviews* 92(4), 727-747.

Cameron L.A. (2000), Poverty and inequality in Java: examining the impact of the changing age, educational and industrial structure, *Journal of Development Economics* 62, 149-180.

Caminada K. and K. Goudswaard (2001), International trends in income inequality and social policy, *International Tax and Public Finance* 8(4), 395-415.

Capeau B. and A. Decoster (2003), The rise or fall of world inequality: big issue or apparent controversy?, *Unpublished manuscript.*

Cheng Y-S. (1996), A decomposition analysis of income inequality of Chinese rural households, *China Economic Review* 7(2), 155-167.

Commander A., A Tolstopiatenko and R. Yemtsov (1999), Chanells of redistribution: inequality and poverty in the Russian transition, *Economics of Transition* 7(2), 411-447.

Cornia G.A. and J. Court (2001), Inequality, growth and poverty in the era of liberalization and globalization, Policy Brief No. 4, Helsinki: UNU/WIDER.

Cornia G.A. and S. Kiiski (2001), Trends in income distribution in the post WWII period: evidence and interpretation, WIDER Discussion Paper 2001/89, Helsinki: UNU/WIDER.

Cowell F.A. (2000), Measurement of inequality, in Atkinson A.B. and Bourguignon F. (Eds), Handbook of Income Distribution, Volume 1, North Holland, chapter 2, 87-166.

Datt G. and M. Ravallion (1992), Growth and redistribution components of changes in poverty measures: A decomposition with applications to Brazil and India in the 1980s, *Journal of Development Economics* 38, 275-295.

Deininger K. and L. Squire (1996), A new data set measuring income inequality, *World Bank Economic Review* 10(3), 565-591.

Deininger K. and L. Squire (1998), New ways of looking at old issues: inequality and growth, *Journal of Development Economics* 57, 259-287.

Demurger S., J.D. Sachs, W.T. Woo, S. Bao, G. Cheng and A. Mellinger (2002), Geography, Economic Policy, and regional development in China, *NBER Working Paper* 8897.

Dikhanov Y. and M. Ward (2002), Evolution of the global distribution of income in 1970-99. Unpublished manuscript presented at the *International Workshop on Income Distribution and Welfare*, Bocconi May 30 to June 2 2002.

Dollar D. and A. Kraay (2001), Trade growth and poverty, Development Research Group, The World Bank.

Donaldson D. and J.A. Waymark (1980), A single-parameter generalization of the Gini index of inequality, *Journal of Economic Theory* 22, 67-86.

Fedorov L. (2002), Regional inequality and regional polarisation in Russia, 1990-99, *World Development* 30(3), 443-456.

Fields G.S. (2000), Measuring Inequality Change in an Economy with Income Growth, The International Library of Critical Writings in Economics: Income Distribution, (Edward Elgar).

Gottschalk P. and T.M Smeeding (1997), Cross-national comparisons of earnings and income inequality, *Journal of Economic Literature* 35, 633-687.

Gottschalk P. and T.M. Smeeding (2000), Empirical evidence on income inequality in industrialized countries, in Atkinson A.B. and Bourguignon F. (Eds), *Handbook of Income Distribution*, Volume 1, North Holland, chapter 5, pp.261-308.

Goudie A. and P. Ladd (1999), Economic growth, poverty and inequality, *Journal of International Development* 11, 177-195.

Gustafsson B. and L. Shi (2001a), The anatomy of rising earnings inequality in Urban China, *Journal of Comparative Economics* 29(1), 118-135.

Gustafsson B. and L. Shi (2001b), The effects of transition on the distribution of income in China: a study decomposing the GINI coefficient for 1988 and 1995, *Economics of Transition* 9(3), 593-617.

Gustafsson B. and L. Shi (2002), Income inequality within and across counties in rural China 1988 and 1995, *Journal of Development Economics* 69(1), 179-204.

Gustafsson B., L. Shi, L. Nivorozhkia and K. Katz (2001), Rubles and Yuan: wage functions for urban Russia and China at the end of the 1980s, *Economic Development and Cultural Change* 50(1), 1-17.

Gustafsson B. and W. Zhong (2000), How and why has poverty in China changed? A study based on microdata for 1988 and 1995, *The China Quarterly* 164, 983-1006.

Hasegawa H. and H. Kozumi (2003), Estimation of Lorenz curves: a Bayesian nonparametric approach, *Journal of Econometrics* 115, 277-291.

Heshmati A. (2004a), Growth, Inequality and Poverty Relationships, IZA Discussion Paper 2004:1338.

Heshmati A. (2004b), The Relationship Between Income Inequality, Poverty and Globalization, *IZA Discussion Paper* 2004:1277.

Heshmati A. (2004c), Measurement of a multidimentional index of globalization and its impact on income inequality, *IZA Discussion Paper* 2004:1263.

Heshmati A. (2005), Continental and Sub-continental Income Inequality, ICFAI *Journal of Applied Economics* 5(6), 7-52.

Heshmati A. (2006a), The World Distribution of Income and Income Inequality, *Journal of World Systems Research* 12(1), 60-107.

Heshmati A. (2006b), Measurement of a multidimensional Index of Globalization, Global *Economy Journal* 6(2), Paper 1.

Hossain M.A. (2001), Inter- and intraregional incidence of inequality and poverty in Thailand's Northeast region, including comments by I. Sarntisart, Regional Development Dialogue 22(2), 185-197.

Ivaschenko O. (2002), Growth and inequality: evidence from transitional economics, CESIFO Working Paper 2002:746.

Jha R. (2000), Reducing poverty and inequality in India: Has liberalization helped?, *Working Papers* 2000/204, Helsinki: UNU/WIDER.

Jian L.R. and Tendulkar (1990), Role of growth and distribution in the observed change of headcount ratio-measure of poverty: a decomposition exercise for India, *Technical report no. 9004* (Indian Statistical Institute, Delhi).

Kakwani N. (1980), On a class of poverty measures, *Econometrics* 48, 437-446.

Kakwani N. and M. Krongkaew (2000), Introduction: Economic growth, poverty and income inequality in the Asia-Pacific region, *Journal of the Asia Pacific Economy* 5(1/2), 9-13.

Kakwani N. and K. Subbarao (1990), *Rural Poverty and its alleviation in India, Economic and Political Weekly*, March 31, 1990.

Kanbur R. and X. Zhang (1999), Which regional inequality? The evolution of rural-urban and inland-coastal inequality in China from 1983 to 1995, *Journal of Comparative Economics* 27(4), 686-701

Kaplow L. (2002), Why measure inequality?, *NBER Working Paper Series* 2002:9342.

Kopczuk W., J. Slemrod and S. Yitzhaki (2002), Why world distribution fails, *NBER Working Paper Series* 2002:9186.

Kuznets S. (1955), Economic growth and income inequality, *American Economic Review* 45, 1-28.

Lee J. (2000), Changes in the source of China's regional inequality, *China Economic Review* 11(3), 232-245.

Lerman R.I. and S. Yitzhaki (1985), Income inequality effects by income source: a new approach and applications to the United States, *Review of Economics and Statistics* 67(1), 151-156.

Lerman R.I. and S. Yitzhaki (1989), Improving the accuracy of estimates of Gini coefficients, *Journal of Econometrics* 42(1), 43-47.

Li H., Squire L. and H. Zou (1998), Explaining international and intertemporal variations in income inequality, *Economic Journal* 108(466), 26-43.

Liebbrandt M., C. Woolard and I. Woolard (2000), The contribution of income components to income inequality in the rural former homelands of South Africa: a decomposable Gini analysis, *Journal of African Economies* 9(1), 79-99.

Lindert P.H. and J.G. Williamson (2001), Does globalization make the World more unequal?, *NBER Working Paper* 2001:8228.

LondoNo J.L. and M. Szekely (2000), Persistent poverty and excess inequality: Latin America, 1970-1995, *Journal of Applied Economics* III(1), 93-134.

Lorenz M.O. (1905), Methods of measuring the concentration of wealth, *Journal of the American Statistical Association* 9, 209-219, reprinted in S. Subramanian (ed) Measurement of inequality and poverty, Oxford University Press, pp. 71-80.

Luttmer E.F.P. (2001), Measuring poverty dynamics and inequality in transition economies: disentangling real events from noisy data, *The World Bank Policy Research Working Paper* 2001:2549.

Maddison A. (2001), The world economy: A millennial perspective, Development Centre Studies, Paris: OECD.

Mahler V.A. (2001), Economic globalization, domestic politics and income inequality in the developed countries: a cross-national analysis, *Luxembourg Income Study Working Paper 273*, Luxembourg.

Milanovic B. (2001), World income inequality in the second half of the 20th century, World Bank, Development Research Group.

Milanovic B. (2002), True world income distribution, 1988 and 1993: First calculation based on household surveys alone, *Economic Journal* 112(476), 51-92.

Milanovic B. and S. Yitzhaki (2001), Decomposing world income distribution: does the world have a middle class?, WB 2001:2562.

Mishra P. and A. Parikh (1997), Distributional inequality in Indian states, *Journal of Income Distribution* 7(1), 89-108.

Moffitt R.A. and P. Gottschalk (2002), Trends in the transitory variance of earnings in the United States, *The Economic Journal 112*, March C68-C73.

Morduch J. and T. Sicular (2002), Rethinking inequality decomposition, with evidence from rural China, *Economic Journal* 112(476), 93-106.

Ogwang T. and U.L.G. Rao (2000), Hybrid models of the Lorenz curve, *Economics Letters* 69, 39-44.

O'Rourke K.H. (2001), Globalization and inequality: historical trends, *NBER Working Paper 8339*, Cambridge MA: NBER.

O'Rourke K.H. and J.G. Williamson (2000), Globalization and history: the evolution of a nineteenth-century Atlantic economy, Cambridge MA: MIT Press (see Review Essay by A.G. Frank (2002), *Journal of World-Systems Research* 8(2), 276-290).

Park D. (2001), Recent trends in the global distribution of income, *Journal of Policy Modeling* 23, 497-501.

Park A., S. Wang and G. Wu (2002), Regional poverty targeting in China, *Journal of Public Economics* 86, 123-153.

Partridge M.D., D.S. Rickman and W. Levernier (1996), Trends in U.S. income inequality: evidence from a panel of states, *The Quarterly Review of Economics and Finance* 36(1), 17-37.

Persson T. and G. Tabellini (1994), Is inequality harmful for growth? *American economic Review* 84, 600-621.

Pyatt G. (1976), On the interpretation and disaggregation of Gini coefficient, *Economic Journal 86*(342), 243-255.

Quah D. (1999), Some dynamics of global inequality and growth, London School of Economics, London School of Economics, mimeo.

Quah D. (2001), Some simple arithmetic on how income inequality and economic growth matter, Paper presented at WIDER conference on Growth and Poverty, 25-26 May 2001, Helsinki.

Quah D. (2002), One third of the world's growth and inequality, LSE, Economics Department, CEPR Discussion Paper 2002:3316.

Ravallion M. (1998), Does aggregation hide the harmful effects of inequality on growth?, *Economics Letters* 61, 73-77.

Ravallion M. (2001), Growth, inequality and poverty: looking beyond averages, World Development 29(11), 1803-1815.

Ravallion M. and S. Chen (1999), When economic reform is faster than statistical reform: measuring and explaining income inequality in Rural China, *Oxford Bulletin of Economics and Statistics* 61, 33-56.

Ravallion M. and S. Chen (2003), Measuring pro-poor growth, *Economics Letters* 78, 93-99.

Ravallion M. and G. Datt (2000), When is growth pro-poor? Evidence from the diverse experience of Indian states, *World Bank Policy Research,* WP 2263

Ryu H.K. and D.J. Slottje (1999), Parametric approximation of the Lorenz Curve, in S. Silber and A. Sen (eds), Handbook of Income Distribution, Chapter 10, 291-314, Kluwer Academic Press.

Sacks J. and A. Warner (1995), Economic reform and the process of global integration, *Brookings Papers on Economic Activity* 1:95.

Sala-i-Martin X. (2002a), The disturbing "Rise" of global income inequality, *NBER Working Paper Series* 8904.

Sala-i-Martin X. (2002b), The world distribution of income (estimated from individual country distribution), *NBER Working Paper* 8933.

Schultz T.P. (1998), Inequality in distribution of personal income in the world: how is it changing and why?, *Journal of Population Economics* 11(3), 307-344

Shorrocks A.F. (1980), The class of additively decomposable inequality, Econometrica 48(3), 613-625.

Shorrocks A.F. (1982), Inequality decomposition by factor components, *Econometrica* 50(1), 193-211.

Shorrocks A.F. (1983), The impact of income components on the distribution of family incomes, *Quarterly Journal of Economics* 98(2), 311-326.

Shorrocks (1984), Inequality decomposition by population subgroups, *Econometrica* 52(6), 1369-1385.

Shorrocks A. and S. Kolenikov (2001), Poverty trends in Russia during the transition, Unpublished manuscript.

Shorrocks A. and G. Wan (2004), *Spatial decomposition of inequality*, Unpublished manuscript.

Silber J. (1999), Eds, Handbook of Inequality Measurement, Kluwer Academic Publishers.

Solimano A. (2001), The evolution of world income inequality: assessing the impact of globalization, Unpublished manuscript, ECLAC, CEPAL – Serie Macroeconomica del desarrollo No. 11, Santiago, Chile.

Stiglitz J.E. (1998), More instruments and broader goals: moving towards the Post-Washington consensus, *WIDER Annual Lecture 2*, Helsinki: UNU/WIDER.

Subramanian S. (1997a), (ed.), Measurement of inequality and poverty, Readers in Economics, Oxford University Press.

Subramanian S. (1997b), Introduction: the measurement of inequality and poverty, in S. Subramanian (ed), Measurement of inequality and poverty, Readers in Economics, Oxford University Press, pp. 1-53.

Summers R. and A. Heston (1991), The Penn World Table (Mark 5): an expanded set of international comparisons, 1950-1988, *Quarterly Journal of Economics* 106, 327-368.

Svedbery P. (2002), Income distribution across countries: how is it measured and what do the results show?, *IIES Seminar Papers,* SWoPEc 2002:698.

Tsui K-Y. (1993), Decomposition of China's regional inequalities, *Journal of Comparative Economics* 17(3), 600-627.

Tsui K-Y. and Y. Wang (1998), Polarisation ordering and new classes of polarisation indices, memo, The Chinese University of Hong Kong.

Van der Hoeven R. and A. Shorrocks (2003), Eds., *Perspectives on growth and poverty,* United Nations University Press, Tokyo, Japan.

Wan G.H. (2002), Regression-based inequality decomposition: Pitfalls and a solution procedure, *WIDER Discussion Paper* 2002/101, Helsinki: UNU/WIDER.

Warr P. (2001), Poverty in Thailand: a regional perspective, including comments by S. Jayasuriya, Regional Development Dialogue 22(2), 142-159.

Williamson J.G. (2002), Winners and losers over two centuries of globalization, *WIDER Annual Lecture 6*, Helsinki: UNU/WIDER.

Wolfson M.C. (1994), Conceptual issues in normative measurement: when inequalities diverge, *American Economic Review* 84(2), 353-358.

Wood A. (1997), Openness and wage inequality in developing countries: the Latin American challenge to East Asian continental wisdom, *World Bank Economic Review* 11(1), 33-57.

Xu K. (2000), Inference for generalized Gini indices using iterated-bootstrap method, *Journal of Business and Economic Statistics* 18, 223-227.

Xu L.C. and H-F. Zou (2000), Explaining the changes of income distribution in China, *China Economic Review* 11, 149-170.

Yemtsov R. (2002), Quo Vadis: inequality and poverty dynamics across Russian regions in 1992-2000, Paper prepared for WIDER project meeting Microsimulation of Tax Benefit Reform in Russia, 2-3 August 2002, Helsinki.

Yitzhaki S. (1983), On an extension of the Gini inequality index, *International Economic Review* 24(3), 617-628.

You I. (1998), Income distribution and growth in East Asia, *Journal of Development Studies* 34(6), 37-65.

Zhang X. and R. Kanbur (2001), What difference do polarisation measures make? An application to China, Journal of Development Studies 37(3), 85-98.

Zhang Z., A. Liu and S. Yao (2001), Convergence of China's regional incomes, 1952-1997, *China Economic Review* 12(2/3), 243-258.

Zitikis R. and J.L. Gastwirth (2002), The asymptotic distribution of the S-Gini index, *Australian and New Zealand Journal of Statistics* 44, 439-446.

INDEX

A

B

C

D

E

H

I

N

O

P

Q

R

S

T